S.P.G. PAPERS
IN THE
LAMBETH PALACE
LIBRARY

S. P. G. PAPERS

IN THE
LAMBETH PALACE
LIBRARY

———

CALENDAR AND INDEXES

———

PREPARED BY

WILLIAM WILSON MANROSS

Professor Emeritus of Church History
Philadelphia Divinity School

OXFORD
AT THE CLARENDON PRESS
1974

Oxford University Press, Ely House, London W. 1

GLASGOW NEW YORK TORONTO MELBOURNE WELLINGTON
CAPE TOWN IBADAN NAIROBI DAR ES SALAAM LUSAKA ADDIS ABABA
DELHI BOMBAY CALCUTTA MADRAS KARACHI LAHORE DACCA
KUALA LUMPUR SINGAPORE HONG KONG TOKYO

ISBN 0 19 920065 3

*Printed in Great Britain
at the University Press, Oxford
by Vivian Ridler
Printer to the University*

CONTENTS

INDEXES

INTRODUCTION

THE S.P.G. Papers in Lambeth Palace Library include the minutes, financial records, and correspondence of the Society for the Propagation of the Gospel in Foreign Parts from 1701 (the year of its founding) through 1711 and a later section of minutes extending from 1737 through 1750. They also include some later correspondence of the Archbishops of Canterbury relating to overseas (chiefly American) affairs. In this last group, the most important documents are those relating to the conferring of the episcopate on the Protestant Episcopal Church in the United States after the Revolution.

The early minutes and correspondence were probably deposited with the president of the society, Archbishop Tenison, before the organization had any headquarters of its own. They cover the formative years of the S.P.G., which were also the formative years of modern missions. It is not always realized how innovative is the (until lately) generally accepted modern practice of supporting missionary work through voluntary societies which usually have their headquarters in, and derive most of their support from, countries remote from those in which their work is carried on. The first such society, in the non-Roman Catholic world, was the Corporation for the Propagation of the Gospel of Jesus Christ in New England, chartered by the Long Parliament in 1649. The S.P.G. was the second and, with its broader area of activity, was probably the first to encounter many of the problems of overseas administration and to set important precedents in solving them. Anyone studying these documents with a background in missionary history can readily recognize this process at work. To take a single example, the society, in its early optimism, appointed its missionaries for three years, hoping that local support would be sufficient at the end of that period. Finding that the actual result was to leave its missionaries without support, it adopted a rule that missionaries should serve during the society's pleasure, which ordinarily meant until they died, resigned, or were dismissed for misconduct or neglect of duty. The problem of mission weaning remains unsolved, with disastrous results in revolutionary situations.

Missionary history is only one of the fields in which the documents are important. They provide a basic source for the social history of the American colonies in the early eighteenth century and furnish significant information about the history of Great Britain and the European Continent in the same period. The second set of minutes, in addition to illuminating the work of the society at a slightly later period, have an important bearing on the educational history of the American colonies and, in particular, the West

Indies, for they give an account of the society's actions in the founding of Codrington College in Barbadoes.

The aim of the present work, as of my calendar of the Fulham Papers, is to enable any researcher to locate readily any information which the documents may have in his field of interest. For this purpose, the effort has been made to note in the summaries all significant facts supplied by the document summarized. The papers have been arranged for binding (which it is hoped funds may become available to complete) and numbered by leaves. The numbers are shown in the margin of the summaries. There are two indexes. The first is a name and subject index to the summaries, but keyed to the original documents. The second is an index of names appearing in the papers but not mentioned in the summaries. Experience with a similar index provided for the Fulham Papers has shown that researchers may find even this limited information about a person in whom they are interested useful. A reference to the relevent summary will show the nature of the document to which the name is attached, and this is often enough to indicate the significance of its presence. For example, take such an entry as: 'Desbrow, Henry, xiv. 185, 265'. A glance at the summaries shows that both references are to lists of scholars supplied by a school-master in Westchester, N.Y. In other cases it may be necessary to consult the original document.

The papers have been microfilmed and, when publication of the calendar has been arranged, positives of the film will be available for purchase by libraries or others who may be interested.

Abstracts of correspondence are attached to the earlier minutes (1701–11). As the originals of these letters are in the correspondence section, and are summarized there, it was not thought necessary to summarize them here. Abstracts of missionary reports (but not of general correspondence) are appended to the later minutes (1737–50). As the originals of these are not in the present collection, any matters of general interest mentioned in them are noted in the summaries of the minutes. Most of them provide only parochial information. For the benefit of those interested in local records, all the reports are listed at the end of the summaries for volume v (p. 32) and their location shown, both under the names of the reporting clergymen and of their parishes.

Identifying dates during the first quarter of the year presents something of a problem under the Julian calendar (which applies to all but the latest documents in the collection), because of uncertainty as to whether the year began on 1 January or the Feast of the Annunciation. Frequently both years are indicated (e.g. 1708/9). In that case, the later year is the one that agrees with modern usage and which is in sequence with the subsequent dates for that year. When only one year has been shown, I have, with some misgivings, taken it as given, but added a notation when subsequent references show that it is really the year following.

The same name is often spelt differently in different documents. In the summaries, I use the spelling in the particular document being abstracted. In the indexes, where some standardization is necessary, I give preference to the spelling in actual signatures, if there are any. Otherwise, I adopt the spelling that seems to be used most often.

In addition to letters received, the correspondence includes copies of many of Secretary Chamberlayne's outgoing letters. These are fair copies which he evidently made or had made for the files, but there is always a possibility of accidental deviation from the letters actually sent. They are, therefore, designated as 'copy' in parenthesis following the date. In the correspondence relating to the consecration of American bishops there are fair copies of letters to and from Granville Sharp, evidently made for the benefit of Archbishop Moore.

In a few cases there are what appear to be original drafts of letters to be sent. These are identified by the word 'draft'. Most of the letters from Europe in volume ix, and a few from non-English-speaking correspondents in the American colonies, are in languages other than English. Secretary Chamberlayne provided translations for the most important of these, or had them made. (As he was a noted linguist, it seems probable that the translations are his own.) Other letters appear only in the original language. In every case, the original language is shown in parenthesis. If there is a translation, that is indicated also.

In index 1, letters from a person or place (and documents from a colony) are listed first, and letters to a person second. Other sub-headings are arranged in order of first reference, in accordance with standard practice. All the minutes have lists of attending members at the beginning. Their names are included in index 2, but where they appear so often as to indicate regular attendance over a period covered by a volume, or a large part of it, I have indicated the fact by an asterisk (*) following the volume number, as to list each attendance would multiply references without providing any additional information. A similar device has been used in referring to the numerous notes and vouchers bearing the names of Secretary Chamberlayne and the treasurer, John Hodges, in volume vi.

The letters in the correspondence section (vols. vii to xvii) are arranged by geographic division and by date within each division. Volumes vii and viii contain letters from the British Isles and volume ix contains those from the European Continent, plus a few relating to China and India. Volume x is composed of letters and documents relating to the American colonies or the United States, but not identified with a particular colony or state. The remaining documents are arranged by colony or state, the continental colonies first and then the West Indies. The provinces within each group are in alphabetical order.

The four men who, as shown by these documents, provided the society with its active leadership during its formative years were: the Archbishop of Canterbury, Thomas Tenison; the Bishop of London, Henry Compton; its first secretary, John Chamberlayne; and its first treasurer, John Hodges. To describe Archbishop Tenison as the first president of the S.P.G. is to understate his role. He was, next to Thomas Bray, its principal founder and its powerful backer in high places. He continued to provide active leadership throughout his life, whereas, so far as can be judged from these documents, Bray's active interest did not continue long after the founding. It is probably inaccurate to describe Tenison, as is sometimes done, as a Latitudinarian, but his advocacy of a conciliatory approach to Protestant dissenters caused him to be distrusted by the High Church party. This distrust, strengthened, perhaps, by the high favour that he had enjoyed with her bro⁻her-in-law, led to his being discountenanced by Queen Anne to such an extent that he gave up attendance at court. It is possible that this fact lessened royal support for the society, though the Queen did authorize some special collections for it, and presented church furnishings to some of its early missions.

Bishop Compton was the first Bishop of London to make any systematic attempt to exercise his supposed colonial jurisdiction, acting under an Order in Council that he believed to have been issued by James II. From evidence in the Fulham Papers, I am inclined to think that his efforts in this respect were less ineffective than those of any of his successors, including Bishop Gibson, who obtained a formal commission from George II. His interest in and active support of the society are shown both by the minutes and by his numerous notes to the secretary, preserved in volumes vii and viii.

John Chamberlayne, the first secretary, as the society's chief administrative officer, was probably more responsible than any other one person for shaping its operational pattern. Born in 1666, he was a younger son of Edward Chamberlayne, author of a work, well known in its day, on *The Present State of England*. He studied at Trinity College, Oxford, and the University of Leyden, where he specialized in languages, of which he was reputed to have mastered sixteen. In addition to continuing his father's work, he translated Brandt's *History of the Reformation in the Low Countries* and some other continental works into English and contributed articles to the *Transactions of the Royal Society*, of which he was a fellow. His earliest work, published in 1685, was in somewhat lighter vein, being devoted to *The Manner of Making Tea, Coffee, and Chocolate*. . . . He held a number of posts at court, which explains why some of his letters in the collection are dated from Windsor Castle, though most are dated from his residence in Petty France, Westminster. This information is from the *Dictionary of National Biography*, which also mentions that he was first secretary of the Society for the Promotion of Christian Knowledge, a post which he held only briefly, but seems to have been ignorant of his important and formative work with the S.P.G.

His correspondence reveals him as a dedicated and hard-working, if slightly pedestrian administrator, coping as best he could with the then novel problem of directing missions from a distance. He certainly meant to be fair, but his zeal for maintaining the standards of the society probably led him to be occasionally unjust to missionaries under accusation. In a letter to John Bartow, minister in Westchester, N.Y., while admitting that a charge against him has proven unfounded, he refuses to name his accuser and warns him that the society has spies all around him of whom he knows not. The strictness of his moral views is also suggested by a letter resigning his post as justice of the peace in Westminster because his fellow justices were not sufficiently zealous in repressing prostitution. Like Archbishop Tenison, he favoured a conciliatory attitude toward Protestant dissenters, and sometimes rebuked missionaries, such as John Talbot of Burlington, N.J. and John Thomas of Hempstead, N.Y., for showing too much zeal for their conversion. Some letters betray the fact that he shared the then widespread English prejudice against the Scotch, though some of the best missionaries were of that nationality. He seems to have had friendlier feelings toward the Welsh. Did he have Welsh connections? The available sources do not say.

I have been unable to find any biographical information concerning the treasurer, John Hodges. His name does not even appear in the index to either Pascoe's *Two Hundred Years of the S.P.G.* or Thompson's *Into All Lands*, yet he certainly performed a major service in organizing the society's finances. Two biographical scraps can be garnered from the documents. Notes exchanged between him and Secretary Chamberlayne show that they were cousins, and correspondence relating to the posting of his bond indicates that his brother, Danvers Hodges, was a country gentleman of substantial property.

It is a pleasure to acknowledge the help of many in the preparation of this work. E. G. W. Bill, Esq., Librarian of Lambeth Palace Library, first suggested the project, and has given me friendly support throughout. The Right Reverend Stephen F. Bayne, S.T.D., sometime Executive Officer of the Anglican Communion, obtained a generous gift which enabled us to begin work. The (American) Church Historical Society, through its President, the Reverend Professor Massey H. Shepherd, Ph.D., has made a generous gift to aid in publication, and sponsored us in an unsuccessful attempt to obtain a Federal grant.

18–19. 21 Jan. 1705. (Committee.) Approved Auchinleek for South Carolina, but left parochial appointment to governor.

20. 31 Jan. 1705. (Committee.)

21–2. 1 Feb. 1705.

23–4. 11 Feb. 1705. (Committee.) A report by Mr. Thomas that an act of South Carolina subjected rectors to removal by lay commissioners referred to Archbishop of Canterbury and Bishop of London.

25–7. 15 Feb. 1705.

28. 18 Feb. 1705 (Committee.)

29–30. 20 Feb. 1705. Meeting of subcommittee to prepare a new system of accounting.

31–2. Duplicate of 29–30.

33–4. 25 Feb. 1705. (Committee.) Recommends that society consider increasing allowance for Mr. Brooke as he reports that he has no local support and Talbot confirms this.

35–6. 28 Feb. 1705. Advance one year's salary (£30) to Mr. Rudman. Gift of books to Mr. Rea, appointed by Bishop of London to Jamaica.

37–40. Duplicate of 35–6 with committee report appended.

41. 4 Mar. 1705. (Committee.) Recommends some gratuity to Mr. Huddleston, schoolmaster in New York, but hold it improper to grant an annual salary to a schoolmaster not employed by society. Renders opinion that £60 is due to Mr. Jackson.

42. 6 Mar. 1705. (Committee.)

43. 11 Mar. 1705. (Committee.)

44. 13 Mar. 1705. (Committee.)

45–6. 15 Mar. 1705. Committee appointed at request of Archbishop of Canterbury to meet with him to consider destruction of college in Virginia. Gift of books to Cyprian and Paul Appia of Piedmont.

47. Committee reports to above meeting.

48. 18 Mar. 1705. (Committee.) Richard Townsend recommended to Bishop of London for deacon's orders, having volunteered to go as schoolmaster to the colonies. Committee recommends that missionaries be required to give exact account of local contributions. Recommends sending Bibles, Prayer Books, and tracts to Long Island. On information from clergy in New York that William Bradford was printing Book of Common Prayer and Tate and Brady, committee recommends that he be requested to send over a specimen. Reports request of Mr. Bartow for payment of salary. Recommends that Mr. Crawford be allowed to move from Dover Hundred to Hopewell for reasons of health.

S.P.G. PAPERS

VOLUME I

MINUTES, 1701–1708

NOTE. Some of the minutes are endorsed as of the 'society' and some as of the 'committee'. In the latter case the word is inserted in parenthesis before the summary.

In abstracting the minutes the effort has been made to take note of all missionary appointments and actions affecting missions, but measures deemed to be of a routine or procedural nature are not noted.

1–2. 27 Feb. 1701. Bishop of London asked to recommend a missionary for Narragansett. Governor designate of New Jersey asked to divide colony into parishes. George Keith granted £200 per annum travelling allowance and immediate payment of £50.

3–4. 8 July 1701.

5. 10 July 1701.

6–7. 18 July 1701.

8. 28 Apr. 1702.

9. 22 Mar. 1703. (Committee.) Mr. Smith told that if he refuses appointment to North Carolina, he must wait for another. William Vesey asked to supervise work of Elias Neau as catechist in New York. John Thomas, formerly assistant to Evan Evans in Philadelphia, appointed to Hempstead, N.Y.

10. 21 Jan. 1703/4.

11–12. 11 Feb. 1704.

13. 14 Mar. 1703/4. (Committee.) Gift of books to William Johnson, appointed by Bishop of London to Jamaica, W. I. Elias Neau granted £15 for catechisms.

14–15. 14 May 1704. Agreed to repay £20 advanced by Bishop of London to Mr. Barclay, sent to Braintree. Voted £50 allowance for Mr. Lockier, minister at Newport. Christopher Bridge attended and reported on his dispute with Samuel Myles in Boston. Granted £10 to Mr. Clubb, schoolmaster in Philadelphia.

16–17. 18 Jan. 1705. Received letter from Samuel Myles introducing Gersham Rawlins, who has come to England for orders. Preliminary action on Andrew Auchinleek as missionary to South Carolina.

49–50. Duplicate of 48.

51. 7 May 1705. (Committee.) Receives testimonials of William Guy.

52. 14 May 1705. Preliminary action on James (Jacob) Rice and Thomas Lloyd as missionaries to Newfoundland and Bermuda respectively.

53. 21 May 1705. (Committee.) Further action on Rice and Guy.

54. 4 June 1705. (Committee.) Requires further testimonials of Rice.

55. 11 June 1705. (Committee.)

56–7. 15 June 1705. Further testimonials required of Guy.

58. 18 June 1705. (Committee.) Gift of books to Edward Brice, appointed by Bishop of London to a school in Barbadoes.

59. 2 July 1705. (Committee.) Proposal to establish a Protestant minister at Leghorn referred to society.

60–1. 20 July 1705. Guy appointed to Narragansett and Muirson to Rye.

62. 23 July 1705. (Committee.)

63. 6 Aug. 1705. (Committee.)

64–5. 17 Aug. 1705.

66–7. 21 Aug. 1705. Samuel Thomas presented testimonial and letter from Governor N. Johnson of South Carolina, and reported donation from Col. Nicholson to buy books for parishes in S.C.

68. 14 Oct. 1705.

69. 5 Nov. 1705. (Committee.) Gift of books to Mr. Trockerman appointed by Bishop of London to Leeward Islands.

70. 6 Nov. 1705. (Committee.) Recommends allowance to Andrew Rudman. Directs Dunn and Auchinleek to obtain further testimonials.

71. 12 Nov. 1705. Dr. Le Jau presented a paper concerning religion in the Caribee Islands.

72–3. 16 Nov. 1705. Grants £50 (third year) allowance to Samuel Thomas in South Carolina and £60 to John Talbot in New Jersey.

74. 19 Nov. 1705. (Committee.) Dr. Le Jau granted £50 allowance at Goose Creek, S.C., and £33 to aid in moving his family. William Dunn directed to produce additional testimonials, and recommended to Stone River, S.C. with an allowance of £25, if they are satisfactory. Auchinleek recommended to North Carolina.

75. 10 Dec. 1705. (Committee.)

76–7. 21 Dec. 1705. Grants £50 to Samuel Thomas if he remains at his station in South Carolina; £20 to Thomas Hassel as catechist and schoolmaster in Charleston.

78. 31 Dec. 1705.

79. 7 Jan. 1705/6. (Committee.)

80. 13 Jan. 1706. (Committee.)

81. 20 Jan. 1706. (Committee.) On receiving petition of Robert Keith, directs inquiry into support of ministers in Maryland. Receives testimonials from Robert Maule.

82. 27 Jan. 1706. (Committee.) Authorizes payment of 'some part' of half year's salary to Cordiner.

83–4. 31 Jan. 1706. Robert Maule appointed missionary at £50 a year.

85. 10 Feb. 1706. (Committee.)

86. 3 Mar. 1706. (Committee.) Recommends that Bishop of London appoint Le Jau to Charleston, if vacant, and send Robert Maule to Goose Creek. Grants Le Jau an advance of half year's salary to move his family.

87–8. 25 Mar. 1706. (Committee.) Proposes to transfer Talbot to North Carolina and Moor from Albany to Burlington.

89–90. 28 Mar. 1706.

91. 1 Apr. 1706. (Committee.)

92. 8 Apr. 1706. (Committee.)

93–4. 19 Apr. 1706. Townsend appointed Schoolmaster on Staten Island with allowance of £20. £5 granted to Rawlins.

95. 22 Apr. 1706. (Committee.)

96. 29 Apr. 1706. (Committee.) Rules that it would not be proper to grant an allowance to Bondet in New York unless he conformed to the Church of England.

97. 6 May 1706. (Committee.) Receiving reports of great need of ministers in North Carolina, recommends that next applicants for missionary appointments be sent there. Recommends gift of communion service and Prayer Books to Rye.

98–9. 17 May 1706. Gift of £10 to Bondet. Archbishop of Canterbury asked to urge Lord Cornbury to secure payment of arrears of salary from Province of New York.

100. 20 May 1706. (Committee.)

101. 27 May 1706. (Committee.)

102. 3 June 1706. (Committee.)

103. 10 June 1706. (Committee.) Refers to society a memorial of Samuel Thomas refuting charges brought against him in a pamphlet written by Marston.

104. 17 June 1706. (Committee.)

105–6. 21 June 1706.

107. 24 June 1706. (Committee.)

108. 1 July 1706. (Committee.) In the interest of Cleator, appointed school-master at Rye, the Bishop of London is asked if royal bounty applies to school-masters.

109. 8 July 1706. (Committee.) Learns that bounty has been granted to Cleator. Adopts an instruction that schoolmasters teach children of Indians and Negroes when they have an opportunity.

110. 15 July 1706. (Committee.) Receives testimonials of Lord.

111–12. 19 July 1706. Archbishop of Canterbury has agreed to take care of Rawlins for a year, placing him under Dr. Woodward. Committee reports that Robert Lord's testimonials have not been found satisfactory.

113–14. Duplicate of 111–12.

115. 22 July 1706. (Committee.) Further testimonials required of Thomas Jenkins.

116. 12 Aug. 1706. (Committee.)

117–18. 16 Aug. 1706. Jackson granted £5 or £10 for relief of want.

119. 7 Sept. 1706. (Committee.) Votes to remove Christopher Bridge from Boston to Newport.

120. 16 Sept. 1706. (Committee.) Recommends that society ask Bishop of London to appoint Black as successor to Bridge in Boston.

121–2. 20 Sept. 1706. Society confirms above proposals. Votes £10 for relief of Jackson and approves payment of £50 salary to Bartow.

123. 14 Oct. 1706. (Committee.) Receives recommendation from Bishop of London to send Black to Narragansett and Roberts to Salem.

124–5. 18 Oct. 1706.

126. 28 Oct. 1706. (Committee.) Receives some proposals from Samuel Weale concerning administration of society's funds and testimonials from Cordiner and Black.

127. 4 Nov. 1706. (Committee.) Refers Weale's proposals to society.

128. 11 Nov. 1706. (Committee.)

129–30. 15 Nov. 1706. Appoints Black to Narragansett and directs committee to ask Bishop of London what other posts are vacant.

131–2. Duplicate of 129–30.

133. 18 Nov. 1706. (Committee.)

134. 25 Nov. 1706. (Committee.) Receives testimonials of Thomas Jenkyns.

135. 27 Nov. 1706. (Committee.)

136. 9 Dec. 1706. (Committee.) Receives testimonials from Robinson.

137. 16 Dec. 1706. (Committee.)

138–9. 20 Dec. 1706. Votes £10 to Talbot on learning the Bishop of Gloucester had deprived him of his living in that diocese. Directs Mr. Stubbs to ask the bishop the reason for his action. Jenkins appointed to Apoquimininck. Votes £10 present subsistence to Lubominsky, formerly Roman Catholic missionary in China, now a proselyte. Cordiner appointed missionary, post to be determined.

140. 30 Dec. 1706. (Committee.)

141–2. 16 Jan. 1707. Vestry of Pascotank, N.C. to be informed that society has anticipated their request by sending two ministers into colony. (Note: It seems probable, from later minutes, that this should be dated 1708, but 1707 is the date shown.)

143–4. 17 Jan. 1706/7. Reply of Bishop of Gloucester and rejoinder of Talbot considered. Apparently the issue was one of residence (cf. vii. 232). Talbot is asked if he will consider returning to service of the society. He also presents a petition for colonial bishops. Archbishop of Canterbury is asked to present Jackson's case to the Lord Keeper.

145. 19 Jan. 1707. (Committee.)

146. 9 Feb. 1707. (Committee.) Receives letter from Moore, reporting his arrest by Lord Cornbury.

147–8. 14 Feb. 1706/7. Receives report from committee on case of Robert Keith, who asked help on ground that his Maryland salary of 25,000 lb. of tobacco was only worth £35 sterling.

149–50. 17 Feb. 1706/7. (Committee.) Asks society to rule on case of Auchinleek, who has gone to Bermuda instead of to Carolina as directed. Decides that Daillé, French minister in Boston, is not eligible for employment, as his congregation did not conform, and he had not been sent by society.

151–2. 21 Feb. 1706/7.

153. 24 Feb. 1706/7. (Committee.)

154. 1 Mar. 1707. (Committee.)

155–6. 7 Mar. 1706/7. (Committee.) Cordiner allowed £20 to transport his family. Maule appointed to Elizabeth and Rahway.

157. 8 Mar. 1707. (Committee.)

158. 15 Mar. 1707. (Committee.) Recommends suspending salary of Robert Keith for failing to comply with the society's condition.

159. 17 Mar. 1706/7. Gift of books to Edward Shanks, appointed by the Bishop of London to Jamaica.

160–1. 21 Mar. 1706/7. Dismisses Auchinleek and approves committee's decision concerning Daillé.

162–3. Duplicate of committee's report with society's action noted.

164. 24 Mar. 1706/7. (Committee.)

165. 31 Mar. 1707. (Committee.) Recommends that Black be sent to Sussex, Del., as Bishop of London has appointed Bridge to Narragansett.

166–7. 3 Apr. 1707. Lubominski held to be no longer worthy of the society's encouragement. Keith allowed £50 to supplement his salary. (Probably refers to Robert Keith.)

168–9. Duplicate of committee's report.

170. 7 Apr. 1707. (Committee.)

171–2. 18 Apr. 1707. Talbot re-employed on condition of returning to Burlington at first opportunity. Black appointed to Sussex. Moore to Hopewell and Maule to South Carolina.

173. 21 Apr. 1707. (Committee.)

174. 28 Apr. 1707. (Committee.)

175. 5 May 1707. (Committee.)

176. 12 May 1707. (Committee.)

177–8. 16 May 1707.

179–80. Duplicate of 187–8.

181. 26 May 1707. (Committee.) Recommends appointment of Alexander Wood to North Carolina, if his testimonials are satisfactory.

182–3. 30 May 1707. Bridge's appointment changed from Newport to Narragansett. Half-year's salary granted to widow of Samuel Thomas.

184–5. Duplicate of 182–3.

186. 16 June 1707. (Committee.)

187–8. 20 June 1707. Cordiner granted half year's salary because of his difficulty in obtaining passage.

189–90. Duplicate of 187–8.

191. 23 June 1707. (Committee.) Recommends vacating appointment of Richard Townsend as schoolmaster on Staten Island, as he has not gone there.

192. 30 June 1707. (Committee.) Recommends payment of £25 to Mrs. Thomas.

193. 7 July 1707. (Committee.)

194. 14 July 1707. (Committee.)

195–6. 18 July 1707. Townsend suspended.

197. 21 July 1707. Gideon Johnston directed to produce additional testimonials.

198. 28 July 1707. (Committee.)

199. 11 Aug. 1707. (Committee.)

200–1. 15 Aug. 1707.

202. 1 Sept. 1707. (Committee.) Francis Milne and William Glen, recommended by Bishop of London, directed to secure required testimonials. Johnston's testimonials approved.

203. 8 Sept. 1707. (Committee.) Recommends Black and Jenkins to Society's consideration because of their difficulty in securing passage.

204. 15 Sept. 1707. (Committee.) Recommends Johnston for appointment. Directs Gordon, recommended by Bishop of London, to obtain testimonials.

205. 22 Sept. 1707. (Committee.) Receives testimonials from James Adams.

206. 29 Sept. 1707. (Committee.) Informs two candidates that society's funds do not allow any new appointments.

207. 6 Oct. 1707. (Committee.)

208–9. 17 Oct. 1707. Agrees to repay £50 advanced by Evan Evans to Andrew Rudman.

210. 27 Oct. 1707. (Committee.)

211. 3 Nov. 1707. (Committee.)

212. 17 Nov. 1707. (Committee.)

213–14. 21 Nov. 1707. Votes £50 to Gideon Johnston, appointed rector of Charleston.

215. 1 Dec. 1707. (Committee.)

216. 8 Dec. 1707. (Committee.)

217–18. 19 Dec. 1707. Adopts standing order (to be confirmed at next meeting) that treasurer should not pay bills drawn by missionaries before their salary was due.

219. 26 Jan. 1707/8. (Committee.)

220–1. 11 Feb. 1707/8. Letter from Picket and Turretin of Geneva, asking aid in securing toleration for Protestant inhabitants of Prageles Valley, lately conquered by Duke of Savoy, referred to archbishops and Bishop of London. Inquiry ordered into leaving of their posts by Gordon, Nichols, Ross, and Jenkins.

222–4. 18 Feb. 1708.

225–6. 20 Feb. 1707 (8).

227. 23 Feb. 1707/8. (Committee.)

228–9. 5 Mar. 1707/8. Votes £10 to Cordiner, taken prisoner by the French. Bishop of London reports appointment of Harris as assistant at Boston.

230–1. 14 Mar. 1708. (Committee.) Appoints Vaughan to Elizabeth and other stations in New Jersey. (In view of 261 and 264–8, this date is probably 1709.)

232–3. 18 Mar. 1708.

234–5. 19 Mar. 1707/8. Discontinues salary of Robert Keith for failing to comply with conditions. Continues Honeyman's case on offer of Col. Nicholson to allow him £30 pending investigation.

236. 22 Mar. 1707/8. (Committee.) On offer of special contribution from Col. Nicholson, agrees to recommend sending a missionary to Connecticut.

237. 5 Apr. 1708. (Committee.)

238–9. 16 April. 1708.

240. 17 May 1708. (Committee.)

241–2. 21 May 1708. Votes £20 relief to William Cordiner, who was taken prisoner by the French while trying to get to the plantations.

243. 31 May 1708. (Committee.)

244–5. 4 June 1708.

246–7. Duplicate of 244–5.

248–9. 14 June 1708. (Committee.) Decides that Honeyman has been cleared of charges and that Bridge has unjustly driven him out of his church.

250–1. 18 June 1708. Votes to transfer Muirson from Rye to Connecticut.

252. 28 June 1708. (Committee.)

253–4. 1 July 1708. Secretary directed to write Bridge that his salary would be stopped unless he returns to Narragansett.

255–6. 13 July 1708. (Committee.)

257–8. 16 July 1708.

259–60. 20 Aug. 1708.

261. 13 Sept. 1708. (Committee.) Receives testimonials from Edward Vaughan.

262–3. 17 Sept. 1708.

264–5. 11 Oct. 1708. (Committee.) Reports that Vaughan fulfills all conditions of employment, except that he is not yet 24 years old.

266–8. 15 Oct. 1708. Vaughan notified that he would be accepted as soon as he has satisfied canonical requirements.

269–70. 15 Nov. 1708. (Committee.) Receives request from governor and council of South Carolina for aid in securing ratification of revised establishment act.

271–2. 13 Dec. 1708. (Committee.) Recommends Marsden for appointment by society on learning that he has voluntarily resigned church in Charleston to Johnston.

273–4. 17 Dec. 1708. Allowances of £50 each granted to Wood and Marsden in South Carolina.

VOLUME II

MINUTES, 1708–1711

1–2. 17 Jan. 1708/9. (Committee.) Votes £40 to Vandereyghen to aid in publishing Spanish New Testament.

3–6. 20 Jan. 1709. On recommendation of Archbishop of Canterbury, votes £10 to Gignillat to aid him in transporting himself to South Carolina. Votes £50 for one year's salary to Beys as minister in Harlem, N.Y., hoping that his congregation will conform to Church of England. Gov. Bass asked to give information about lands in New Jersey which he has advised society to purchase. Receives offer of Micajah Perry to donate tenth of his lands in New Jersey. Votes gift of books and £10 to William Guthrie appointed by Bishop of London to Jamaica.

7–9. 21 Jan. 1708/9.

10–11. 30 Jan. 1709 (Committee.)

12–14. 6 Feb. 1709. (Committee.) Votes £20 to Maule for loss of effects.

15. 7 Feb. 1708/9. (Committee.)

16–17. 13 Feb. 1709. (Committee.) Recommends appointment of Humphreys as schoolmaster in Burlington as proposed by Talbot.

18. 14 Feb. 1708/9. (Committee.)

19–20. 17 Feb. 1709.

21–2. 20 Feb. 1709. (Committee.)

23–4. 4 Apr. 1709. (Committee.) Receives testimonials from James Reynolds. Informs Samuel Wallis that he cannot be employed by society until ordained in Church of England.

25–6. 11 Apr. 1709. (Committee.) Wallis, having been ordained by Bishop of London, directed to produce testimonials. Reynolds recommended for appointment.

27–8. 15 Apr. 1709. Death of Muirson reported. Vaughan appointed to New Jersey and Reynolds to Rye, N.Y.

29–30. 9 May 1709. (Committee.) Receives testimonials from Edward Hudson.

31–2. 16 May 1709. (Committee.) Hudson is rejected because of unfavourable report on his reading of the service and preaching. Nichols has moved from Chester, Pa., to Maryland. Salary to be paid to date of departure.

33–5. 20 May 1709. Club appointed to Trinity Church, Oxford, Pa., succeeding Rudman, deceased. Efforts made to prevent sailing of Reynolds because of reports unfavourable to his character.

36–7. 30 May 1709. (Committee.) Refers applications of Robert MacNoe and Andrew Boyd to society, because of their youth and the fact that they are not yet ordained. Directs Jacob Rice to produce testimonials.

38–9. 3 June 1709. Bondet appointed missionary to New Rochelle, N.Y.

40–1. 13 June 1709. (Committee.) Robert Sinclair directed to produce testimonials.

42–3. 17 June 1709. As Reynolds had sailed before he could be stopped, secretary is directed to write Governors Lovelace of New York and Dudley of New England, informing them of his dismissal.

44–5. 11 July 1709. (Committee.) Receives testimonials from Sinclair.

46–7. 15 July 1709. Thomas Hassel, schoolmaster in South Carolina, having returned for priest's orders, is voted an allowance of £50 on condition of his returning to South Carolina.

48–9. 8 Aug. 1709. (Committee.) Bridge appointed to Rye, N.Y.

50–1. 15 Aug. 1709. (Committee.) Recommends Sinclair as missionary to Newcastle, Del. Receives testimonials from Urmiston.

52–5. 19 Aug. 1709. Urmiston appointed to North Carolina, replacing Gordon who is sent to Chester, Pa. Sinclair appointed to Newcastle.

56. 12 Sept. 1709. (Committee.) Declines to consider case of Rice, as he was not in employ of society while in Newfoundland.

57–60. 16 Sept. 1709. Clauses in North Carolina establishment act allowing dismissal of ministers by vestries referred to Archbishop of Canterbury. Difficulty encountered in appointing Gordon to Newcastle, as Ross is already there, though his allowance has been stopped. Appointment of Maule to St. John's Parish, S.C., approved.

61–2. 10 Oct. 1709. (Committee.) Recommends a gift to Muirson's widow.

63–6. 17 Oct. 1709. (Committee.) Recommends sending French prayer books to de la Pierre, French minister recently arrived in South Carolina.

67–73. 21 Oct. 1709. Missionaries to be notified that their salaries will be stopped unless they report to secretary twice a year, in accordance with previous order. Thomas Barclay appointed missionary and schoolmaster at Albany and Schenectady, N.Y.

74–5. 7 Nov. 1709. (Committee.)

76–7. 14 Nov. 1709. (Committee.)

78–9. 18 Nov. 1709.

80–3. 28 Nov. 1709. (Committee.) Recommends paying £25 to Muirson's widow. Receives testimonials from Thomas Poyer.

84–7. 2 Dec. 1709.

88. 12 Dec. 1709. (Committee.) Recommends ordination of John Frederic Hager, so that he can be sent as minister with the Palatines who are emigrating to New York. Recommends appointment of Poyer to Jamaica, N.Y., on learning of death of Urquhart. Reports that there is no evidence that Dutch congregation at Harlem, N.Y., wants Henry Beys sent them as a minister of the Church of England, and that he has failed to clear himself of charges brought before the Classis of Amsterdam by the town of Kingston.

89–90. 16 Dec. 1709. Votes £50 allowance to Hager.

91–5. 26 Dec. 1709. (Committee.) Recommends appointment of Gordon to Chester, Pa.

96–9. 30 Dec. 1709. Directs secretary to inform vestry of Apoquimininck that Black has been named missionary there.

100–1. 16 Jan. 1709/10 (Committee.) Recommends temporary appointment of Beys to Harlem.

102. 22 Jan. 1710. (Committee.)

103–4. 29 Jan. 1710. (Committee.)

105–6. 1 Feb. 1710.

107–8. 3 Feb. 1710. (Committee.)

109–10. 3 Feb. 1709/10.

111–12. 10 Feb. 1709/10. Beys sent to Harlem.

113–14. 13 Feb. 1710. (Committee.)

115–16. 27 Feb. 1709/10. (Committee.) Permits Mackenzie to move from Staten Island, N.Y., to Stratford, Conn.

117–18. 3 Mar. 1709/10.

119–20. 6 Mar. 1709/10. (Committee.)

121–2. 13 Mar. 1709/10. (Committee.)

123–4. 17 Mar. 1709/10.

125–6. 17 Apr. 1710. (Committee.)

127–8. 21 Apr. 1710. Appoints a special committee to consider petition of Indians for missionaries.

129-30. 24 Apr. 1710. (Committee.) Receives testimonials from Robert Griffith, recommended by Bishop of London for Apoquimininck.

131-4. 28 Apr. 1710. Receives deputation of Indian sachems. Approves report of special committee recommending sending two missionaries to Indians and general policy of giving priority to conversion of the heathen.

135-6. 15 May 1710. (Committee.)

137-8. 19 May 1710. Resolutions of previous meeting (131-4) concerning Indian missions referred to committee.

139. 5 June 1710. (Committee.)

140-1. 12 June 1710. (Committee.)

142-3. 16 June 1710. Appointment of Griffith rejected because of objections of Archbishop of Canterbury to some expressions in a pamphlet of his which the archbishop regarded as tending to popery.

144-5. 3 July 1710. (Committee.)

146-7. 17 July 1710. (Committee.) Receives letter from Maule reporting destruction of his house by fire.

148-9. 21 July 1710. Committee reports death of Urquhart.

150. 31 July 1710. (Committee.)

151-8. 14 Aug. 1710. (Committee.) Received testimonials from Jacob Henderson.

159-60. 18 Aug. 1710.

161. 28 Aug. 1710. (Committee.)

162. 11 Sept. 1710. (Committee.)

163-4. 15 Sept. 1710. Thomas Halliday appointed to take over some of the stations served by Vaughan in New Jersey. Allowance granted to Wood, rector of Ashley River Parish, S.C. Benjamin Dennis appointed schoolmaster in Goose Creek Parish, S.C. Jacob Henderson appointed to Dover Hundred, Del.

165-6. 9 Oct. 1710. (Committee.)

167-8. 16 Oct. 1710. (Committee.)

169-76. 20 Oct. 1710.

177-8. 6 Nov. 1710. (Committee.)

179-80. 10 Nov. 1710. £10 each voted for two schoolmasters employed by Mackenzie on Staten Island.

181. 13 Nov. 1710. (Committee.) Recommends restoration of Ross to society's employment, as he left Newcastle before receiving society's order against removals.

182-5. 17 Nov. 1710.

186. 27 Nov. 1710. (Committee.)

187–91. 15 Dec. 1710. Restores Ross to society's employment. Receives report of removal of Black to Virginia.

192–3. 24 Dec. 1710. (Committee.)

194–5. 11 Dec. 1710. (Committee.)

196. 18 Dec. 1710. (Committee.)

197–201. 19 Dec. 1710. Select committee appointed to deal with Codrington bequest.

202. 1 Jan. 1710/11. (Committee.)

203–4. 5 Jan. 1710–11. Reminded by Indians of promise to send a missionary.

205. 8 Jan. 1710/11. (Committee.)

206–8. 15 Jan. 1710/11. (Committee.)

209–12. 19 Jan. 1710/11. Petition from officers forming council of war in Annapolis Royal, N.S., for a missionary to Indians in that colony.

213–14. 26 Jan. 1710/11.

215–16. 5 Feb. 1710/11. (Committee.) Concerned with measures for securing the estate that Gen. Codrington had left to the society in Barbadoes.

217–18. 7 Feb. 1710/11. (Committee.) Concerned with the same.

219–22. 8 Feb. 1710/11. Instructions to John Smalbridge, appointed manager of Codrington estate approved. At request of Archbishop of Canterbury, secretary is directed to furnish the archbishop with a list of missionaries from whom he might select one to be sent to the Indians.

223–4. 16 Feb. 1710/11. Motion of Sir John Philips that society's attorneys be directed to treat slaves on Codrington estate with more than customary humanity referred to committee.

225–6. 26 Feb. 1710/11. (Committee.)

227. 5 Mar. 1710/11. (Committee.)

228–9. 12 Mar. 1710/11. (Committee.)

230–1. 16 Mar. 1710/11. (Committee.)

232–5. 19 Mar. 1710/11.

236–9. 22 Mar. 1710/11. (Committee.) George Ross, appointed missionary to Chester, Pa., has been taken prisoner by the French.

240–1. 26 Mar. 1711. (Committee.)

242–3. 9 Apr. 1711.

244–6. 16 Apr. 1711. (Committee.)

247–52. 20 Apr. 1711.

253. 23 Apr. 1711. (Committee.)

254–5. 30 Apr. 1711. (Committee.)

256–8. 7 May 1711. (Committee.)

259–60. 14 May 1711. (Committee.) Receives testimonials from Theophilus Hill and directs him to produce more.

261–2. 17 May 1711. (Committee.)

263–70. 18 May 1711. Prayer books and tracts to be sent to Le Jau for any of his Negro converts who can read.

271. 28 May 1711. Gratuity of £10 granted to Swedish minister, Erinus Burk, for supply church at Apoquimininck in absence of English minister.

272. 11 June 1711. (Committee.) David Duncan directed to produce testimonials.

273–4. 15 June 1711.

275–8. 18 June 1911. (Committee.)

279–84. 22 June 1711.

VOLUME III

MINUTES, 1711–1712

1. 2 July 1711. (Committee.) Testimonials of David Duncan found insufficient.

2. 16 July 1711. (Committee.)

3–6. 20 July 1711. Because of objections of Archbishop Tenison to Dutch–English prayer book, all copies are to be sent to him to be destroyed, and his advice is sought in preparing another. Henderson allowed to move from Dover to Lewes, Del.

7. 13 Aug. 1711. (Committee.)

8–11. 17 Aug. 1711. Testimonials received from Giles Rainsford. Attorneys report difficulty in obtaining possession of Codrington estate.

12. 20 Aug. 1711. (Committee.)

13. 27 Aug. 1711. (Committee.)

14. 17 Sept. 1711. (Committee.) Rowland Ellis, recommended by Bishop of Bangor as schoolmaster, directed to procure further testimonials.

15–16. 21 Sept. 1711. New edition of Dutch prayer book considered.

19–20. 8 Oct. 1711. (Committee.) Advises Bishop of London that it cannot take any action towards the appointment of Ebenezer Taylor, former dissenting minister from South Carolina, until he is in episcopal orders. Recommends Ellis for appointment and receives testimonials from Daniel Mennadier.

21–2. 15 Oct. 1711. (Committee.)

23–30. 19 Oct. 1711. Appoints a special committee on the society's affairs in Barbados on receiving a letter from the Archbishop of Canterbury expressing concern about them. Rainsford appointed to North Carolina. Ellis named schoolmaster in Burlington. Mennadier appointed to Narragansett.

31. 22 Oct. 1711. (Committee.)

32–9. 2 Nov. 1711. Receives report of committee on Barbadoes and approves draft of agreement with Col. Codrington for surrender of estate.

40. 5 Nov. 1711. (Committee.)

41–2. 12 Nov. 1711. (Committee.) Recommends Ebenezer Taylor for appointment.

43–4. 16 Nov. 1711. Select committee authorized to seal agreement with Col. Codrington's attorneys. Taylor appointed to St. Andrew's Parish, Ashley River, S.C.

45. 19 Nov. 1711. (Committee.)

46–53. Votes £50 allowance to Gideon Johnston on receiving petition from his wife, saying that he could not stay in Charleston without aid. Agrees to provide him with a schoolmaster. Gift of £50 and library to Alexander Adams, rector of Stepney Parish, Md. Barclay granted £15 for an Indian interpreter and £5 for an Indian boy. Halliday admonished, on complaint of Vaughan that his behaviour was indiscreet.

54–5. 3 Dec. 1711. (Committee.)

56. 10 Dec. 1711. (Committee.)

57–62. 21 Dec. 1711. Barbadoes committee reports sealing agreement with Col. Codrington. Maule allowed to move to some other station in South Carolina if governor and rest of the clergy approve. Mennadier appointed to Christ Church, S.C., at his request, instead of Narragansett.

63–71. 31 Dec. 1711. (Committee.) Recommends appointment of Philips and Bishop as missionaries.

72–5. 4 Jan. 1711/12. Agents of Col. Codrington have suggested that society might obtain grant of all of Barbadoes from the Queen. Philips appointed to Stratford.

76–8. 7 Jan. 1711/12. (Committee.) Approves draft of petition to the Queen for Barbadoes.

79–80. 14 Jan. 1711/12. (Committee.) Receives testimonials from William Guy and recommends his appointment as schoolmaster at Charleston if he receives deacon's orders.

81–2. 18 Jan. 1711/12. Barbadoes committee reports its opinion that society has present title to one fourth of the island.

85–8. 25 Jan. 1711/12. Guy appointed. Archbishop of Canterbury asked to obtain a missionary for the Indians as soon as possible, as Col. Nicholson reports that one chapel will be ready in spring.

89–90. 4 Feb. 1711/12. (Committee.)

91–4. 8 Feb. 1711/12.

95–6. 11 Feb. 1711/12. (Committee.)

1736–1739

97–102. 18 Mar. 1736. Committee reports paying £30 to widow of John Fullerton, missionary in South Carolina, and £10 back salary to his administrator. Has asked vestry in Burlington, N.J., to explain discrepancy between their statement of finances and that of the rector, Robert Weyman. People of Newark, N.J., have petitioned for a missionary and John Beach is willing to be transferred there from Newtown, Conn., but society is not in position to erect a new mission. Roe appointed to St. George's Parish, S.C.

103–4. 22 Mar. 1736.

105–14. 20 Jan. 1737. Wetmore reports legal difficulties of Churchmen in Horseneck and Greenwich, Conn., where he has officiated during illness of Henry Caner, missionary at Fairfield. He has started action against the tax collectors, and society agrees to give him what support it can. Declines request of Archibald Cummings for an assistant in Christ Church, Philadelphia. Directs inquiry into conduct of Boyd, missionary in North Carolina. Votes gratuity of £10 to Kilpatrick, missionary in Newfoundland, as poor fishing season has led to a falling off in local contributions. Collin Campbell appointed to Burlington, N.J. Henry Barclay appointed missionary to the Mohawks.

115–20. 17 Feb. 1737. Edward Vaughan, missionary at Elizabeth, N.J., reports death of Robert Weyman, missionary at Burlington, leaving wife and six children unprovided for. Before his death, Weyman had reported that Rowland Ellis. schoolmaster at Burlington, neglected his duties to hold public office. Ellis presented a certificate of wardens and vestry to the performance of his duties. Matter referred back to committee. Henry Jones, minister at Bobavista, N.F., granted £40. Trinity, Boston, asks allowance for Davenport, who is to become their rector.

121–6. Ellis dismissed and inquiry instituted into conduct of schoolmasters elsewhere. John Beach renews appeal for Newark and describes some hardships of Churchmen in Connecticut.

127–30. 15 Apr. 1737. William Johnson of Barbadoes, reports difficulties in instructing slaves. Bishop of London reports removal of Davenport from Scituate and recommends appointment of Brockwell to succeed him. William Davidson, seeking appointment to North Carolina, is informed society is not in position to start any new missions.

131–4. 20 May 1737. Letter from Vesey reporting on Standard and some other missionaries. Brockwell appointed to Scituate.

135–8. 16 Sept. 1737. Letter from Archibald Cummings, reporting on several missionaries. Hughes, missionary at Radnor, Pa., has resigned to go to Barbadoes. Votes £10 to James Houston, schoolmaster at Chester, Pa. Clergy of New York complain that justices of the peace are allowed to perform marriages.

139–44. 21 Oct. 1737. Henry Barclay, catechist to the Mohawks, will be appointed missionary when he has received orders. Morris has resigned his mission at Winnyaw, S.C., while under charges. Thomas Benison is recommended for the post and directed to produce testimonials. Accounts of Codrington plantation considered and some action taken.

145–51. 18 Nov. 1737. Report of Ferdinand John Paris, asked to investigate license issue (135–8): Complaining ministers failed to supply proof of the fact or to specify precisely what change they wanted in the wording of marriage licences.

152–6. 16 Dec. 1737. Brockwell granted leave to move to Salem, Mass., as soon as a replacement can be obtained for Scituate. Millechamp of Goose Creek, S.C., granted leave to return to England for six months, if he arranges supply for his parish.

157–62. 19 Jan. 1738. Paris again asked to inquire into colonial marriage licences. Ross is sending his son home for orders and hopes he will be appointed missionary. Dismissal of Ellis reaffirmed, in spite of further defence from him. Watts has removed from Annapolis Royal, N.S., to Bristol, R.I., where he has become master of episcopal school founded through the bequest of Nathaniel Kay. Desires continuance of allowance. Committee reports against taking action until report received of Watts removal from Annapolis Royal. Pigot permitted to come home to prosecute an appeal to King in Council against adverse judgment in a civil action. Committee has received a letter from Roger Price, rector of King's Chapel, opposing aid to Trinity Church, Boston.

163–70. 16 Feb. 1738. Henry Jones, minister at Bonavista, N.F., granted £40. Request for aid to Thomas Roberts, schoolmaster in Horseneck, Greenwich township, Conn., rejected. Report from F. J. Paris on history of governor's power to grant marriage licences: though there is an implied sanction for it in the standard form of instruction to governors, he has been unable to find that it was ever expressly authorized by law or commission.

171–2. 16 Mar. 1738.

173–8. 21 Apr. 1738. Checkley to be appointed missionary to Providence, R.I., when he has received orders. Small appointed missionary to Christ Church

Parish, S.C. Plant, missionary at Newbury, Mass., granted leave to visit England after fourteen years' service. Petition from inhabitants of Hebron, Conn., to share in services of Seabury, missionary at New London. Richard Caner, brother of Henry, employed as lay reader at Norwalk, Conn.

179–82. 19 May 1738. Decides to maintain two resident missionaries in North Carolina, in place of one itinerant. Marsden named as one of them. Checkley confirmed as missionary to Providence on presenting evidence of ordination.

183–8. 16 June 1738. Millechamp, of St. James Church, Goose Creek, S.C., obliged to return home because of ill health. John Boyd, serving as itinerant in North Carolina, to be second of two settled missionaries.

189–90. 21 July 1738. Marsden has been refused a licence by the Bishop of London.

191–4. 18 Aug. 1738. Allowance of £15 voted for schoolmaster at New Providence, Bah.

195–8. 15 Sept. 1738. Harrison, missionary on Staten Island, N.Y., granted leave to visit England. Archibald Cummings requests grant to aid in expenses as commissary. Bishop of London says he will not obstruct Marsden's going to North Carolina, but cannot grant him a licence until he has a report from his commissary. Gratuity of £10 granted to Millechamp to aid him in returning to his cure.

199–202. 20 Oct. 1738. People at Newport desire Samuel Johnson as successor to Honeyman, who is dying.

203–8. 17 Nov. 1738. Mary Varnod, widow of missionary, granted £25. Addington Davenport says he has informed the founders of Trinity Church, Boston, that he cannot do anything for them in his present situation (assistant at King's Chapel), except by agreement with Roger Price, the rector. Beckett, missionary at Lewes, Del., and Harrison, missionary on Staten Island, would like to exchange stations. On recommendation of Archibald Cummings, Commissary in Pennsylvania, votes to appoint Aeneas Ross to a vacancy when one occurs.

209–14. 15 Dec. 1738. John Vaughton, manager of the society's plantation on Barbadoes, has had trouble with the slaves, who complain of ill treatment.

215–20. 18 Jan. 1739. Resolves not to appoint a missionary to Staten Island vacated by death of Harrison. Votes £10 additional salary to Kilpatrick on condition that he reside the whole year in Newfoundland. Agrees to consider Theophilus Morris, brother to deputy secretary of New York, on first vacancy. Archibald Cummings, commissary in Pennsylvania, reports concerning incomes of missionaries in his jurisdiction. George Ross advised to send his son Aeneas over for ordination. Roe, St. George's Parish, S.C., asks removal for reasons of health.

221–4. 15 Feb. 1739.

225–8. 21 Mar. 1739. Archibald Cummings, Commissary in Philadelphia, recommends Aeneas Ross for ordination and gives some account of Whitefield's preaching there. Watts, schoolmaster in Bristol, R.I., again asks for an allowance. (Cf. 157–62.)

229–38. 13 Apr. 1739. Philip Bearcroft elected secretary, succeeding Dr. Humphreys, deceased. Petitions received from Price and members of Church in Hopkinton, Mass., asking his appointment as missionary there, but society unable to open any new mission. Committee reports having granted a gratuity of £10 to Arnold, itinerant in Connecticut, and recommends him for first vacant parish. McSparran gives some account of school in Providence and of prosecution of his suit. Brockwell reports that he has moved to Salem, Mass., because of ill treatment in Scituate. Society agrees to his settlement in Salem. Votes gratuity of £10 to William Lindsay, itinerant in Pennsylvania.

239–42. 18 May 1739. John Garzia appointed to succeed Boyd in North Carolina.

243–8. 15 June 1739. Gabriel Johnson, governor of North Carolina, reports death of Boyd and recommends Garzia to succeed him. Mitchell appointed schoolmaster in New Providence, Bah., replacing Squire, who is reported by Smith, the local missionary, to have ceased teaching.

249–52. 20 July 1739. Dismisses Marsden after receiving letters about him from Bishop of London and Commissary Garden of South Carolina.

253–8. 17 Aug. 1739. On receiving complaints from clergy and laymen in Massachusetts and Connecticut of unjust taxation, the society authorizes Arnold to come to England and present the case. Massachusetts clergy complain specifically that Governor Belcher has secured exemption of Quakers and Baptists but not Churchmen from ecclesiastical taxes. On petition from Georgia trustees, society agrees to re-establish mission at Frederica. Refuses request of Auchinleek, minister in Bermuda, for an allowance. Authorizes Barbadoes attorneys to make needed repairs on Barbadoes plantation. Vesey reports on missionary incomes in New York. James Moir, recommended by Garden, appointed to replace Marsden in North Carolina, if Bishop of London will ordain him.

259–60. 21 Sept. 1739.

261–6. 19 Oct. 1739. Account of missionary incomes in his jurisdiction from Commissary Price of Massachusetts. Moir's appointment confirmed on proof of ordination. F. J. Paris complains of mistreatment by Brown, missionary at Brookhaven. Brown directed to answer.

267–70. 16 Nov. 1739. Price offers to supplement salary of Arnold if they will settle him in Hopkinton. Society refuses to restore Ellis as schoolmaster at Burlington, N.J.

271–4. 21 Dec. 1739. Letters from Vesey and others describe complications in calling a successor to Harrison on Staten Island because there are rival vestries there. As Pigot is unwilling to return immediately to Marblehead, Mass., society dismisses him and appoints Alexander Malcolm in his place.

VOLUME IV

MINUTES, 1740-1744

1–4. 16 Jan. 1740. Honeyman speaks of Whitefield's visit to Newport, R.I. Society votes £10 to widow of Watts, schoolmaster in Bristol, on recommendation of New England clergy. Agrees to appoint Aeneas Ross assistant to his father when he receives priest's orders.

5–8. 20 Feb. 1740. Agrees that Aeneas Ross is to officiate in Bristol, Pa., and again refuses to reinstate Ellis as schoolmaster in Burlington, N.J.

9–14. 20 Mar. 1740. Arnold, Staten Island, N.Y., and Beach, Newtown, Conn., permitted to exchange stations. Society agrees to appoint an Indian schoolmaster to assist Barclay, missionary at Albany, N.Y.

15–20. 18 Apr. 1740. Campbell, missionary at Burlington, N.J., directed to supply church at Bristol, Pa., and Vaughan, missionary at Elizabeth, N.J., to supply Newark. Arnold appointed missionary to Staten Island, on condition that he supply Newark one Sunday a month. (These entries make it appear that 9–14 should be dated 1741.) Thompson, missionary at St. Bartholomew's Parish, S.C., granted leave to return to England for a short time. Theophilus Morris appointed itinerant in Connecticut, succeeding Arnold.

21–2. 16 May 1740. Funds do not permit complying with request of Gov. Edward Trelawney of Jamaica, W.I., to appoint a catechist to reside among 'late rebellious' Negroes on that island.

23–4. 20 June 1740. No action on request of Auchinleek and Horton, ministers in Bermuda, for stipends. Smith, New Providence, Bah, describes effect of hurricane.

25–8. 18 July 1740. William Johnson reports death of Vaughton, the society's manager in Barbadoes, and appointment of Abel Alleyne to succeed him. Leslie has resigned from St. Paul's parish, S.C., because of ill health.

29–30. 15 Aug. 1740. Griffith Hughes and James Bruce added to society's attorneys in Barbadoes.

31–6. 19 Sept. 1740. Clergy of New England defend organizers of church in Hopkinton, Mass., from aspersions of 'dissenting teacher', but society is unable to start a mission there. Temple appointed schoolmaster in Hempstead, N.Y., succeeding Gildersleeve, deceased. Request of Brockwell for larger allowance rejected. Commissary Garden of South Carolina proposes a plan for the instruction of Negroes.

37–40. 17 Oct. 1740. Garden, with Hassel and Guy, authorized to buy two young Negroes to inaugurate his plan. Abel Alleyne, Barbadoes, reports death of William Johnson.

41–4. 21 Nov. 1740. Attorneys in Barbadoes directed to select two of the most promising Negro boys for religious instruction. Cummings writes to refute charges brought against Arnold by Whitefield. Becket, reporting from Lewes, Del., describes Whitefield's preaching.

45–50. 19 Dec. 1740. Gov. Robert Bing of Barbadoes recommends the 'useful sciences' be added to instruction given on Codrington estate. Jenney, missionary at Hempstead, N.Y., granted leave to return to visit his father, Archdeacon of Dromore.

51–2. 14 Jan. 1741. Special committee meeting because plantation accounts from Barbadoes for 1740 have been seized by French.

53–60. 15 Jan. 1741. Applications for missionaries from Norwalk and Hebron, Conn., rejected. Gratuity of £10 to Beach, Newtown, Conn., for extra services, including instruction of Negroes. Inquiry into complaint of Brockwell, Salem, Mass., that treasurer rejected some of his bills.

61–6. 19 Feb. 1741. Resolved that in future all parishes applying for missionaries be required to furnish glebes, as recommended by McSparran.

67–70. 1 Mar. 1741. Special committee on Barbadoes affairs, works out an agreement with solicitors of Lady Codrington concerning payment of her annuity from estate of Gen. Codrington.

71–2. 19 Mar. 1741. Foregoing agreement approved by society. Grant of £20 to Nathaniel Whitaker of Maryland, stricken with smallpox while in England for orders.

73–4. 15 Apr. 1741. Report of committee giving draft of address to King for a special collection.

75–8. 17 Apr. 1741. Several letters and reports concerning Barbadoes estate appended. Resolved not to open mission in Scituate, Mass. Aeneas Ross granted £10 towards expense of returning to America.

79–82. 15 May 1740. Orr, assistant in Charleston, appointed to St. Paul's Parish, S.C., succeeding Leslie, resigned. Durand appointed to succeed Small in Christ Church Parish, S.C.

83–6. 17 July 1741.

87–90. 18 Sept. 1741.

91–6. 16 Oct. 1741. As house in Burlington, N.J., is in poor repair and of no use to society, Parish is directed to see if it can legally be sold.

97–102. Charles Fortescue appointed schoolmaster in Chester to succeed Houston who has gone to Maryland.

103–4. 4 Dec. 1741. Special committee on Barbadoes estate.

105–6. 15 Dec. 1741. Another meeting of special committee. They are dissatisfied with the plantation's yield.

107–12. 18 Dec. 1741. Death of Kilpatrick reported from Trinity Bay, N.F. Garden reports concerning estate of Ludlam, former missionary to Goose

Creek, left to support a school there. Norris has returned, resigning his mission in Georgia. Henry Caner, Fairfield, Conn., recommends his brother Richard for ordination. Society agrees to appoint Richard to assist his brother when ordained.

113-14. 23 Dec. 1741. Special committee on Barbadoes.

115-16. 21 Jan. 1742. Presley appointed missionary to Bonavista, N.F.

117-22. 18 Feb. 1742. Seabury moved from New London, Conn., to Hempstead, N.Y., succeeding Jenney, who has been elected rector of Christ Church, Philadelphia. Aeneas Ross appointed to mission at Oxford, Pa., vacated by Howie, who is seeking a parish in Jamaica, W.I.

123-6. 18 Mar. 1742. Grant of £50 to Trinity Church, Boston, to assist in finishing church. Gratuity of £10 to Pugh, Apoquimininck, Del., for supplying Duck Creek.

127-8. 1 Apr. 1742. Special committee on Barbadoes.

129-34. 9 Apr. 1742. John Moore appointed schoolmaster at Jamaica, N.Y., succeeding Willet, resigned.

135-40. 21 May 1742. Price gives some account of Great Awakening in Boston. Nathaniel Hodges appointed to succeed Smith, deceased, in Bahamas.

141-2. 18 June 1742.

143-4. 16 July 1742. Garden and associates have purchased two Negro boys for instruction.

145-8. 20 Aug. 1742.

149-54. 17 Sept. 1742.

155-6. 14 Oct. 1742. Special committee on Barbadoes considers complaints of Bolton against their agent, Moore.

157-62. 15 Oct. 1742. Report of above committee, exonerating Moore.

163-4. 19 Nov. 1742.

165-74. 17 Dec. 1742. Andrew Wright appointed schoolmaster on Staten Island, N.Y., succeeding George Taylor, deceased. Peat, James Town, Jamaica, W.I., recommends sending a missionary to Musketo Indians. Roe permitted to set up a catechetical school in Boston, Mass., instead of returning to his parish. Millechamp, St. James's Parish, Goose Creek, S.C., granted leave to return to England. Long report of Barbadoes committee seems to reflect tension between committee, plantation manager (Abel Alleyne), and town agent (Daniel Moore).

175-8. 20 Jan. 1743. £10 per annum added to Peasley's salary (Bonavista, N.F.) on condition that he continue to teach poor children gratis.

179-84. 17 Feb. 1743.

185-90. 16 Mar. 1743 (or 1744?). Hildreth appointed schoolmaster in New York, succeeding Noxon, resigned, on recommendation of Vesey. Death of Becket, missionary at Lewes, Del., reported. Peasley to be moved to St. Johns, N.F. Committee reports rules of order for Codrington College.

191–6. 15 Apr. 1743. Society decides to discontinue school in New York, on receiving resignation of Noxon, the schoolmaster. Morris appointed to succeed Seabury at New London and James Lyons to succeed Morris as itinerant in Conn.

197–8. 20 May 1743. Thompson, a graduate of Yale, authorized to come to England for orders, with prospect of being appointed to New Rochelle, N.Y.

199–200. 17 June 1743.

201–2. 23 June 1743. To comply with certain clauses in Gen. Codrington's will, Barbadoes committee recommends that number of Negroes on plantation be increased to 300 and a schoolmaster be employed to teach poor children gratis.

203–4. 6 July 1743. Barbadoes committee recommends sending a schoolmaster and usher to Codrington estate.

205–8. 15 July 1743. Both of the foregoing reports approved.

209–14. 19 Aug. 1743. Committee recommends appointment of missionary to Warwick, R.I., which McSparran has been visiting monthly, but society defers action. Price reports that provision has been made for a glebe in Hopkinton, Mass.

215–20. 16 Sept. 1743. Testimonials for Ebenezer Thompson received from missionaries in New England. As Addington Davenport has donated his own estate for a parsonage and glebe in Scituate, Mass., society agrees to reopen mission there, and appoints Thompson to the post.

221–6. 21 Oct. 1743.

227–32. 18 Nov. 1743. Recommendation of committee for establishing a catechetical school under Roe in Boston postponed to next meeting. Backhouse, missionary in Chester, Pa., granted £10 additional salary to serve as schoolmaster, as Fortescue, who held that post, has moved to Philadelphia. Society decides to send a missionary to Moskito Indians on recommendation of Gov. Edward Trelawney and a petition from their 'king'.

233–4. 16 Dec. 1743. Thomas Rotheram appointed schoolmaster in Codrington College.

235–40. 18 Jan. 1744 (1745). On recommendation of Vesey, Basil Bartow, son of late Thomas Bartow, appointed schoolmaster in Westchester, N.Y., succeeding Forster, dismissed. Christopher Robert Reynolds appointed schoolmaster and Thomas Thompson missionary in Monmouth County, N.J. William Cattel appointed physician in Codrington College.

241–2. 11 Feb. 1744 (1745?) Special meeting of Barbadoes committee recommends appointment of Floyer Sydenham as President and Professor of Divinity in Codrington College.

243–6. 15 Feb. 1744 (1745). Appointment of Sydenham confirmed.

247–8. 25 Feb. 1744 (1745?) Barbadoes committee appoints a subcommittee to consider how income of college can be improved.

249–52. 15 Mar. 1744 (1745?). Notice of death of Hassel received from vestry of St. Thomas's Parish, S.C. Alexander Garden, Jr., recently ordained son of Commissary Garden, appointed to succeed him. Barbadoes committee reports that Sydenham has declined appointment.

253–6. 20 Apr. 1744. John Miln dismissed as missionary in Monmouth County, N.J., because of failure to report and charges of drunkenness and neglect of duty by wardens of Freehold.

257–62. 18 May 1744. Church at Newbury, Mass., divided. Leaders of new church allege that Plant promised to allow part of his salary for its minister, but now refuses. Plant ordered to answer charge, and to officiate alternately at the two churches for the time being. Clement Hall, who has come from North Carolina for orders, will be appointed an itinerant in that colony, if he is ordained.

263–6. 15 June 1744.

267–70. 20 July 1744. Checkley, son of missionary at Providence, appointed missionary to Newark, N.J.

271–4. 17 Aug. 1744. Gibbs appointed to Simsbury, Conn.

275–6. 17 Aug. 1744. Barbadoes committee arranged for departure of Rotheram, schoolmaster, and Brewsher, usher for Codrington College.

277–84. 21 Sept. 1744. Hezekiah Watkins appointed missionary to New Windsor. Resolution adopted to discourage candidates from coming over for ordination without previous authorization. Boschi appointed to St. Batholomew's parish, S.C., vacated by removal of Thompson to St. George's, Dorchester, S.C. Roe dismissed as catechist in Boston because of charges of sexual misconduct brought by Price.

285–8. 19 Oct. 1744. On recommendation of committee, directs Henry Barclay, missionary at Albany, to report on character of John Jacob Oel, Dutch missionary to the Mohawks, who has requested a gratuity. Report from Commissary Price that Roe had got his landlady's daughter with child, and had been ordered by the govenor to leave the colony. Secretary reported death by smallpox of the younger Checkley.

289–92. 23 Oct. 1744. (Barbadoes committee.)

293–8. 16 Nov. 1744. Brockwell writes from Salem, Mass., that Prince, late professor of mathematics at Harvard, asked the clergy of New England to recommend him for orders, but that Brockwell opposed him because of the scandals that had led to his dismissal. Society agrees to pay bills arising from illness and burial of young Checkley. Barbadoes committee directed to proceed with plans for the erection of a college, in accordance with the will of Gen. Codrington.

299-302. 21 Dec. 1744. Death of Smirk, catechist in Barbadoes, reported. Roe reports being captured by French on return voyage. Lyons, itinerant in Connecticut, authorized to settle in Northbury if he thinks best. Resolved that a physician be sent to Codrington plantation.

303-4. 31 Dec. 1744. Barbadoes committee recommends appointment of William Cattell as surgeon and apothecary for Codrington College.

VOLUME V

MINUTES, 1745-1750

1-2. 17 Jan. 1745. £10 added to Peasley's salary on condition that he continue to officiate at Petty Harbour, N.F., as often as he can. At request of Georgia trustees, society appoints Zouberbuhler missionary to Savannah, replacing Bosomworth, who has returned without leave. Resolved in the future not to appoint any missionary unless he applies to the society in person.

3-8. 21 Feb. 1745 (1746). Thompson, missionary to Monmouth County, N.J., authorized to take legal action to obtain possession of church at Shrewsbury, padlocked by Miln and his party. Church was bequeathed to society by Leeds. Usual gift voted to widow of Pugh, missionary at Apoquimininck, Del. Philip Reading to succeed him when ordained. Gratuity of £10 to Gabriel Falk, Swedish minister in Pennsylvania. Duties of Bryant, lately appointed professor of philosophy and mathematics at Codrington College, defined.

9-12. 21 Mar. 1745 (1746). Reading's appointment confirmed on notice of his ordination. Price granted £60 for catechetical lectures in Boston, but they are to be discontinued after next August on his recommendation. Standard allowed to return to England for his health. Society agrees to found a catechetical school for Negroes in Philadelphia. Bluet appointed missionary to Dover, Del.

13-14. 16 Apr. 1745. (Barbadoes committee.) Recommends that separate accounts be kept for Codrington College and the plantation.

15-20. 19 Apr. 1745. Foregoing report approved. Fordyce allowed to return to England for his health.

21-4. 17 May 1745. Joseph Halliday to be appointed missionary of Bahamas on ordination. Joseph Samson appointed assistant to Wetmore, to serve Bedford and North Castle, N.Y., and granted a special gratuity because of losses when captured by French. Conditions set for renting Barbadoes estate.

25-8. 21 June 1745. Gratuity to widow of Garzia, deceased missionary to North Carolina. Complaints of vestry of St. Andrew's Church, Staten Island, N.Y., against Arnold, forwarded by Vesey, allege drunkenness, disorderly behaviour, and neglect of duty. Vesey says there is a rumour that he is 'distracted'. Society votes to dismiss him. Samson's appointment confirmed.

29-34. 19 July 1745. Lindsay, itinerant in New Jersey, dismissed on basis of charges brought by inhabitants of Trenton and supported by Campbell and by various affadavits, though not proven before the commissary (Jenney). Richard Locke appointed to succeed him. Richard St. John appointed missionary to Bahamas, replacing Holiday, who is going to Bermuda.

35-6. 16 Aug. 1745.

37-40. 20 Sept. 1745. Death of Lewis Jones of St. Helen's Parish, S.C., reported. Orr transferred there from St. Paul's Parish, as vestry of St. Paul's had failed to provide a parsonage or elect Orr rector.

41-4. 18 Oct. 1745. On recommendation of Pundarson, £5 per annum is voted for schoolmaster in North Groton, Mass. Plant directed to allow £20 for an assistant to supply second parish in Newbury, Mass. Brown transferred from Brookhaven, N.Y., to Newark, N.J. 8 Nov. 1745 (on same sheet). No business transacted because of absence of any vice-president.

45-8. 8 Nov. 1745. (Barbadoes committee.)

49-52. Stoupe permitted to resign mission in New Rochelle. £40 voted for missionary and catechist to Moskito Indians. Governor of Jamaica asked to secure additional support from the legislature. Lyons transferred to succeed Brown at Brookhaven, N.Y. Barzillai Dean to succeed Lyons as itinerant in Connecticut. Bryant appointed professor of philosophy and mathematics in Codrington College.

53-6. 20 Dec. 1745.

57-60. 16 Jan. 1746 (1747). Guy allowed to return to England for his health. Quincy appointed to St. George's Parish, Dorchester, S.C., succeeding Thompson, resigned. As the governor of Bahamas is holding parish there for his secretary (Snow), St. John is authorized to move to South Carolina and accept any vacant parish there.

61-6. 20 Feb. 1746 (1747). Wardens and vestry of Trinity Church, New York, report death of Vesey and election of Henry Barclay as rector. Moir authorized to move from Cape Fear to northern North Carolina.

67-74. 20 Mar. 1746. Charlton appointed to succeed Richard Caner, deceased, as missionary on Staten Island. Received answers to charges against Lindsay. Found some of them insufficiently supported, but held that his conduct on the whole made him unworthy to continue as missionary. Approved some arrangements for Codrington College.

75-80. 18 Apr. 1746. Petitioners from New Brunswick, N.J., notified that a missionary would be appointed when they set apart a glebe and parsonage and pledged at least £40 per annum currency towards his salary. Arnold admits but seeks to extenuate some of the charges against him. Society agrees to pay his salary to Michaelmas, but to restore him to employment only on certificate from Vesey of good behaviour for twelve months.

81-6. 16 May 1746. Miln's defence is received, but nothing can be done for him until he yields the church at Shrewsbury.

87-90. 20 June 1746. Brockwelll is leaving Salem, Mass., to become lecturer in King's Chapel, Boston. On receiving defence of Nathan Prince from charges brought by Brockwell and testimonial of other New England clergy, society decides that he may be a suitable person to go as a missionary to Moskito Indians.

91-4. 18 July 1746. Boschi withdrawn from St. Bartholomew's Parish, S.C., because vestry refused to elect him rector. Parish will be discontinued as a mission unless it agrees to accept anyone who is sent.

95-100. 15 Aug. 1746. Barbadoes attorneys report resignation of Abel Alleyne as manager, because of ill health, and appointment of John Payne to succeed him.

101-4. 19 Sept. 1746. Allowance of Hildreth, schoolmaster in New York, increased by £5 on condition that he instruct any Negroes who come to him. William Macgilchrist, formerly assistant at St. Philip's Church, Charleston, S.C., appointed to Salem, Mass., to succeed Brockwell. Gratuity of £20 to Bryant because of delays in obtaining passage.

105-8. 17 Oct. 1746.

109-12. 21 Nov. 1746. Honeyman, in consultation with Johnson, authorized to select a graduate of Yale for ordination to serve as catechist and assistant in Newport, R.I.

113-16. 19 Dec. 1746. Cotes appointed to St. George's Parish, S.C., to succeed Quincy, who has become assistant in St. Philip's Church, Charleston.

117-20. 15 Jan. 1747 (1748). St. John appointed to St. Helen's Parish, S.C.

121-4. 19 Feb. 1747 (1748?) Jones, Trinity Bay, N.F., granted leave to return to England for the winter.

125-6. 18 Mar. 1747.

127-30. 10 Apr. 1747. John Snow appointed missionary to Bahamas. St. John transferred to South Carolina.

131-6. 15 May 1747. Henry Caner has resigned as missionary in Fairfield, Conn., to accept post as rector of King's Chapel, Boston, succeeding Roger Price, resigned. Sampson appointed to Fairfield. Thomas Bradbury Chandler appointed catechist at North Castle and Bedford, N.Y., assisting Wetmore, missionary at Rye. Temple, schoolmaster in Hempstead, N.Y., authorized to employ an assistant. Mathew Graves appointed missionary to New London, Conn. Sturgeon named catechist in Philadelphia.

137-40. 19 June 1747. Title to part of the society's lands in Burlington, N.J., having been challenged, committee recommends defending it, though property is unused and in ruinous condition.

141-4. 17 July 1747. Death of Richard Caner, missionary on Staten Island, reported. Samuel Auchmuty, son of Robert Auchmuty, judge of admiralty in

Boston, appointed catechist to Negroes in New York, succeeding Charlton, who is appointed to Staten Island. Nathan Prince recommended to Bishop of London for orders.

145–7. 21 Aug. 1747.

148–52. 18 Sept. 1747. Missionaries in vicinity of Duck Creek, Del., directed to officiate there as often as they can.

153–6. 10 Oct. 1747. Miln having surrendered the property in Shrewsbury, society agrees to pay his salary to midsummer, 1744, the quarter's end following his dismissal. Timothy Millechamp's leave in England for his health extended on recommendation of Lord Digby. Slingsby Bethel elected treasurer, succeeding Thomas Tryon, deceased.

157–60. 20 Nov. 1747. Backhouse, missionary in Chester, authorized to exchange with Locke, itinerant in Pennsylvania, if Locke agrees. Society agrees to appoint missionary to Derby, Conn., succeeding Dean, who died on way over, if people agree to provide house and glebe and pledge £20 sterling towards salary. Richard Mansfield will be appointed, if he comes to England for orders. Dibble will be appointed to Norwalk, Conn., on the same condition.

161–6. 18 Dec. 1747. Malcolm, Marblehead, Mass., granted leave to return to England. Year's salary advanced to Nathan Prince, appointed missionary to Moskito Indians. Long report from Barbadoes committee gives details of operation of college and management of estate.

167–70. 20 Jan. 1748. Gov. Trelawney reports death of Prince shortly after his arrival. George Craig appointed itinerant in Pennsylvania, succeeding Locke, resigned.

171–4. 17 Feb. 1748. Samuel Seabury, Jr., appointed catechist at Huntington, N.Y., under direction of his father.

175–8. 17 Mar. 1748. Plant directed to select some young graduate of one of the New England colleges to be ordained to serve the second church in Newbury, Mass., as his assistant. John Ogilvie appointed missionary at Albany and to the Mohawk Indians on ordination. Jones, formerly missionary to Trinity Bay, N.F., appointed missionary to Moskito Indians. Robert Cuming appointed to St. John's Parish, S.C. and Robert Stone to St. James's Parish, Goose Creek, S.C.

179–82. 15 Apr. 1748. Quincy reports leaving St. George's Parish, Dorchester, S.C., to become assistant to Garden in Charleston. Hopkinton, Mass., erected as a mission and Price appointed to it.

183–8. 20 May 1748. Death of Vaughan, Elizabeth, N.J., reported. Vestry have invited Chandler to come and reside among them as lay reader until he is old enough to be ordained. He is appointed catechist there by society. Death of Pierson, Salem, N.J., reported by Commissary Jenney. Thompson, formerly of St. George's Parish, S.C., appointed to Salem. Moir has left Cape Fear and settled in Edgecomb Parish, N.C. Millechamp dismissed from St. James's, Goose Creek, having accepted position as rector of Colesborne in the Diocese of Gloucester.

189–90. 17 June 1748. Jeremiah Leaming, selected by Honeyman and Johnson as assistant in Newport, to be appointed when ordained.

191–4. 15 July 1748. Charlton reports death of Wright, schoolmaster on Staten Island. Seabury reports that Keeble, schoolmaster at Oyster Bay, has gone insane. Dible appointed missionary to Stamford and Greenwich, Conn., on ordination. Mansfield appointed to Derby, Waterbury, Oxford, and Westbury, Conn.

195–8. 16 Sept. 1748.

199–206. 21 Oct. 1748. Report of Barbadoes committee concerned mainly with relations of college faculty to plantation manager and attorneys.

207–10. 18 Nov. 1748. Jenney asked to investigate charges against Bluet, missionary in Duck Creek, Del., with power of dismissal, if he finds them justified.

211–12. 16 Dec. 1748.

213–16. 19 Jan. 1749 (1750?). Usher, missionary in Lewes, Del., granted six months' leave to settle affairs in Ireland, following death of his elder brother.

217–22. 16 Feb. 1749 (1750?). Malcolm has resigned as missionary at Marblehead, Mass., to accept call to Annapolis, Md. Death of Boschi, St. Bartholomew's Parish, S.C., reported by widow.

223–8. 16 Mar. 1749 (1750?). William Langhorne appointed to St. Bartholomew's Parish, S.C. Hugh Neill appointed to Dover, Del., vacated by death of Bluet. Amyl, missionary to Nova Scotia, directed to return home to answer charges.

229–30. 14 Apr. 1749. (Special meeting.) A previous special meeting (minutes not with these papers) had been held 7 April to consider request of Lords Commissioners of Trade and Plantations for ministers for colonists being sent to Nova Scotia. In a series of resolutions, reproduced here in the form of a letter to the Commissioners, it agreed to provide six missionaries and six schoolmasters for Nova Scotia, as the progress of settlement required, and to pay them maximum salaries (£70 and £15 a year respectively). It was noted that this commitment exceeded the present income of the society. The provision of a bishop for Nova Scotia was also recommended. Tutty appointed first missionary and Halhead first schoolmaster.

231–2. 19 Apr. 1749. (Special meeting.) Appointed Amyl missionary to Nova Scotia.

233–6. 21 Apr. 1749. Wardens at Rye, N.Y., directed to repair church and provide glebe and parsonage. Jane Caner, widow of Richard, acknowledges gift of half-year's salary on his death. Gen. Oglethorpe asked to obtain Parliamentary grant to support a minister in Georgia.

237–8. 19 May 1749.

239–40. 16 June 1749. Dr. Cutler reports poor attendance at catechetical lectures given by Boston clergy at society's request, but is asked to continue a little longer. Brockwell and Hooper refuse to participate. Edward Holyoke, President of Harvard, acknowledges gift of books from the society.

241–4. 21 July 1749. Death of Charles Taylor, schoolmaster on Staten Island, reported. Robert Carter, appointed missionary to the Bahamas succeeding Snow, deceased.

245–8. 15 Sept. 1749. Browne, missionary to Newark, N.J., allowed to return to England for his health. Orr allowed to visit northern colonies for the same purpose. Wood appointed missionary to New Brunswick and Elizabeth, N.J., on ordination. German prayer books presented to John Glessendanner, ordained to officiate among German-speaking Swiss in Orangeburg, S.C.

249–52. 20 Oct. 1749. On complaint of Thompson, their missionary, Churchmen in Salem, N.J., told that mission will be withdrawn if they do not provide a parsonage and glebe within twelve months. Peasley transferred to St. Bartholomew's Parish, S.C., because he has encountered opposition in St. John's, N.F. Tutty, missionary to Nova Scotia, granted leave to return to England for a month.

253–6. 17 Nov. 1749. New Cambridge and Cornwall, Conn., added to mission at Simsbury. Boschi, having been disappointed in application for a chaplaincy, is continued at St. Bartholomew's, S.C., and Peasley's appointment there cancelled.

257–62. 15 Dec. 1749. St. John, St. Helen's Parish, S.C., granted leave to return to England for his health. Barbadoes attorneys asked to explain why they refused to let Blenman see their minutes.

263–8. 18 Jan. 1750 (1751). Jenney authorized to enter first vacant mission, as he complains that Christ Church, Philadelphia, fails to pay his salary. Petrus Paulus, son of Abraham, a Mohawk Indian who has been acting as lay preacher, appointed schoolmaster to the Indians. Peasley appointed to St. Helen's Parish, S.C.

269–72. 15 Feb. 1750 (1751). Thompson, Monmouth County, N.J., authorized, at his request, to go as missionary to Guinea. Ottolenghi appointed schoolmaster to Negroes in Georgia.

273–8. 15 Mar. 1750 (1751?). Michael Houdin, converted Roman Catholic priest, voted gratuity for officiating to churches in New Jersey. Commissary Barclay asked to inspect his orders. Samuèl Cooke appointed missionary to Monmouth County, N.J.

279–80. May 1750. An incomplete minute prepared for printing containing explanations designed to allay colonial opposition to bishops.

281–4. 15 June 1750. Leaming, catechist in Newport, granted an additional £10 a year because of extra duties resulting from Honeyman's infirmity. Death of Amwyl reported.

285–92. 20 July 1750. John Jacob Oel appointed assistant to Ogilvie as missionary to Mohawks. Thompson transferred from Salem, N.J., to Chester, Pa. Chandler appointed missionary to Elizabeth, N.J. Benjamin Lindsay appointed missionary to Trinity Bay, N.F., on ordination. Death of Thomas Duke, town agent in Barbadoes, reported. Gov. Trelawney has appointed Jones to a parish in Jamaica, as Moskito Shore is too unhealthy for an elderly man with a family.

293–6. 21 Sept. 1750. Barrington appointed schoolmaster on Staten Island, N.Y., replacing Taylor, deceased. Sachem Abraham granted £5 gratuity for preaching to Indians.

297–300. 19 Oct. 1750. Henry Caner reports death of Honeyman.

301–4. 16 Nov. 1750. Copp appointed missionary to Augusta, Ga., on ordination. John Rotheram, brother to Thomas, schoolmaster in Codrington College, appointed usher, succeeding Brewsher, who has been obliged to return to England for his health.

305–8. 21 Dec. 1750. Gibbs to be removed from mission at Simsbury, Conn., at first opportunity because of failure of church there to meet society's conditions.

Missionaries whose reports are abstracted in the minutes, 1736–50, volumes III, 97 through V (cf. Introduction, p. viii):

Arhold, Jonathan, iii. 131–4, 199–202, 261–6, iv. 135–40, 165–74, 191–6, 221–6, 257–70, 277–84.

Auchmuty, Samuel, v. 183, 189, 207, 224, 235, 264.

Backhouse, Richard, iii. 135–8, 229–38, iv. 45–50, 53–60, 97–102, 157–62, 227–32, 243–6, 257–62, v. 93, 157, 208, 242, 254.

Barclay, Henry, iii. 199–202, 229–38, 261–6, iv. 9–20, 61–6, 122–6, 129–34, 149–54, 179–84, 221–6, 235–40, 277–84, v. 17, 49, 62, 76, 121, 179, 183, 191, 207, 234.

Barrington, v. 294.

Bartow, Basil, v. 78, 128, 129, 234, 287.

Beach, John, iii. 121–6, 215–20, iv. 41–4, 145–8, 215–20, 253–6, v. 29, 128, 195, 245, 286.

Becket, William, iii. 155–6, 249–52, iv. 41–4, 53–60, 83–6, 97–102, 191–6.

Bluet, Thomas, v. 114, 200.

Boschi, Charles, v. 92, 103, 122, 157, 240.

Bosomworth, iv. 299–302.

Brewsher, v. 55, 260, 295.

Brockwell, Charles, iii. 105–14, 191–4, 199–202, 215–20, 262–70, iv. 1–4, 21–2, 37–40, 83–6, 91–6, 135–40, 145–8, 157–62, 209–14, 221–6, 277–84, v. 87, 93, 127.

Brown, Isaac, iii. 92–102, 203–8, 215–20, iv. 41–4, 53–60, 129–34, 145–8, 179–84, 215–20, 277–84, v. 22, 102, 155, 245, 276, 307.

Browne, Arthur, iii. 145–51, 163–70, iv. 53–60, 163–4, 221–6, 299–302, v. 41, 63, 147, 169, 253.

Browne, Joseph, iii. 179–82, 191–4, 215–20, iv. 53–60, 91–6, 165–74, 221–6, 271–4, 277–84, v. 29, 82, 95, 154, 189, 195, 245, 293.

Bryant, William, v. 164, 202, 259.

Willet, iii. 179–82, 229–38.
Wright, Andrew, iv. 271–4, v. 179.
Zouberbuhler, Bartholomew, v. 59, 157, 173.

Parishes from which the foregoing reports were sent:

Albany, N.Y., iii. 199–202, 227–38, 261–6, iv. 9–20, 61–6, 123–26, 129–34, 149–54, 179–84, 221–6, 235–40, 277–84, v. 17, 59, 62, 76, 224, 264.

Amboy, N.J., iii. 127–30, iv. 91–6, 129–34, 165–74, 179–84, 191–6, 221–6, v. 17, 21, 50, 76, 102, 154, 192, 235, 250, 298.

Apoquimininck, Del., iii. 135–8, 229–38, iv. 53–60, 83–6, 149–50, 227–34, v. 17, 138, 150, 192, 200, 253, 301.

Bahamas, iii. 243–8, iv. 227–32, v. 126.

Barbadoes, iv. 15–20, 29–30, 45–50, 83–6, 285–8, v. 47, 52, 54–5, 73, 114, 163–4, 202, 205, 215, 259–60, 289, 295.

Bonavista, N.F., iii. 221–4, iv. 79–82, 175–8, 221–6.

Boston, Mass, iii. 105–14, 121–6, 203–8, 243–8, 261–6, iv. 25–8, 37–40, 83–6, 91–102, 123–6, 135–40, 157–62, 165–78, 191–6, 209–20, 253–6, 285–8, v. 10, 25, 41, 88, 105, 109, 113, 127, 131, 146, 189, 195, 199, 211, 237, 285, 297.

Braintree, Mass., iii. 243–8, 261–6, iv. 1–4, 53–60, 97–102, 135–40, 157–62, 199–200, 221–6, 285–8, v. 22, 43, 88, 126, 213, 274.

Bristol, Pa., iii. 145–51, 189–90.

Bristol, R.I., iv. 1–4, 143–4, 157–62, 175–8, 215–20, 263–6, v. 15, 43, 113, 127, 249, 306.

Brookhaven, N.Y., iii. 92–102, 215–20, iv. 41–4, 67–70, 129–34, 145–8, 165–74, 177–84, 215–26, 277–84, v. 22, 118, 146, 191, 225, 242, 249, 275.

Burlington, N.J., iii. 199–202, 243–8, iv. 7–20, 91–6, 165–74, 221–6, 235–40, 277–84, v. 10, 31, 137, 200, 213, 250, 258.

Cape Fear, N.C., v. 258.

Charleston, S.C., iv. 87–90, 123–34, 163–74, 179–84, 249–52, v. 37, 118, 151, 167, 179, 266.

Chester, Pa., iii. 135–8, 229–38, 267–70, iv. 45–50, 53–60, 97–102, 157–62, 179–84, 227–32, 243–6, 257–62, v. 93, 157, 208, 242, 254.

Christ Church Parish, S.C., iii. 215–20, iv. 135–40, 149–54, 249–52, v. 58, 82, 119, 151, 196, 211, 246, 251.

Connecticut, iv. 37–40, 209–20, 253–6, 271–84, 299–302, v. 15, 39.

Derby, Conn., v. 285.

Dover, Del., iii. 203–14, iv. 5–8, 53–68, 97–102, 185–90, 197–8, 227–34, 243–6, v. 10, 29, 36, 114, 200, 269.

Elizabeth, N.J., iii. 115–20, iv. 9–20, 135–40, 253–6, v. 21, 134, 225, 235, 246, 289.

Fairfield, Conn., iii. 131–4, 173–8, 229–38, iv. 15–20, 53–66, 107–12, 165–74, 191–6, 215–20, 253–6, v. 5, 15, 110, 128, 132, 157, 223, 233.

Frederica, Ga., iv. 31–6, 299–302.

Goose Creek, S.C., iv. 61–6, 165–74, 197–8, 209–14, 263–6.

Hempstead, N.Y., iii. 145–51, iv. 15–20, 31–6, 45–50, 135–40, 149–54, 235–40, 277–84, v. 5, 16, 68, 103, 106, 134, 145, 173, 192, 234, 237, 245, 287.

Hopkinton, Mass., v. 218, 239, 257, 275, 302.

VOLUME VI

FINANCIAL RECORDS

1. Form of subscription dated 17 Oct. 1702.

2–3. Report of committee to examine Dr. Bray's accounts.

4–5. Copy of subscription form with subscribers for 1702.

6–8. Subscribers to the charges of the charter. (1702?)

9–12. Members who have not subscribed.

13–14. Annual subscribers.

15–16. Members who have neither subscribed annually nor to the expenses of the charter.

17. Subscriptions collected by John Evans.

18–20. Printed copy of subscription form.

21. Written copy, dated 3rd Anne, with names of subscribers.

22. Another printed copy, dated 1703.

23–4. Memorandum of secretary to a subcommittee, giving estimate of annual subscriptions and answering some other inquiries, dated 8 Mar. 1705. Mentions estates in Virginia and New Jersey donated to society by Col. Bond and Sergeant Hook.

25–6. Report of auditing committee, 23 Sept. 1706.

27–8. List of subscribers appended to (25–6).

29. Receipt to Francis Tweed, 18 Oct. 1706, for payment of 2nd quarter's land tax.

30. Tweed's account as the society's tenant, 1705–7.

31–4. Two copies of report of auditing committee, 26 Jan. 1707 (8).

35–6. Account of money received by the society's messenger, William Carter, from members since 14 June 1707.

37–41. Account of members' subscriptions and arrears as of 25 Dec. 1707 (2 copies).

42. General view of the income and disbursements of the society as they appeared to auditors in their inspection, 26 Jan. 1707 (8).

43–4. Auditors' report, 4 June 1707.

45–6. Account of subscriptions with arrears to 25 Mar. 1707.

47–54. Receipts and vouchers for 1707.

55–8. Auditors' report, 26 Jan. 1708 (9).

59–62. Account of money received from members by William Carter, messenger, from 26 Jan. 1707 (8) to 16 Jan. 1708 (9).

63–5. Account of annual subscriptions with arrears to 25 Dec. 1708.

66. General view of income and disbursements as they appeared to auditors 26 Jan. 1708 (9).

67–105. Receipts and vouchers for 1708.

106–9. Auditors' report, 31 Jan. 1709 (10).

110–11. Account of money received from members by William Carter, messenger, to 31 Jan. 1709 (10).

112–14. List of subscriptions with arrears to 25 Dec. 1709.

115–16. General view of income and disbursements as seen by auditors 31 Jan. 1709 (10).

117–238. Receipts and vouchers, 1709.

239–349. Receipts and vouchers, 1710.

350. Summary account of receipts and disbursements for 1739.

351. Fragmentary account, showing entries for 1732, 1733, and 1740.

352. Fragmentary account, showing entries for 1744–8.

353–65. Fragmentary accounts of Barbadoes plantation with some queries about them. Dates range from 1732–57.

366. Account of cash in the general account from 31 Jan. 1754 to 29 Jan. 1767. (Totals only.)

367. Cash on American bishops' account, 1754–67.

368–74. Account of payments to American Loyalist clergy from fund raised for their relief, 1779–80.

375–7. Unidentified wrappers.

378. Copy of advertisement for subscriptions for relief of American Loyalist clergy, inserted in London Papers in 1779.

379–88. Account book listing subscriptions to fund for relief of American clergy, 1776. Names of some beneficiaries given at end (386–7). (Note: Due to an error in numbering the manuscripts, the numbers 371–9 are repeated in the opening pages of this account book. These duplicate numbers are shown in parenthesis in the index.)

389–90. Another list of Loyalist clergy who received benefits from the fund.

391–2. Wrappers.

393–4. Subscribers (mostly bishops) to the Archbishop of Canterbury's fund for rebuilding the churches in Barbadoes, 1781.

395–6. Summary of the society's finances, July 1783.

397. Balances with various bankers to the credit of the fund for American clergy, 7 Feb. 1797.

398–415. Notebook containing historical account of the offices of secretary and assistant secretary, ending with lists of these officers and treasurers. Last date shown is 1782.

416–26. Auditors' report, 1796.

427. Summaries of society's benefactions, 1772–9 and 1785–96.

428. Comparative statement of income and disbursements, undated.

429. Abstract of account of fund for American clergy.

430–2. Unexplained figures.

433–4. Annual expenses of Codrington College, undated.

435. Account of money paid to missionaries. Undated, but names belong to first decade of eighteenth century.

436. Fragments of undated accounts.

437. Undated bill of V. Edwards.

438. Fragmentary account, undated.

VOLUME VII

CORRESPONDENCE

BRITISH ISLES, 1679–JUNE 1707

1–3. Duplicate of Order in Council, 25 Apr. 1679, permitting clergy serving as chaplains at sea or in the plantations to retain benefices in England.

4–7. 'Proposals for propagating the Gospel in all Pagan contries.' The first proposal, published in Gordon's *Geographical Grammar*, is for raising a fund to train clergy in pagan languages and send them out as missionaries. Supplementary proposals, designed for a future edition, are for establishing missionary schools in various Indian communities to train them in English and Christianity, as he is convinced that the multiplicity of their languages makes his first proposal impractical. Dated 6 Jan. 1701/1 in notation.

8–9. Proposals for more effective fund raising. Dated 6 Mar. 1701/2 in notation.

10. List of Lord Mayor and aldermen, dated 13 Mar. 1701/2.

11–12. By-laws and standing orders of S.P.G., dated in margin. Last date is 17 Sept. 1702.

13. Joshua Walker to Secretary (John Chamberlayne), Great Billing, near Northampton, 5 Mar. 1702. Unwilling to commit himself to a subscription because of family responsibilities, but asks for printed material concerning society. (Note: As Chamberlayne is secretary throughout the present correspondence, he will henceforth be identified simply as 'Secretary'.)

14. Bishop Compton to Archbishop Tenison, 15 Mar. 1702, suggesting some tracts with which he thinks George Keith should be supplied.

15–16a. Draft of address by society to Queen Anne on her accession. Dated 27 Mar. 1702 in notation.

17. Bishop Compton to Secretary, 27 Mar. 1702, recommending John B. Soroseil for mission to Staten Island.

18. L. Gordon to Dr. Bray, 17 Apr. 1702, saying he has experienced delay in getting (New) York money and in obtaining Queen's Bounty.

19. Draft of recommendation of Bishop Compton to Lords Commissioners for Trade and Plantations concerning support of the Church in New York.

20–1. William Stephens to Dr. Beveridge, Hadstock, 11 May 1702. Testimonial for John Bartow. Endorsed by Edward Norton.

22. Bishop of Ely to —, Melton, near Doncaster, 16 May 1702 (slightly damaged), refers to subscription and says he is in Melton for his health.

23. Sir William Russell to Secretary, 19 May 1702. Most country gentlemen feel that present taxes make them unable to do much for society.

24. Sir William Whichcote to Secretary, Lin Hall, 4 June 1702, promising to support society.

25. Bishop of Salisbury to Secretary, 13 July 1702. Archdeacons will be the best persons to solicit subscriptions from clergy.

26. Bishop of Ely to Secretary, Ely, 14 July 1702, naming persons who might manage subscriptions.

27. Bishop of Chichester to Secretary, 15 July 1702. He will inquire among the clergy to see who might undertake the work.

28–9. Bishop of Chester to Secretary, Chester, 15 July 1702. Listing possible managers of the subscription.

30. Bishop of Bath and Wells to Secretary, Bath, 25 July 1702, with a similar list.

31. Sir Edmund Turner to the Secretary, Stoke, near Post Wytham in Lincolnshire, 17 Aug. 1702. He has sent Mr. Hodges (the treasurer) £107/4/6 collected by John Adamson, Rector of Burton-Coggley.

32. Do. to Secretary, 14 Sept. 1702, speaks of sending list of subscribers and names persons who might be appointed collectors.

33. Do. to do., same date. He has distributed copies of charter and abstracts and could use some more.

34. John Adamson to Secretary, Burton Coggley, 16 Sept. 1702, suggesting that collectors be listed in order of seniority.

35. Richard King to Secretary, Exon, 19 Sept. 1702, asking that official forms be sent for collection.

36. Draft of letter from Secretary to all 'deputies' (collectors), 6 Oct. 1702.

37. Richard King to Secretary, Exon, 7 Oct. 1702, enclosing some subscriptions.

38. A. Charlett to Secretary, University College, Oxford, 18 Oct. 1702. He has received a parcel of papers and given them to those for whom they were intended.

39. Sir John Philipps to Secretary, Picton, 20 Oct. 1702, concerning appointment of collectors in Diocese of St. Davids.

40. W. Buxhill to Secretary, Dedham, 3 Nov. 1702, recommending — Thomas as missionary to South Carolina.

41. Jenkin Williams to Secretary, Taunton, 9 Oct. 1702. Unspecified obligations at home prevent his accepting appointment as missionary.

42. George Bond to Secretary, 12 Dec. 1702, promising support.

43. Bishop Compton to Secretary, 18 Dec. 1702. He has received requests for ministers from Swansea, Mass., Westchester, N.Y., and an unnamed location between Philadelphia and Newcastle.

44. Nathaniel Marwick to Secretary, Taunton, 23 Dec. 1702. He is willing to go as missionary, if he can obtain his parents' consent, if his terms are met, and if he is sent to New York.

45. John Osmond to Secretary, Exeter, 16 Dec. 1702, acknowledging appointment as collector.

46. William Brown to Secretary, Haverford West, 17 Dec. 1702, acknowledging similar appointment.

47-8. Nathaniel Markwick to Secretary, Taunton, 4 Jan. 1703. As his parents oppose his going to America, he has accepted a benefice in the Diocese of Bath and Wells.

49. Joshua Walker to Secretary, Great Billing, near Northampton, 11 Jan. 1702/3. He has sent a gift of £5.

50. John Mackqueen to Secretary, Dover, 16 Jan. 1702/3, recommending George Mackqueen as missionary.

51. George Thorp to Dr. Beveridge, 28 Jan. 1702/3, authorizing him to subscribe £10 per annum in his name.

52. Bishop Compton to Secretary, 19 Feb. 1702/3, enclosing some papers.

53. George Thorp to Secretary, Christ Church, Canterbury, 11 Mar. 1702/3, subscribing fifty shillings a quarter.

54. A. Torriano to Secretary, Farnham Castle, 29 Mar. 1703. He will distribute the society's material at next visitation.

55. Bishop of Sarum to Secretary, Salisbury, 5 Apr. 1703. He is distributing appeal, but will not press for subscriptions until he learns what the 'trading towns' have done.

56. James Fall to Secretary, York, 5 Apr. 1703. Is sending contributions.

57. Bishop of Chester to Secretary, Chester, 10 Apr. 1703. He will have the society's material distributed at the forthcoming visitations, and will pay his own subscription.

58. James Gordon to Secretary, 13 Apr. 1703, concerning a bill drawn on the society by his deceased brother.

59. Bishop of Lichfield and Coventry to Secretary, 14 Apr. 1703. He will distribute appeal at next visitation.

60. Philip Stubs to Secretary, Wadham College, Oxford, 14 Apr. 1703, concerning collection.

61. Bishop of Ely to Secretary, 15 Apr. 1703. Sorry to hear that none of those he recommended has answered the Secretary's letters.

62. John Vaughan to Secretary, Carnarvon, South Wales, 15 Apr. 1703. Thinks it will help subscriptions there if he knows what has been subscribed elsewhere.

63. Richard King to Secretary, Exon, 24 Apr. 1703, reporting progress.

64. Bishop of Bristol to Secretary, Bristol, 28 Apr. 1703. He will ask his archdeacon to inquire in his next visitation for possible collectors in Dorsetshire.

65. John Thrale to the Archbishop of Canterbury, Exchequer, 30 Apr. 1703. As agent for the Colony of New York, he has been asked to remind the Archbishop of the request of the Lords Commissioners that he name a clergyman for that province.

66. Thomas Willis to the Secretary, Adderbury, near Banbury, 6 May 1703. On behalf of the Bishop of Llandaff, who is ill with the gout, he says the bishop will do what he can for the society when he goes to his diocese next March.

67. Bishop Compton to Secretary, Fulham, 11 May 1703, asking aid for Jackson, minister at St. John's, N.F.

68. Jonathan Edwards to Secretary, St. John's College, Oxford, 15 May 1703. He is sending testimonials for Nichols.

69. Francis Cooke to Secretary, Exeter, 17 May 1703. Writes on behalf of Bishop of Exeter to say that material arrived too late for distribution at archdeaconal visitation.

70. Archbishop of York to Secretary, Bishops-thorp, 26 May 1703. John Brook, a young clergyman whom he recommends, is willing to serve in the colonies, but his relatives will let him go only if they know where he is to be sent, and what his support is to be.

71. Francis Wyndham to Secretary, Clowerswall, 28 May 1703. Acknowledging election to membership.

72. Bishop of Oxford to Secretary, Worcester, 31 May 1703. He has arranged for distribution of the society's material.

73. Archbishop of York to Secretary, Bishops-thorpe, 7 June 1703, recommending Thompson, who offers to go to the colonies as schoolmaster.

74. Richard Wroe to Secretary, Manchester, 22 June 1703, enclosing a contribution.

75. Bishop of Chester to Secretary, Wigan, 29 June 1703, asking to whom he should pay subscription.

76. Archbishop of York to Secretary, 30 June 1703. Asks forms for testimonials and application for Brook, but doubts that Thompson, who is not a university man, is qualified for the post at New York, where Bishop Compton proposes to send him.

77–8. William Ashurst to Secretary, London, 30 June 1703. Doubts that his Corporation (for the Propagation of the Gospel in New England) will be able to aid the society in sending a missionary to the Mohawks, as they are already supporting three Dutch ministers among them.

79. Richard Wroe to Secretary, 9 July 1703. He, Joseph Yates, and Joseph Hooper are willing to serve as collectors.

80. Sir Edmund Turner to Secretary, Stoke, near Port Witham, 7 Aug. 1703, concerning collection in Lincolnshire.

81. Richard King to Secretary, Exon, 1 Sept. 1703. Has collected £20 for the society.

82. Richard Wroe to Secretary, 24 Sept. 1703, asking for more material to distribute.

83. John Evans to (Mr. Adamson, notation), 19 Sept. 1703. He has collected more than he expected, but thinks more could be done if the bishops and other leaders would push the work.

84. Francis Hildyard to Secretary, York, 11 Oct. 1703, transmitting some subscriptions.

85–6. John Adamson to Secretary, Burton, 1 Nov. 1703. Reports success of local subscription and urges a general collection.

87. Richard Wroe to Secretary, Burton, 1 Nov. 1703, acknowledging receipt of appointment as collector.

88. Codicil in will of John Robinson of Ruabon in the county of Denbigh, signed 26 Nov. 1703, leaving £50 in books and cash to society.

89. Charles Smith to Secretary, Ashelworth, near Gloucester, 14 Dec. 1703, asking further information concerning his appointment as missionary to Mohawks.

90. Thomas Tye to Secretary, 15 Dec. 1703. He is a candidate for appointment as missionary.

91. Do. to Secretary, Burton, 29 Dec. 1703. Finds some difficulty in obtaining additional testimonials as required.

92. Bishop Compton to Secretary, 8 Jan. 1703/4, asking aid for Urquhart, who is going to Jamaica, N.Y., Crawford, who is going to Dover Hundred, Del., and Stewart, who is going to Bedford, N.Y.

93. James Davis, Rector of Heyden in Essex, 3 Feb. 1703/4. Testimonial to Alexander Stuart, who has been studying with him at request of Dr. Bray. Letter to Stuart on reverse side.

94. Michael Bridges to Secretary, Burnsley, 7 Feb. 1703/4, asking for information on how to seek a missionary appointment.

95. John Adamson to Secretary, Burton-Coggsley near Stamford, 10 Feb. 1703/4, concerning collection in Lincolnshire.

96–7. William Popple to Secretary, Whitehall, 13 Feb. 1703/4. On behalf of Lords Commissioners of Trade and Plantations, he says that Queen allows a bounty of £20 to any minister going to the plantations. Commissioners think it would encourage ministers to go to colonies if they were assured of a benefice in England after a certain time. Suggests inquiring how funds are raised for Corporation for Propagation of the Gospel in New England.

98. Richard King to Secretary, Exon, 23 Feb. 1703/4. His recollection of the amount of his recent remittance differs from that reported by Hodges.

99. List of vice presidents, 1701–3/4.

100–1. Charles Smith to Secretary, Ashellworth, 19 Mar. 1703/4. Society rejected him for Indian mission because he is married, but proposed to send him to Roanoke, N.C. He is unwilling to go there, because it is too unhealthy, but will accept an appointment to South Carolina.

102. Bishop Compton to Secretary, Fulham, 18 Mar. 1703/4, introducing Thomas, who is willing to go to New York or New Jersey.

103. Do. to do., 10 Apr. 1704, introducing Wall, who would like some books to take to his parish in Virginia.

104. Michael Bridges to Secretary, Barnsley near Doncaster, 10 Apr. 1704, again seeking information about an application. He is a friend of Thorogood Moore's.

105. Bishop Compton to Committee, 17 Apr. 1704, recommending unnamed bearer to a mission.

106. W. Melmouth to Secretary, 21 Apr. 1704, with some paper that he wants to have presented to the society.

107. Anonymous note, London, 25 Apr. 1704, accompanying a gift of books.

108. Richard Wroe to Secretary, Manchester, 5 May 1704. Has not received sermons that were sent to him.

109. H. Gower to Dr. Stanley, St. John's College, Cambridge, 20 May 1704, describing efforts to organize trustees of charity bequeathed by Mr. Oley.

110. Draft of letter from Secretary to non-attending members, Petty France, Westminster, 12 May 1702.

111. Richard Wroe to Secretary, Manchester, 12 May 1704. The sermons have been received. The delay was caused by their being given to the Wigan carrier instead of to the Manchester carrier.

112. Bishop Compton to Committee, 13 May 1704. Berkley, whom he recommended for Braintree, Mass., has been obliged to return for want of support, but he has applied to the Queen for a grant to support ministers there and at Swansea and Narragansett.

113. W. Popple to Secretary, Whitehall, 23 May 1704. Lords Commissioners desire a copy of the society's charter and an account of what has been done under it.

114–15. H. Gower to Dr. Stanley, St. John's College, Cambridge, 23 May 1704 (two copies), relating to the Oley charity (109).

116–17. Thomas Bray to Secretary, Sheldon, near Birmingham, 24 May 1704, concerning payment of allowance to Lockier.

118. Thomas Locke to Secretary, 6 June 1704, concerning the Oley charity.

119. Thomas Bray to Secretary, 11 June 1704. He has received favourable reports of Lockier's work in Rhode Island.

120. Thomas Locke to Secretary, 6 July 1704. Oley's will made no reference to the society, which was not in existence when it was drawn, but allows trustees to give a considerable sum towards the propagation of the Gospel.

121–2. Extract of a letter from Gov. Dudley of Massachusetts to Lords Commissioners, 13 July 1704, saying colonial authorities are sending a delegation to conciliate the Iroquois, as is customary every five years, and expressing fear that their alliance will be lost if a missionary is not sent among them.

123. G. Barnsley, Selscomb, 21 July 1704 and James Cranston, Hasting, 23 July 1704 to Secretary, acknowledging appointment as collectors.

124. William Turner to Secretary, Stamford, 12 Aug. 1704. Testimonial to Moore.

125–6. Richard Wroe to Secretary, 14 Aug. 1704. Reports sending contributions collected in his area.

127. John Evans to Secretary, Uffington, 2 Sept. 1704. He does not know Buckton, about whom the Secretary has inquired, but has obtained a testimonial from head of school in Stamford, where Buckton was an usher.

128. Bishop Compton to Treasurer, 7 Sept. 1704, asking that Jackson's allowance be paid to bearer, his agent.

129. J. Sayer to Secretary, Whitnisham, 5 Oct. 1704, enclosing a contribution and offering to serve as collector.

130–1. Thomas Bray to Secretary, Sheldon, 11 Nov. 1704. He does not know who is responsible for paying Gov. Nicholson's benefaction to the society.

132–3. John Blair to Committee, London, 20 Nov. 1704. He is in debt as the result of being taken by the French on way to North Carolina.

134. Secretary to Primate of Ireland and Archbishop of Dublin, St. Martin's Library, 15 Dec. 1704 (draft), enclosing material relating to the society.

135–6. Thomas Bray to Secretary, Sheldon, 23 Dec. 1704. In response to an inquiry occasioned by a petition from the wife of Robert Keith, he says that Keith was not granted an allowance when he went to Maryland in 1701, because local support was deemed sufficient.

137. George Barnsley to Secretary, Selscomb, 26 Dec. 1704, reporting collections.

138. Bishop of Londonderry to Bishop Compton, 11 Jan. 1704/5, asking him to find a post for son of Col. Blayer.

139. Bishop Compton to Committee, Fulham, 12 Jan. 1704/5, asking them to examine Marston, whom he proposes to send as catechist to New York.

140. Archbishop of Armagh to Secretary, 30 Jan. 1704/5, acknowledging receipt of material relating to society.

141. William Popple to Bishop Compton, Whitehall, 3 Feb. 1704/5, enclosing 121–2.

142. Bishop Compton to Committee, 5 Feb. 1704/5, introducing Aeneas Mackenzie, recommended for appointment to New York or New Jersey.

143. Do. to Secretary, 15 Feb. 1704/5. Knows no one to recommend for an unspecified mission, unless they send Bondet there instead of to New York. Urges that assistance be provided for Evans in Philadelphia.

144. William Turner to Secretary, Stamford, —— Feb. 1704/5. If Buckton ever had a serious defect in speech, he has overcome it, and he has maintained a good character since he has been in that area.

145–7. Archbishop of Dublin to Secretary, 26 Feb. 1704, asking gift of books for Rea, who is going to Jamaica, W.I.

148. Bishop Compton to Committee, 2 Mar. 1704/5, introducing Ross, who is seeking an appointment to New York.

149. Do. to Secretary, 4 Mar. 1705, asking allowance for Talbot at Burlington, N.J.

150. Do. to do., Fulham, 14 Mar. 1705, introducing 'the two Appia's', Vaudois missionaries.

151–2. Thomas Bray to Secretary, Sheldon, 14 Mar. 1704/5. In answer to an inquiry as to who is responsible for continuing allowance to Tibbs in Maryland, he says that, in order to obtain support of deputies from the poorer parishes for the establishment act, he had to promise help in supplying them with ministers. When this act was disallowed, and he sent back the draft of an act that would be approved, six ministers were sent over with it, three of them, including Tibbs, with an allowance. He originally made himself responsible for this, but as the subscriptions originally made for that purpose were transferred to the society, he thinks it should accept responsibility for continuing the allowance.

153. Bishop Compton to Committee, Fulham, 7 May 1705, asking them to examine William Guy whom he thinks may be the proper person to send to Rye, N.Y.

154. Do. to do., Fulham, 11 May 1705, introducing Thomas Lloyd, recommended by the Bishop of Bangor for Bermuda.

155. Do. to Secretary, Fulham, 17 May 1705, introducing Jacob Rice, who may be a good person to send to Newfoundland, as the government is recalling Jackson.

156. Josua Walker to Secretary, Great Billing, near Northampton, 19 May 1705, enclosing a contribution.

157. Bishop of Peterborough to Secretary, Peterborough, 9 June 1705, naming clergy who may be qualified to serve as collectors.

158. Archbishop of York to Secretary, Bishops-thorpe, 23 June 1705. He ordained Guy ten years ago and was favourably impressed by him then, but has only seen him once since.

159. Bishop Compton to Secretary, 30 June 1705. As the people in Muirson's former parish (unnamed) resent his having come home for orders, Compton recommends sending him to Rye, N.Y., where the people have been discouraged by Pritchard. He recommends continuing Honeyman on Long Island.

160. Archbishop of York to Secretary, Bishops-thorpe, 23 July 1705. He has been told by resident of parish in Nottinghamshire where Guy was a curate, that he left parish without notice to rector, because of a scandal caused by his drinking.

161. Vigerius Edwards to Secretary, Old Bayley, 17 Aug. 1705. Prevented by rheumatism from attending meeting, he reports that he and Dr. Bradford have audited the treasurer's accounts.

162. Memorandum listing 'matters of the Society Adjourn'd on various dates'. Latest date 3 Sept. 1705.

163. Humphrey Hody to Secretary, Monks Risborough in Bucks., 13 Sept. 1705, having retired to the country, he is discontinuing his subscription.

164. Charles Smith to Secretary, Ashellworth, near Gloucester, 3 Oct. 1705. He is willing to go as missionary to Iroquois instead of to South Carolina as formerly proposed.

165. William Hamilton to Secretary, Callidon, near Armagh, 10 Oct. 1705. Testimonial to Andrew Auchinleek.

166. George Keith to Secretary, London, 16 Oct. 1705, listing previous payments by the society to Talbot.

167–9. Extract from the will of Jane Brown, 3 Nov. 1705, bequeathing £100 in trust to be paid to the society in five annual instalments.

170. Bishop Compton to Committee, 5 Nov. 1705, introducing Tuckerman, who is going to the Leewards and solicits books.

171. George Keith to Secretary, London, 13 Nov. 1705. He has received a letter from Talbot, who asks continuance of his allowance.

172. Archbishop of Dublin to Bishop Compton, Pall Mall, 13 Nov. 1705, recommending William Dun.

173. Bishop Compton to Committee, Fulham, 6 Dec. 1705, recommending Roberts for Salem, N.J.

174. James Cranston to Secretary, Hastings in Sussex, 8 Dec. 1705. He has had poor success as a collector but has a chance to obtain a benefaction from a nobleman.

175. Bishop Compton to Committee, Fulham, 10 Dec. 1705, asking gift of books for Wright, who is going to the Leewards.

176. Undated note from Bishop Compton that appears to have been included with (175), asking that Talbot be established at Burlington, N.J., and that books be sent him.

177. Bishop Compton to Secretary, Fulham, 17 Dec. 1705, asking that a gift be made to Evan Evans in Philadelphia, who is inadequately supported by local contributions, and that an assistant be sent him. Suggests Roberts for the post. Lord Cornbury has asked that a missionary be sent to eastern Long Island. Honeyman asks that his allowance be continued in Rhode Island.

178. George Keith to Treasurer, Eburton, 17 Dec. 1705, concerning publication of his journal.

179–80. Do to do., 29 Dec. 1705, recommending allowance for Andrew Rudman.

181. Do. to Secretary, 27 Dec. 1705, concerning publication of his journal.

182–3. Standing orders of the society. Marginal dates extend through 1705.

184. Secretary to Bishop Compton, Petty France, 2 Jan. 1706 (copy), asking him to obtain Queen's bounty for Jenkins, who is going to Apoquimininck, Del.;

to seek a royal allowance for a minister at Albany, and to propose a place for Cordiner.

185. Bishop Compton to Secretary, Fulham, 7 Jan. 1706. There are legal difficulties in the way of obtaining a chaplain's stipend at Albany. If the society will send Cordiner there, with an allowance as schoolmaster, Compton will undertake to obtain another £50 from some source. Recommends continuing Honeyman in (Newport) Rhode Island, as Bridge has gone to Narragansett.

186. Do. to Committee, 18 Jan. 1706, introducing Maul, who is recommended by the Archbishop of Dublin.

187–8. Do. to Dr. Maplecroft, 16 Jan. 1706. Urges sending Cordiner to Albany and appointing Black to assist Brooks. Regrets that stipend of Bartow has been stopped, as he has done good work in Westchester.

189. Draft of letter of thanks for contributions, 22 Jan. 1705/6.

190–1. William Ashurst to Secretary, London, 26 Jan. 1705/6, describing financial and other arrangements of the Corporation for the Propagation of the Gospel in New England.

192. Bishop Compton to Christopher Bridge, Fulham, 4 Feb. 1706, advising him to leave Boston, because of friction, and accept appointment in Rhode Island.

193. Treasurer to Secretary, 6 Feb. 1706. He needs the secretary's alphabetical list of members to compile a list of members trading with the colonies, as requested by the committee.

194. Bishop Compton to Secretary, Fulham, 13 Feb. 1706. Discusses several possible appointments.

195. Bishop of Bangor to Secretary, 21 Feb. 1706, asking for a gift of books to Sheppard, who is going to Virginia.

196. Archbishop of Dublin to Secretary, Dublin, 25 Feb. 1706. In answer to an inquiry, he says that Lord Cutts died insolvent.

197. James Chalmers to Secretary, 27 Feb. 1705/6. Testimonial to James Ray.

198. George Wheeler to Secretary, Durham, 14 Mar. 1706, enclosing a bill for £5. Recommends Theophilus Pickering, Sir Ralph Carre, and John Smith for membership.

199. Secretary to Col. Yeate, 9 Apr. 1706 (copy), asking how to proceed in seeking aid for the society from the City of Bristol.

200. Certificate of John Harding, bookseller, and William Cooper, his assistant, 7 and 13 Apr. 1706, saying that after buying some books from an unidentified clergyman, they found the society's seal in them.

201. George Barnsley to Secretary, Selscomb, 15 Apr. 1706, returning commission sent to him and to Cranston to collect for society.

202. Bishop Compton to Secretary, 15 Apr. 1706. Received unspecified charge too late to stop Wright from sailing, but will write him to see what answer he can give.

203-4. George Wright to Bishop Compton, Plymouth, 3 May 1706. The charge is selling the society's books, which he admits, but seeks to extenuate.

205. Secretary to Mr. Yate, Petty France, 24 Mar. 1706, resigning as justice of the peace in Westminster because he feels that his colleagues are lax in punishing prostitution.

206. Do. to Barnsley, Petty France, 28 May 1706, thanking him for remittance (copy).

207. Bishop Compton to Secretary, 13 June 1706, recommending Roberts for Salem or Apoquimininck.

208. John Adamson to Secretary, Burton, 13 June 1706. Sir Edmund Turner has withdrawn his subscription because age requires him to close his London house, but will probably contribute the same amount voluntarily. Adamson proposes a general collection for the society.

209. Sir Jeff. Jeffreys to Secretary, London, 27 June 1706. He sent the society's books to Pritchard, but they were lost, as the ship was taken by the French. Pritchard left no estate.

210. Bishop Compton to Secretary, 29 June 1706, introducing Black, who is well recommended.

211. William Turner to Secretary, Stamford, 2 July 1706. He would like to go to the colonies as a schoolmaster, but has not yet been able to obtain his wife's consent.

212. Secretary to Archbishop of Cashel, Petty France, 2 July 1706, acknowledging contribution.

213. Bishop Compton to Secretary, 4 July 1706, concerning several appointments.

214. Frideni Bonet to Secretary, 22 July 1706 (in French), recommending Benedict Picket as a member.

215. George Keith to Secretary, Eburton, 1 Aug. 1706, concerning publication of his journal.

216. C. Whiting to Stubbs, Ross, 10 Aug. 1706. He has received a gift of £5 and a silver flagon for Communion as the result of a sermon on behalf of the society.

217. Henry Newman to Treasurer, 16 Aug. 1706, asking aid for J(ackson?) a former missionary, now unemployed, though the Queen has promised to do something for him sometime.

218. C. Congreve to Secretary, Portsmouth, 19 Aug. 1706, asking if any action has been taken concerning appointment of John Humphreys as schoolmaster at Albany.

219. Do. to do, Portsmouth, 20 Aug. 1706. He has put in writing some proposals for promoting the Church in America, and will send them to the committee if requested. Two of them appear on the reverse of sheet. They are: that vacant lands in New York and other colonies be held in trust for the support of bishops, and that glebe lands be provided in several colonies.

220. C. Whiting to Stubbs, Ross, 18 Sept. 1706. Refers to a contribution to the society, but is chiefly concerned with apprenticing a poor relation to some trade.

221. Bishop Compton to Secretary, 26 Sept. 1706. Agrees to send Black to Boston.

222. John Osmond to Secretary, 14 Oct. 1706, enclosing contributions.

223. Bishop Compton to Secretary, 14 Oct. 1706. An unnamed visitor from New England thinks Black too young for the lectureship in Boston, so why not send him to Narragansett? Recommends Roberts for Salem.

224. Do. to do., 18 Oct. 1706. Proposes Sir Charles Hobby, a rich planter from Jamaica, W.I., as a member and wonders if anything can be done for Innes in New Jersey and Rice in Newfoundland.

225. Do. to do., 25 Oct. 1706, introducing unnamed bearer, who has a testimonial from the Bishop of Londonderry.

226. Do. to do., Fulham, 15 Nov. 1706. As the shortness of the day and the badness of the road prevent his attending the committee, he inquires about its action on several matters in which he is interested.

227. Do. to do., 27 Nov. 1706, introducing Robinson, a prospective missionary.

228–9. Do. to do., 29 Nov. 1706, asking that committee be patient with some person unnamed.

230. Bonet to Secretary, Suffolk St., 9 Dec. 1706, introducing Lubominski a Polish convert from Roman Catholicism.

231. Bishop Compton to Secretary, 20 Dec. 1706. Recommends Cordiner for Albany, Black and Robinson for North Carolina, and Jenkins for Apoquimininck.

232. Bishop of Gloucester to Secretary, 23 Dec. 1706, explaining deprivation of Talbot (cf. i. 138–9, 143–4). As the living was a poor one, he thought the curate should have the full income. Talbot had resigned, but refused to put his resignation in legal form, and the patron grew impatient.

233–4. William Black to Secretary, Plymouth, 3 Jan. 1707 (probably 1708). He and Jenkins have run out of money because of delays in sailing.

235. Bishop Compton to Secretary, Fulham, 18 Jan. 1706/7. Suggests sending Cordiner to Albany and Bridge to (Newport) Rhode Island, transferring Honeyman to Narragansett.

236. Secretary to Archbishop of Dublin, Petty France, Westminster, 3 Feb. 1706/7, thanking him for recommending Maule.

237. Wilt. Stanley to Secretary, Hadham, 3 Feb. 1706/7. He is unwilling that a hastily written piece of his be used in a projected work by Dr. Woodroff.

238. Secretary to Whistler, Petty France, Westminster, 5 Feb. 1706/7 (copy), acknowledging a benefaction.

239–40. Bishop Compton to Secretary, 6 Feb. 1706/7, with a memorandum of recommendations to be presented to committee.

241–2. Archbishop of Cashel to Secretary, Dublin, 25 Feb. 1706/7. He does not find the bishops of his province much inclined to support the society, but thinks they might be if written to individually.

243. Archbishop of Armagh to Secretary, Dublin, 4 Mar. 1706. He did not press collection for society when he first received material, as the bishops of his province were concerned with building manses, authorized by a recent act of Parliament, and he was concerned with founding a public library, which he stocked by purchasing Bishop Stillingfleet's library. These pressures being lessened, he is prepared to send a gift of £300.

244. Bishop Compton to Secretary, Fulham, 22 Mar. 1706/7, asking that an unnamed person be recommended to committee.

245. Secretary to Archbishop of Dublin, Petty France, Westminster, 25 Mar. 1707, again thanking him for recommending Maule.

246. Bishop Compton to Secretary, 29 Mar. 1707, recommending Black for Sussex County, Del.

247. Secretary to Archbishop of Cashel, Petty France, Westminster, Mar. 1706/7 (copy). His letter (241–2) was presented to society. Most members think that an appeal to the Irish bishops would have more weight if it came from the archbishops.

248. Do. to Archbishop of Armagh, acknowledging contribution referred to in (243). Undated draft, but evidently authorized at March meeting.

249. Another, much corrected draft of the same letter.

250. George Keith to Committee, Eburton, 4 Apr. 1707, asking aid for Talbot.

251. Extract from will of Edward Clifford, dated 4 Apr. 1707, leaving £100 for the advancement of the Protestant religion in the West Indies.

252. Bishop Compton to Secretary, 12 Apr. 1707. He is surprised to learn that Maule has sailed for Carolina, as he thought that he was to be sent to New Jersey with Brooke.

253–5. Talbot to Secretary, London, 16 Apr. 1707. Asks society to return him to America. Hints that he has been beset by rumours.

256. Archbishop of Armagh to Secretary, Dublin, 23 Apr. 1707. He is remitting the £300.

257. Bishop Compton to Committee, Fulham, 28 Apr. 1707, asking grant for Walker, who is going with Cordiner to be schoolmaster in his parish.

258. Do. to Secretary, 3 May 1707, suggesting applying to American merchants and planters for contributions.

259. Secretary to Dr. Edwards, Petty France, Westminster, 6 May 1707 (copy). As Nichols, one of the missionaries, says he is not receiving income from a travelling fellowship at Oxford, Edwards is asked to ascertain the facts.

260. Bishop Compton to Secretary, Fulham, 12 May 1707. Asks gift of books to Evans, who is going to Virginia, and inquires when Bridge's salary will start in Narragansett.

261. Jonathan Edwards to Secretary (Jesus College, Oxford), 11 May 1707. Nichols stipend has been regularly paid.

262. Bishop Compton to Secretary, 16 May 1707, asking what decision has been made concerning Bridge, who has been at Narragansett six months.

263. Con. (?) Yeats to Shute, Marlborough, 22 May 1707. Brown, of Cottley, Bradford Parish, Wilts., has left £100 to the society.

264. Bishop Compton to Secretary, 24 May 1707, recommending Wood.

265. Robert Atkyns to Bishop of Gloucester, Lower (?, writing smudged), 29 May 1707, offering gift of £100 to the society.

266. Josiah Woodward to Secretary, 30 May 1707, asking help for widow of (Samuel) Thomas.

267. Bishop Compton to Secretary, 21 June 1707, urging allowance for Bridge.

268. Do. to do., 21 June 1707. Cordiner is in financial difficulties because of delayed sailing.

269. Bishop of Gloucester to (Archbishop Tenison), Little Chelsey, 21 June 1707, enclosing (265).

270-1. Archbishop of Cashel to Secretary, Dublin, 24 June 1707, reports sending a contribution, and says he has received Keith's journal.

VOLUME VIII

CORRESPONDENCE

BRITISH ISLES, July 1707–undated

1. Frideni Bonet to Secretary, Suffolk St., 4 July 1707, enclosing a memorial from Italian converts in Geneva.

2. Bishop Compton to Secretary, 15 July 1707, introducing (Gideon) Johnston, who has come over for orders. Hopes Bridge's affairs can be settled, so Compton can name an assistant for Boston.

3. Maynard Colchester to Secretary, 15 July 1707, Wesbury. He is well acquainted with Danvers Hodges, who is reputed to have a good estate.

4. Bishop Compton to Secretary, 22 July 1707, recommending Johnston for Charleston.

5. Secretary to Archbishop of Cashel, Petty France, Westminster, 26 July 1707 (copy), acknowledging gift and reporting transmission of promotional material for society and S.P.C.K.

6. Robert Atkyns to Bishop of Gloucester, Lower Swell, 28 July 1707. Accepts membership in the society, though his age will keep him from attending meetings.

7. Theodore Vesey to Secretary, Litchfield St., Soho, 18 Aug. 1707, subscribing £20 per annum on behalf of Archbishop of Tuam.

8. Bishop Compton to Committee, 16 Aug. 1707, introducing Mill, who is recommended for North Carolina.

9. John Rogers to Secretary, Leicester, 16 Aug. 1707, asking to whom he could remit a contribution.

10–11. Samuel Weale to Secretary, 25 Aug. 1707, saying he is prepared to present a plan for raising money.

12. Archbishop of Cashel to Secretary, Dublin, 26 Aug. 1707. Parcel referred to in (5) not received.

13. Bishop Compton to Committee, 1 Sept. 1707, introducing Glan, who offers himself for the plantations.

14. Do. to Secretary, 4 Sept. 1707, concerning difficulties of Black and Cordiner in obtaining passage because of war.

15. Do. to Committee, 12 Sept. 1707, introducing Gordon, whom he recommends for North Carolina.

16. John Rogers to Treasurer, Leicester, 13 Sept. 1707, remitting a contribution of £10 from John Alleyne.

17. Bishop Compton to Secretary, 24 Sept. 1707, introducing Winkworth, recommended by Speaker.

18. Do. to do., 25 Sept. 1707, introducing Milne.

19. Do. to do., 25 Sept. 1707. Welsh in Pennsylvania are asking for a missionary who can speak their language, as some do not speak English. Mr. Evans, the bearer, can recommend someone, if the society is willing to send him.

20. Secretary to Archbishop of Tuam, Petty France, Westminster, 25 Sept. 1707 (copy). Acknowledges subscription, but regrets that society cannot at present find a place for Johnson, recommended by the archbishop, as their resources will be strained in fulfilling their commitment to send two missionaries to North Carolina.

21. Humphrey Wanley to Secretary, Duke St., York-buildings, 29 Sept. 1707. Testimonial to Gordon.

22. Secretary to Walker, Petty France, Westminster, 4 Oct. 1707 (copy). Sorry for his misfortunes, but society is unable to do anything for him beyond the gift of £5 already sent.

23. Bishop Compton to Secretary, 17 Oct. 1707. Recommends sending Milne to Choptank, Md., with an allowance, as poor state of tobacco trade has made some Maryland livings inadequate.

24a. Samuel Weale to Secretary, 17 Oct. 1707. He was unprepared to reveal his plan to Taylor, who called on behalf of the archbishop, but will disclose it to the Secretary.

24b. N. W. Edgar to John Hutchinson, Ipswich, 27 Oct. 1707. Will (vii. 251) was one of three drawn by Clifford.

25. Bishop Compton to Secretary, 3 Nov. 1707 asking for books for Cunningham and Thompson, who are going to Jamaica, W.I.

26. J. Woodward to Secretary, Popler, 21 Nov. 1707. Unable to attend meeting, he asks secretary to present a letter from Wallace, minister at Elizabeth City, Va., and a request from Neau for a short catechism for his Indian catechumens.

27. Bishop Compton to Secretary, 27 Nov. 1707. A second request for books for Cunningham and Thompson.

28. Do. to do., 3 Dec. 1707, enclosing unspecified material.

29. James Adams to Secretary, Kingslae, 9 Dec. 1707. Ship on which he was going to Virginia driven into Irish port by unfavourable winds.

30. Secretary to Archdeacon Rogers, Petty France, Westminster, 25 Dec. 1707 (copy), informing him of election as member.

31. Do. to Bishop of Oxford, Petty France, Westminster, 25 Dec. 1707 (copy), asking him to preach at anniversary meeting. Postscript says that in consequence of his accidental discovery of a bequest to the society, he has been instructed to ask all bishops to have their registers checked for such bequests.

32. Do. to Ducket, Petty France, 30 Dec. 1707 (copy), asking about the Clifford will (cf. vii. 251, vii. 24b).

33. Do. to Archdeacons who are members of society, Petty France, Westminster, 2 Jan. 1707/8 (copy), asking them to check registers for bequests.

34. Bishop of Oxford to Secretary, Worcester, 3 Jan. 1707 (8), asking to be excused from preaching because of pressure of business.

35. Evans to Secretary, Wrexham, 6 Jan. 1707/8. Mainly in answer to an inquiry about a book, but also mentions a bequest to society.

36. Copy of codicil in will of Mr. Robinson, referred to in (35). Attested by Richard Davies, 9 Jan. 1707/8.

37. Secretary to Evans, Petty France, 22 Jan. 1707/8 (copy), acknowledging (35 and 36).

38. Do. to Symonds, 22 Jan. 1707/8 (copy), acknowledging gift.

39–40. Bishop Compton to Committee, 31 Jan. 1707/8, asking gift of books for Hindman, who is going to Maryland.

41. J. Shepherd to Dr. Hutchinson, Herringfield, 5 Feb. 1707/8. Defectiveness of Clifford's will (cf. vii. 251, viii. 24b, 32), makes collection of the bequest difficult.

42. Samuel Weale to Secretary, 17 Feb. 1707(8), asking him to present some memorial to society.

43. Archbishop of Dublin to Secretary, Dublin, 18 Feb. 1708, introducing Reynolds.

44–5. The memorial of Samuel Weale referred to in (42), 20 Feb. 1707(8). Does not reveal his plan, but says he will disclose it if a committee will wait on him in Fleet Prison, where he is confined.

46. Archbishop of Cashel to Secretary, Cashel, 21 Feb. 1707/8. He has received the material referred to in (5), but does not have much hope of obtaining support. Still thinks a direct appeal to the Irish bishops would be more effective.

47. Bishop Compton to Secretary, 27 Feb. 1707/8. Recommends restoring stipend to Honeyman.

48. Richard King to Treasurer, Exon, 5 Apr. 1708, concerning his subscription and gift from another.

49. Robert Keith to Secretary, London, 14 Apr. 1708. As his allowance has been discontinued because of failure to sail for America, he offers explanations.

50. Mary Keith to (Secretary?), London, 14 Apr. 1708. She hopes society will not restore her husband's allowance, as she does not want to go to America, but please do not tell him.

51. Robert Wake to Secretary, Pembroke College, 15 Apr. 1708. On behalf of Bishop of Bristol, he says bishop will decide what action to take when he receives papers that are being sent. He has sent return of small livings in his diocese to the Exchequer, as required by the Act.

52. Francis Tweed to Vigerius Edwards, 17 Apr. 1708, excusing delay in payment of rent as society's tenant.

53. Bishop of Gloucester to Secretary, Little Chelsea, 21 Apr. 1708. Financial difficulties oblige him to discontinue subscription.

54. Edward Dummer to Secretary, Middle Temple, 23 Apr. 1708. As circumstances obliged him to leave town, he was unable to present a memorial that he had prepared for the Bishop of Llandaff.

55. Secretary to Bishop of Hereford, Petty France, Westminster, 25 May 1708, acknowledging discontinuance of subscription.

56. Do. to Bishop of Bristol, Petty France, Westminster, 29 May 1708 (copy), acknowledging (51).

57. Do. to Bishop of Gloucester, Petty France, 29 May 1708 (copy), regretting discontinuance of subscription.

58. Bishop Compton to Secretary, 20 May 1708, asking him to present Honeyman's case to the society.

59. Bishop of Hereford to Secretary, Whitborn, 2 June 1708, offering to pay arrears of subscription in annual instalments.

60. George Keith to Secretary, Eburton, 4 June 1708. He has received reports from Talbot concerning Moore and Brooke, who have sailed from New England, and Honeyman, whose continuance in Rhode Island he recommends.

61. Bishop Compton to Secretary, 11 June 1708. Col. Quarry gives a favourable report concerning Honeyman and thinks Bridge is fomenting trouble.

62. Do. to do., 21 June 1708 (by amanuensis, because unable to write). Convinced that Bridge is in the wrong in dispute with Honeyman.

63-4. Do. to do., 9 July 1708. Copy of a letter from Samuel Albro, with whom Bridge lodged at Narragansett, complaining of his abusive behaviour.

65. Robert Cotton to Secretary, Newcastle, 25 July 1708, enclosing a contribution.

66. Bishop Compton to Secretary, 26 July 1708. Recommends sending Bridge to New Jersey or Maryland.

67. Archbishop of Dublin to Secretary, Dublin, 7 Aug. 1708, recommending Fausset.

68. William Taylor to Secretary, 10 Aug. 1708, summarizing some minutes of the society concerning missionaries.

69. Secretary to Archdeacon Rogers, Petty France, 12 Oct. 1708 (copy), acknowledging contribution.

70. Thomas Templeman to Secretary, Arundell, 14 Oct. 1708. Mr. Windham is unable to continue his subscription.

71. Francis Tweed to Vigerius Edwards, 23 Oct. 1708, remitting some payments, but not as much as he would like to.

72. Bishop Compton to Secretary, 23 Dec. 1708. Excuses Nicholls for going from Chester, Pa., to Maryland and Ross for going from Newcastle, Del., to Chester. Blames Jenkins for ousting Ross from Newcastle. Mylne has settled in Virginia. Compton approves aid to Van der Eyghen and would like to see something done for Auchinleek and Eburn in Bermuda.

73. Secretary to Ducket, Petty France, Westminster, 1 Jan. 1708/9 (copy), thanking him for aid in connection with the Clifford will. (Previous ref. 41.)

74. Secretary to Kelshall, Petty France, Westminster, 1 Jan. 1708/9 (copy), thanking him for aid in connection with Clifford legacy, which has finally been paid by Mr. Middleton.

75. Do. to Shepherd, Petty France, Westminster, 1 Jan. 1708/9 (copy), thanking him for aid in the same matter.

76. Do. to Middleton, Petty France, Westminster, 1 Jan. 1708/9 (copy), thanking him for remitting bequest.

77. Bishop Compton to Secretary, 5 Jan. 1708/9, enclosing a petition on behalf of Rudman, who is at point of death.

78. Do. to do., 18 Jan. 1708/9. Prevented by gout from attending meeting, he asks society not to be too hard on offending missionaries.

79. Secretary to Archbishop of Dublin, Petty France, Westminster, 10 Feb. 1708/9. If two or three gentlemen with proper testimonials and the archbishop's recommendation come over immediately, they will have a good prospect of getting appointments.

80. Bishop Compton to Secretary, 12 Feb. 1708/9, enclosing a letter that he wants delivered to Lord Mayor.

81. Do. to do., 19 Mar. 1708/9, urging clemency for offenders. (Cf. 72.)

82. Do. to do., 25 Mar. 1709, introducing Wallace.

83. James Chalmers to Bishop Compton, London, 25 Mar. 1709. Testimonial to Samual Wallace.

84. Bishop Compton to Secretary, 29 Mar. 1709, recommending quick dispatch of Reynolds, as this is the season when ships are in haste to sail, and it is difficult to send missionaries later.

85. James Chalmers to Secretary, St. Martin's Churchyard, 30 Mar. 1709. Testimonial to Samuel Wallace.

86. Bishop Compton to Secretary, 1 Apr. 1709. A second introduction of Wallace.

87. Do. to do., 7 Apr. 1709. He has ordained Wallace a deacon.

88. Do. to do., 4 May 1709, recommending King. Evans reports admonishing Jenkins for abandoning Apoquimininck.

89. Francis Pemberton to Vigerius Edwards, Belchamp St. Pauls, 14 May 1709. He has spoken to Tweed, who agrees to be at next meeting of society to account for his arrears.

90. Secretary to Archbishop of Cashel, Petty France, Westminster, 14 May 1709 (copy). He has heard from Mr. Jones that the archbishop complains of not hearing from him, but it is the archbishop who is at fault, not having acknowledged a recent shipment of books.

91. Schemettau to Secretary, London, 16 May 1709 (in French), recommending Achenbach, chaplain to the King of Prussia, for membership.

92–3. Unsigned proposal, 16 May 1709, asking that a minister who can read German be sent with Palatines going to New York. As they are mixed Calvinist and Lutheran, they would probably unite in the use of the liturgy of the Church of England.

94. Richard Rooth to Secretary, Epsom, 19 May 1709. Missionaries in Pennsylvania frequently desert their posts. Chester and Newcastle are vacant. Minister who should be in Newcastle is trying to get position as assistant and schoolmaster in Philadelphia.

95. Bishop Compton to Secretary, 23 May 1709, introducing Andrew Boyd.

96–7. James Reynolds to Secretary, 29 May 1709. He has been delayed in obtaining passage.

98. Francis Pemberton to Vigerius Edwards, Belcham St. Pauls, 19 May 1709. Tweed is coming to London, but Pemberton thinks it would be better for both tenant and society if accounts were examined and rent collected by a local official in the future.

99. James Chalmers to Secretary, London, 30 May 1709. Testimonial to Andrew Boyd.

100. James Reynolds to Secretary, Plymouth, 30 May 1709. He has obtained passage to Boston.

101. Secretary to Jones, Petty France, Westminster, 26 July 1709 (copy). Jones has been appointed a collector, but secretary presumes he will not start until he has finished collecting for the Palatines.

102. Bishop Compton to Secretary, 13 Aug. 1709, introducing Urmston.

103. William Jones to Secretary, Hourne, 8 Aug. 1709. Acknowledges appointment. Thinks Archbishop of Cashel would be pleased with election as a member.

104. Bishop of Salisbury to Secretary, 8 Aug. 1709, introducing Halliday.

105. Archbishop of Cashel to Secretary, Dublin, 15 Sept. 1709. Says he did acknowledge former shipment. Asks that more material be sent.

106. Josiah Woodward to Secretary, Popler, 21 Oct. 1709. Prevented from attending meeting by shortness of days and bad weather. Neau has submitted a sample catechism for approval and asks assistance for Bondet.

107. Bishop of Bangor to Secretary, 24 Oct. 1709. Nicholas Pitts left £1,000 to society, but died before executing his will. Something may be obtained by application to his heir at law, George Pitts.

108. William Jones to Secretary, Hourne, 16 Nov. 1709. Archbishop of Cashel has indicated that he would be honoured by election as member of society. As the Palatine collection is unfinished, Jones has not started on that for the society.

109. Bishop Compton to Secretary, 17 Nov. 1709, asking books for Gignillat, who is going to a French congregation in South Carolina.

110. Do. to do., 30 Nov. 1709, introducing Coleby.

111. Do. to do., 22 Jan. 1710. Quotes letter from Governor of Virginia suggesting that society aid poorer parishes there during present crisis in tobacco market.

112. Secretary to Capt. Gordon, Petty France, Westminster, 18 Feb. 1709/10 (copy), transmitting a parcel of books in acknowledgement of some favour to the society.

113. Do. to Sinclair, Petty France, Westminster, 28 Mar. 1710 (copy), sending a parcel of books to be distributed among an 'unruly crowd', apparently on shipboard.

114. Archbishop Tenison to Secretary, 19 May 1740, asking that action on appointment of Griffith be deferred until the archbishop can attend, because of Romanizing tendencies detected in Griffith's *Serious and Friendly Call to ye Dissenters*.

115. Edward Bishop to Secretary, Martock, 16 Feb. 1710/11, asking if there has been any decision of proposal to send him as missionary to Iroquois.

116. William Ward to Secretary, Portsmouth, 6 Mar. 1710/11, asking what should be done with a chest of books sent him a year ago, padlocked, without key.

117. Archbishop of Armagh to Secretary, Dublin, 28 Mar. 1710/11. Is sending another contribution of £300. Refers to a plan for establishing charity schools to convert infidels in Malabar, and a similar project, which he is supporting, to provide charity schools which will bring up Irish children as Protestants.

118. John Norris to Secretary, 20 Mar. 1710/11. An unnamed schoolmaster near him in Carolina has offered to teach Indian children free. His school is some distance from the Indians, and Norris wonders if the society could help him to move it nearer.

119. Lord Dartmouth to Archbishop of York, Whitehall, 28 Mar. 1722. Queen has decided not to authorize a general collection for the society on Good Friday, as she is informed that it is customary to make collections for other charities on that day, but she will authorize a collection at some future date.

120. Nathaniel Carpenter to the Secretary, 29 Mar. 1711. Recommends Walter Douglas, who is going as governor of the Leeward Islands, as a member of the society.

121. Edward Bishop to Secretary, Martock, 13 Apr. 1711. He is surprised that recency of his conversion to the Church should be considered an objection to employing him as missionary. He is still willing to go, though he has a prospect of preferment at home.

122. Secretary to Archbishop of Armagh, 21 Apr. 1711 (draft), acknowledging contribution.

123. Francis Pemberton to Dr. Stanley, Belchamp, 29 Apr. 1711. Society's tenant is willing to renew lease, but desires an abatement of the rent.

124. Secretary to Bishop Compton, Petty France, Westminster, 7 May 1711. Queen has authorized a collection for the society in London, Westminster, and Southwark.

125. Edmund Drake to Secretary, Chelsea, 11 May 1711, enclosing Bishop of Winchester's letter to the clergy of Southwark about the collection.

126. Bishop Compton to Secretary, 12 May 1711. He is returning the Queen's letter for printing.

127. Edmund Drake to Secretary, Chelsea, 12 May 1711, quoting a phrase from the Queen's letter relating to extent of collection.

128. Bishop Compton to Secretary, 14 May 1711. He has no authority in Westminster, but has written to the Dean and chapter concerning the collection.

129. Do. to clergy of his diocese, 14 May 1711, urging support of collection.

130. Secretary to ministers of London and Westminster, Petty France, 16 May 1711 (copy), about the collection.

131. Henry Newman to Secretary, Whitehall, 16 May 1711. Acknowledges gift of 600 copies of Bishop of St. Asaph's sermon, presented by the society to the S.P.C.K. Quotes information about Codrington estate from a letter from Woodbridge. West India packet that sailed about three weeks ago has been taken by the French.

132. Edward Bishop to Secretary, Martock, 18 May 1711. Implies that he has been rejected for Indian mission. He is still willing to go anywhere that society may send him.

133. Secretary to the dissenting ministers of London and Westminster, Petty France, 22 May 1711 (copy), asking them to support the collection, as he believes that they agree with the Church in essentials.

134. Henry Newman to Secretary, Whitehall, 30 May 1711, acknowledging gift of 300 copies of Bishop of Norwich's sermon to S.P.C.K.

135. Bishop Compton to Secretary, 31 May 1711, introducing Duncan, whom he recommends for South Carolina, where there are three vacancies.

136–7. Bishop of Winchester's letter to the clergy about the collection, May, 1711.

138. La Mothe to Secretary, Thostleworth, 3 June 1711. He has translated abstract of Bishop of St. Asaph's sermon into French.

139–40. William Carter (Messenger) to Society, 11 June 1711, reporting on his inspection of the society's estate.

141. B. Robinson and Thomas Reynolds (dissenting ministers) to Secretary, London, 13 June 1711, quoting extract from letter of Cotton Mather relating to

dispute between Urquhart and dissenters over title to church building in Jamaica, N.Y.

142. Archbishop Tenison to Secretary, Lambeth, 14 June 1711. Prevented by illness from attending meeting of society, he asks that his objection to Dutch translation of liturgy be made known.

143–4. Thomas Fishwick to Revd. Mr. Shoot (Shute?), Inner Temple, 14 June 1711, offering himself as schoolmaster for the colonies.

145. G. Rawlins to Secretary, St. Thomas's (Southwark), 15 June 1711, objecting to employment of Keen as missionary on ground of character.

146–7. J. Leonhardus to Robert Hales, London, 15 June 1711 (Latin), expressing support of society by 150 Protestant ministers of Geneva and asking that their president, Amoos, be made a corresponding member.

148. R. Hales to Secretary, Ormond St., 15 June 1711, enclosing (146–7).

149. John Humphrey to Secretary. On board H.M.S. *Shoreham*, 27 June 1711. He has obtained a chaplaincy on that ship as a means of securing passage to New York.

150. Bishop Compton to Secretary, 19 June 1711. Glad that Ross is out of the enemy's hands. Society should decide his case quickly, as Compton has applied to admiralty to secure his passage.

151. R. W. Boehm to Secretary, 30 June 1711. He has been told that the Palatines in Carolina have no minister, but only a schoolmaster.

152. William Tong, B. Robinson, and Thomas Reynolds to Secretary, London, 6 July 1711, thanking him for sending information about committee's action in regard to Jamaica, N.Y.

153. John Tayleure to Secretary, 6 July 1711. He, Dr. Stanley, and V. Edwards, a committee appointed to examine the society's estate, recommend granting an abatement to Tweed, if he renews the lease for twelve years.

154. Archbishop Tenison to Secretary, 20 July 1711. He has sent a letter to Harris to be transcribed for presentation to the society, unless he thinks it sufficiently legible as it is. From references to a marked copy of some book, it seems likely that this letter states his objection to Dutch translation of the Prayer Book.

155. Archbishop of Armagh to Secretary, 26 July 1711, acknowledging receipt for his gift.

156. La Mothe to Secretary, Thistleworth, 4 Aug. 1711, proposing Antony Aufrere as a member.

157–8. John Norris to Secretary, 6 Aug. 1711, advocating religious instruction of slaves.

159. Do. to Bishop Compton, 7 Aug. 1711, applying for ordination. Because of

a shortage of ministers in Carolina, he has been accustomed to read service for family and neighbours.

160. Bishop Compton to Secretary, 27 Aug. 1711. Rainsford asked in great haste for a letter to the Lord Treasurer (for Queen's bounty?), but did not say where to send it or post the required bonds. Compton is disturbed by rumours that he is sponsoring Van der Eyghen's translation of the Prayer Book.

161. Archbishop of Armagh to (Bishop Compton), Johnstown, near Dublin, 12 Sept. 1711. Testimonial to Daniel Menadier.

162. Bishop of Bangor to Dr. Bradford, Golden Square, 17 Sept. 1711. Testimonial to Rowland Ellis.

163. R. Mayo to Lazenby, 19 Sept. 1711. Contrary to a report which Lazenby has received, Mayo reported favourably on Rainsford's preaching.

164. Robert Lazenby to Dr. Butler, Epsom, 20 Sept. 1711, enclosing (163) and saying that both he and Mayo approved of Rainsford's preaching and reading prayers.

165. W. Hall to Stubbs, 4 Oct. 1711, on behalf of Bishop Compton, introducing Menadier.

166. Bishop Compton to Secretary, 4 Oct. 1711, introducing Taylor, who has come from South Carolina, well recommended, for orders.

167. Do. to do., 10 Oct. 1711. He has received a request for books and tracts from Mylne, rector of Kingston Parish, Gloucester, Va.

168. Archbishop Tenison to Secretary, Lambeth, 18 Oct. 1711, recommending appointment of select committee on Barbadoes affairs. (Cf. iii. 23–30.)

169. Bishop Compton to Secretary, 3 Nov. 1711. He has ordained Taylor and recommends that he be sent to St. Helen's Parish, S.C.

170. Do. to do., 19 Nov. 1711. Asks allowance to supplement salary of Philips in Shrewsbury, Md., a poor parish. Says this was done for Cordiner.

171. Do. to Mr. Stubbs, 29 Nov. 1711, asking him to delay action on Codrington estate.

172. W. Hall to Secretary, 18 Dec. 1711, on behalf of Bishop Compton, recommending Philips for Stratford and Narragansett.

173. Bishop Compton to Secretary, 31 Dec. 1711, returning some letters and recommending Philips for Stratford and Narragansett.

174. Do. to do., 3 Jan. 1711/12. He doubts that Stratford and Narragansett are strong enough to support two ministers.

175. Do. to do., 12 Feb. 1711/12. Asks gift of church furnishings for Rice, as people of Newfoundland repaired church, which was in ruinous condition, at their own expense.

176–7. Extracts from minutes of Governors of Queen Anne's Bounty, various dates, 1717–37, all relating to appointment of officers. Minute of 11 Nov. 1723 refers to Chamberlayne as deceased.

178. Secretary (Philip Bearcroft) to Archbishop of Canterbury, Charterhouse, 15 Jan. 1739/40, reporting that committee has decided not to appoint a missionary to Staten Island, N.Y., and that it has received notice of sundry bequests.

179. Archbishop Potter to Duke of Newcastle, 10 Mar. 1745–6, reminding him of society's petition for colonial bishops. They did not press for an answer during the late disturbances, but feel entitled to one now that things are normal.

180. J. O. (?) to President and Trustees of Charity School at Bombay, St. Paul's Deanery, London, 2 Mar. 1752. S.P.C.K. strongly approves of their project, and is donating some books.

181. Extract from a letter from a correspondent in Lancaster to Revd. Mr. Waring, 10 June 1757, recommending new school in Old Hutton, Kendal Parish, as location for an S.P.C.K. library.

182. Copy of a letter from same correspondent to J. Waring, 28 June 1757. As S.P.C.K. has apparently approved location of library, he gives some suggestions for setting it up.

183. Transcript of a note of Bishop Gibson concerning blunder of James I in proclaiming canons of 1603–4 before they had been approved by Convocation of York. Copy attested by Archbishop of Canterbury, 22 Aug. 1759.

184. Bishop of Clogher to —— ('My good Lord'), Dublin, 3 Feb. 1778, concerning a proposal to repeal the Test Act.

185. Archbishop of Armagh to (Archbishop of Canterbury?), Dublin, 4 Feb. 1780, concerning tactics to be used in opposing repeal.

186. Irish bishops and archbishops to (Archbishop of Canterbury?), Dublin, 4 Feb. 1780. Repeal of sacramental test has passed Commons, and they ask him to secure its disallowance by Privy Council, or, if that is impossible, to secure the addition of a 'Declatory Provision,' which they hope will lessen its ill effects.

187. Bishop of Bath and Wells to Archbishop of Canterbury, Gros Place, 9 May 1784. Lord Chancellor is reported to be of the opinion that the Bishop of London can ordain American candidates under the present law, if he requires them to swear allegiance. The bishop thinks this illegal, but that an exception could be granted by an Order in Council.

188. Granville Sharp to Benjamin Franklin, Old Jewry, 17 June 1785 (copy). Chiefly concerned with a privately circulated book of Sharp's, which, under pretext of advocating a reform of English government, is really intended to advise Americans in setting up theirs. It also contains a defence of episcopacy and recommendations for shortening the English liturgy.

189. Benjamin Franklin to Granville Sharp, Passy, 5 July 1785 (copy), chiefly concerned with law of inheritance and Franklin's revision of the Prayer Book,

but suggests that, if English bishops do not soon consecrate bishops for America, the Americans may resort to 'election', by which he seems to mean some form of collective ordination.

190–1. Granville Sharp to Archbishop of Canterbury, Old Jewry, 15 Sept. 1785, enclosing (188 and 189). Quotes letter from Benjamin Rush, expressing satisfaction at revival of Episcopal Church (though himself a Presbyterian), and saying that he does not think there would now be any opposition to bishops without civil jurisdiction. Sharp has had similar assurances from Dr. Wither-spoon and Mr. Manning. He mentions application of Seabury to non-juring bishops of Scotland, and Wesley's action in setting apart superintendents for the Methodists as reasons for pressing for authorization for English bishops to con-secrate foreign bishops without oath of allegiance.

192. Do. to Benjamin Franklin, Old Jewry, London, 29 Oct. 1786 (copy), stating objections to non-juring consecration.

193. Do. to Archbishop of Canterbury, Old Jewry, 17 Feb. 1786. He has heard that Connecticut Episcopalians are seeking to obtain various legacies left to an American bishop for Seabury. He thinks the law against non-jurors will prevent this, but such legacies might be claimed for a bishop legally consecrated in England. Having seen Dr. Smith's sermon before the General Convention, he has some hope that Americans may be able to excuse their changes in the liturgy.

194. Examination of legality of consecrating foreign bishops, enclosed with (193). Holds that wording of rubric implies that oaths of allegiance need be required only of persons elected by direction of *congér d'élire*.

195. Granville Sharp to Benjamin Franklin, Old Jewry, London, 19 Aug. 1786 (copy), acknowledging receipt of a copy of proposed American Prayer Book. A rumour had circulated, based on a note of Dr. Price and a letter of Dr. Rush, that General Convention had proceeded on the same plan in its revision as King's Chapel, and this caused grave fears of Socinianism. Having examined the proposed book, Sharp is convinced that Americans have proceeded on a plan recommended by a royal commission, of which his grandfather, later Archbishop Sharp, was a member, in 1689.

196. Jonathan Boucher to Archbishop of Canterbury, Epsom, 9 Mar. 1787, enclosing a confidential petition. From his comments, it would appear that this petition was concerned with co-operation between Bishop Seabury and the pro-posed Bishop of Nova Scotia.

197. William Dickes to Archbishop of Canterbury, Lambeth House, 22 July 1789, with an account of subscription for relief of American Loyalist clergy.

198. Bishop of Bath and Wells to (Archbishop of Canterbury), 5 Feb. 1789. He thinks it would be better for American bishops to procure a full English succes-sion, without any Scottish mixture.

199. John Vardill to Archbishop of Canterbury, 60 Clipstone St., Portland Place, 16 Feb. 1790, concerning ill health of Charles Birtwhistle.

200. Henry Cruger to Archbishop of Canterbury, 13 Craven St., 17 Feb. 1790. Testimonial to Birtwhistle, also noting his ill health.

201. B. Halifax to Archbishop of Canterbury, Clapton Terrace, 17 Feb. 1790. Testimonial to Birtwhistle.

202–10. Opinion of counsel, William Scott and George Harris, 1790, given at request of archbishop, on question whether less than three bishops can confer a valid consecration. They allow it in cases of grave inconvenience or urgent necessity.

211. Thomas Lister to Gisbourne, —— 1790. Testimonial to Birtwhistle.

212–14. Copies of testimonials to John Vardill, Loyalist clergyman, dated from 1783–91.

215–18. Decree of Lord Chancellor, 6 Mar. 1792, concerning distribution of estate of Peter Hugetan van Vryhouwen. S.P.G. was a party to the action.

219. Circular letter of bishops in Ireland to absent Irish bishops, Dublin, 9 Feb. 1794, urging them to return to support the Church in some political crisis.

220. Bishop of Llandaff to Archbishop of Canterbury, St. George's, 5 Mar. 1800. He is opposed to some measure relating to the Irish Church introduced by the Archbishop of Cashel, but thinks a proposal of the Lord Lieutenant for a joint convocation with the Church of England might be sound.

221–6. 'One of the Laity' to Mr. Urban, 1800, apparently intended for publication. Advocates titles for wives of higher ecclesiastics.

227. Undated, unsigned fragment concerning immorality in the Navy.

228–31. Standing orders of S.P.G., two written and one printed copies.

232–3. Undated proposals for better securing the society's libraries.

234. Bishops translated from Ireland to England. Lists six from 1567 to 1692.

235–6. Bishop Compton to Secretary, undated, recommending Roberts for Salem.

237. Do. to do., 14 Feb. ——. As no particular offence is alleged against (Honeyman?), Compton thinks that his allowance should be continued while he remains in Rhode Island.

238. Do. to do., 'Friday', (no other date), urging continuance of Honeyman.

239. Do. to do., 15 Jan. ——, enclosing some material relating to case of Robert Keith.

240. Account of the Church in the colonies, in Bishop Compton's hand and signed with his usual initials, 'H.L.' Undated, but refers to William III as 'his late majesty'. When he came to the see in 1675, Compton found that the Bishop of London had 'by Act of Council a title to the jurisdiction of sending ministers

into all Foreign Plantations', but that it was so defective as to be of little effect. He found there were 'scarce four' chaplains in America. He persuaded Charles II to grant a bounty of £20 to every minister who went over, to pay his passage. He also secured an instruction to the governors not to admit any minister to a regular benefice without his license. It was also ordered that every minister should be admitted as a member of the vestry. After this, colonists in the Leeward Islands, and Jamaica, W.I., started building churches, Virginia and Barbadoes having already done so. He then persuaded the King 'to devolve all Ecclesiastical Jurisdiction upon me and my successors, except Inductions, Marriages, Probate of Wills & Administrations'. The only Church of England clergyman in the northern colonies, prior to the founding of King's Chapel, Boston, was the chaplain in the fort at New York. Compton obtained a grant from William III for the support of a minister in Boston.

241. Undated list of books.

242–3. Proposed declaration promising to take proper care of society's books, to be signed by missionary receiving them.

244. Undated list of letters.

245–6. Undated petition of Sebastian van der Eycken, asking society to purchase copies of his Spanish translation of the New Testament for use among the Yammassee Indians.

247. Undated orders of the society relating to missionaries.

248. Undated list of letters answered.

249. Bridget Loftkin to Society, undated, relating to society's threat to prosecute her absent husband for a bond he signed in behalf of his son-in-law, Gordon.

250. Undated list of books.

251. Robert Dews to Revd. Dr. Johnson (Johnston?), Charleston, 30 June ——, promising support.

252. Undated list of testimonials required of persons seeking appointment as missionaries.

253. Undated list of books.

254–5. Thomas Williams to Ph. Stubbs, undated, introducing Lloyd, who wants to go to Jamaica.

256. Undated list of books.

257. Undated fragment of a letter.

258. Latin description of a book.

259–70. Undated proposals for propagating the Gospel in the colonies, attributed in notation to 'Mr. Johnson'.

271–2. Undated testimonial to John Brook, signed by sundry persons and countersigned by the Archbishop of York.

273. Undated titles of two proclamations.

274–5. List of consecrations copied from Le Neve's *Lives of the Archbishops of Canterbury*.

276–7. Undated list of peculiars in the Deanery of the Arches, London, with names of incumbents and curates.

VOLUME IX

CORRESPONDENCE

EUROPE AND ASIA

1–4. Godfrey Delius to Secretary, Bergen-op-Zoom, 29 May 1702 (translation). Though the governor who persecuted him is dead, his party still controls the council, so Delius does not dare to return to New York as the society requests. He is willing to serve them in England, and to receive episcopal orders for that purpose. Efforts to convert the Indians must be accompanied by civilizing measures and by the prohibition of rum.

5–7. Otto Grassus, Joh. Jacobus, and Johannes Davagius to the Society, 6 June 1702 (Latin). Endorsing work of society and giving some account of their own body.

8–9. Do. to do., same date (Latin). Testimonial to Dr. John Leonhardus.

10–11. J. F. Ostervald to Secretary, Neuchatel, 7 Mar. 1703 (French, with translation), acknowledging thanks of society for his dedication of his catechism to it.

12. Alex. Torriano to Secretary, Farnham Castle, 31 Mar. 1703, on behalf of 'My Lord', saying certain papers need not be sent until nearer time for visitation. (Misplaced, should be in vol. vii).

13–15. Delius to Secretary, Bergen-op-Zoom, 7 May 1703 (French, with translation), declining to go as society's missionary to New York.

16. Copy of (13–15).

17–18. Joh. Leonhardus to Society, Hoven, Rhine Valley, 17 May 1703, asking aid (Latin).

19. D. Cockburn to Secretary, Amsterdam, 7 May 1713. He has been obliged to draw in advance on society's allowance to rent church from the Brownists for another year.

20. L. Tronchin and J. A. Turretin to Secretary, Geneva, 21 May 1703 (French), acknowledging letter from him and agreeing to promote interests of society in Switzerland.

21. Copy of Secretary's reply to (20), 25 May 1703 (Latin).

22–5. Delius to Secretary, Bergen-op-Zoom, 26 June 1703 (French, with translation), stating terms on which he is willing to return to New York.

26–8. John Ossiander to Count of Wartenburg, Tubingen, 18 July 1703 (Latin, with translation), discussing possibilities of union of Reformed and Lutheran churches.

29. Cockburn to Secretary, Amsterdam, 9/20 July 1703. Condition of Church there not very encouraging.

30–1. Delius to Secretary, Bergen-op-Zoom, 11 Aug. 1703 (translation). He had planned to come to London in person for conference with Bishop (of London) and Archbishop, but has been delayed by illness of ministers with whom he had arranged to supply his parish. Defends terms stated in (22–5), which some members of society seem to have thought exorbitant.

32–3. Do. to do., Amsterdam, 20 Aug. 1703 (French, with translation), sent (with book by M. Neau) by hand of Mr. Phillips, who is on his way to America with power of attorney to collect funds claimed by Delius in Boston and New York.

34. John Urmston to Secretary, Archangel, 30 Sept. 1703. Encouraged by possibility of assistance from society, though he does not have license from the Bishop of London. Gives unfavourable account of religion in Russia.

35–6. Delius to Secretary, The Hague, 10 Oct. 1703 (French, with English translation). He came to The Hague planning to sail for England, but the fleet has been delayed. He is sending a translation of the Dutch liturgy.

37. Do. to do., Bergen-op-Zoom, 11 Oct. 1703 (French). Further discussion of terms for returning to America.

38. Cockburn to Secretary, Amsterdam, 19 Oct. 1703, concerning financial problems of his church.

39. Do. to Treasurer, Amsterdam, 27 Nov. 1703. One of his bills on the society has been refused because drawn in advance.

40. Delius to Secretary, Bergen-op-Zoom, 28 Jan. 1704, n.s. (French). Urges continuance of work among Iroquois and asks help in collecting his arrears in Boston and New York.

41. Do. to do., De Brille, 16 Apr. 1704 (French). He has again been prevented by accident from sailing for England.

42. Do. to do., Bergen-op-Zoom, 24 Aug. 1704 (French). He has received favourable reports of the society's mission from the French community in New York.

43. Cockburn to Archbishop of York, 4 Nov. 1704. He has land for a church but is unable to build at present. Asks the archbishop to use his influence to secure continuance of the society's allowance.

44. Joh. Leonhard to Secretary, Geneva, 30 Oct. 1704 (Latin), naming some members of the society with whom he is acquainted.

45-6. J. F. Osterwald to Secretary, Neuchatel, 3 Dec. 1704 (French, with translation). Mentions miscarriage of previous letter from Secretary, and discusses religious situation in Switzerland.

47-8. Osterwald to Society, Neuchatel, 3 Dec. 1704 (French, with translation), acknowledging election to society.

49. John Jacob Scherer to Secretary, St. Gall, 16 Dec. 1704. He speaks of sending several previous letters and books which have not been received, and refers to Leonhard's mission to England on behalf of Protestants in his area, and to previous and expected visit of Hales.

50-1. Tronchin and Turretin to Secretary, Geneva, 19 Dec. 1704 (French, with translation). They have learned from Osterwald of their election to the society, though the letter announcing it miscarried.

52-3. Otto Grassus to Secretary, Tosan, 28 Dec. 1704 (Latin, with translation). As 'Dean of the Upper League', he returns thanks for good will of the society as shown in response to Leonhard's mission.

54-5. Johannes Leonhard to Society, Lesamine, 29 Dec. 1704. Reports conditions among the Grissons as he has found them since his return, noting some improvement.

56-7. Scherer to Secretary, St. Gall, 22 Jan. 1705 (French, with translation). Discusses affairs of the Grissons, and notes that a previous letter, sent in care of Dr. Joaiah Woodward, seems to have miscarried.

58-9. Delius to Secretary, The Hague, 7 Feb. 1705 (French, with translation). Regrets his inability to supply the society with his (Indian?) translation of certain devotions, as this and other papers were lost in his flight from New York.

60. Tronchin and Turretin to Society, Geneva, 17 May 1705 (French). Describe troubles of the Grissons.

61-2. Leonhard to Society, Curiae, 22 Aug. 1705 (Latin, with translation). Thanks for assistance to the Grissons.

63-4. Osterwald to Secretary, Neuchatel, 23 Aug. 1705 (French, with translation). He is sending a copy of their liturgy, and asks intervention on behalf of a co-religionist who has served nineteen years in the galleys for a religious offence.

65-7. Otto Grassus to Society, Tosana, 24 Aug. 1705 (Latin, with translation). Correspondence has been presented to their synod, which returns thanks for aid.

68-9. Osterwald to Secretary, Neuchatel, 27 Aug. 1705 (French, with translation), introducing M. de Montmollin.

70. Abraham Pungelen to ——, 3 Oct. 1705 (Latin). Testimonial to Johann Friedrich Hager.

71. Leonhard to Secretary, 4 Feb. 1706, introducing Dubourdieu.

72-3. Otto Grassus and Joh. Jacob Vedzosin to Society, 8 Feb. 1706 (Latin), seeking aid from Queen.

74. Osterwald to Secretary, Neuchatel, 22 Feb. 1706. Introduces Montmollin again and notes that some members of society have expressed approval of their liturgy.

75. Secretary to Otto Grassus, Westminster, 7 Apr. 1706 (copy, French). Directed by society to express good will for their synod and approval of Leonhard's mission.

76. Do. to Osterwald, Petty France, Westminster, 9 Apr. 1706 (copy). Refers to visit of brothers Appia, and speaks of receiving some documents.

77. Do. to Leonhard, Petty France, Westminster, 10 Apr. 1706 (copy, French). Acknowledges letters and speaks of visit of the Appias.

78-9. Grassus to Society, Tosan, 10 Jun. 1706 (Latin). Thanks for aid.

80. Leonhard to Secretary, 13 Aug. 1706 (Latin), acknowledging letters.

81-2. Osterwald to Secretary, Neuchatel, 21 Aug. 1706 (French with translation). Speaks of Montmollin as representing interests of their group in England.

83. Leonhard to Secretary, Trimonty, 20 Sept. 1706 (Latin), concerning affairs of Grissons.

84. John Jacob Scherer to Society, St. Gall, 30 Nov. 1706 (Latin), with references to brothers Appia and to Leonhard.

85. Frideni Bonet to Secretary, Suffolk St., 9 Dec. 1706 (translation), introducing Lubominsky, Polish convert, who has a letter of recommendation from Professor Monk of the University of Leiden. (A duplicate of vii. 230.)

86-7. B. Picket to Secretary, 31 Dec. 1706 (Latin), with complimentary address to society.

88-9. Delius to Secretary, Bergen-op-Zoom, 28 Jan. 1707, discussing Indian mission and asking aid in collecting arrears. (In English, with numerous corrections, probably a translation.)

90-1. Do. to do., Halveren, 7 Mar. 1707 (French, with translation). Printer at Utrecht wants 25 guilders to print translation of the Bishop of Chichester's sermon.

92-3. Secretary to Osterwald, Westminster, 26 Mar. 1707 (translation). He is sending some of the society's publications by Montmollin, who is returning to Neuchatel.

94-7. Memorial of Italian proselytes, with marginal dates through Mar. 1707 (French, with English abstract), seeking aid of the society.

98. Frideni Bonet to Secretary, Suffolk St., 4 July 1707, enclosing an English version of (94–7).

99–103. The version of the memorial enclosed in (98), dated 12 Apr. 1707. Gives name of first convert as Matthew Bertand de la Logha.

104–5. Werenfels to Secretary, Basel, 23 July 1707, acknowledging election to membership (French, with translation).

106–9. John Rudolf Zwinger to Society (Latin) and to Secretary, 23 July 1707 (French, with translation), acknowledging election as member.

110. Secretary to Delius, 28 July 1707 (copy), saying, in answer to (90–1), that society is willing to pay 25 guilders for printing the translation of the Bishop of Chichester's sermon.

111–12. Otto Grassus to Society, Tosan, 2 Aug. 1707 (Latin). Concerning affairs of his group.

113. Samuel Werenfels to Society, 8 Aug. 1707 (Latin), acknowledging election.

114–16. Osterwald to Secretary, Neuchatel, 6 Aug. 1707 (French, with translation). He has forwarded letters sent in his care to Zwinger and Werenfels and is sending replies by Chaplain Werndley of the English Navy.

117. Pierre de Toullieu to ——, 14 Nov. 1707 (Latin). Testimonial to Johan Friedrich Hager.

118–19. Delius to Secretary, 8 Dec. 1707, Halleren (French, with translation). He is seeking a means of sending the translated sermons to England.

120–2. Picket to Secretary, Geneva, 12 Feb. 1707/8 (French, with translation). Protestants in Geneva have appointed a committee to examine the proselytes (cf. 94–103) and provide for their needs.

123. Delius to Secretary, Halleren, 23 Feb. 1708 (French). Relates difficulties in transmitting printed sermons.

124. Kelsall to Thomas Edwards, Wiebich, 23 Feb. 1708, relating to the Clifford legacy. (Cf. viii. 41.)

125–6. Delius to Secretary, Halleren, 23 Apr. 1708 (French, with translation), concerning possible overcharge by printer of translation of Bishop of Chichester's sermon.

127–8. Secretary to Picket, Westminster, 25 June 1708 (copy). He apologizes for delay in answering (120–2), but he was unable to communicate it immediately to the society, as its spring meetings are taken up with colonial business, since that is the season when the ships sail.

129–30. Kelsall to the Bishop of Ely, Wiebich, 11 Oct. 1708, concerning the Clifford legacy. (Cf. 124).

131. Picket to Secretary, Geneva, 28 Dec. 1708 (French), enclosing address of his organization to the society.

132–3. The address enclosed in (131) (Latin).

134–5. Jacob Bassgne to Society, Rotterdam, — 1708 (Latin), concerning religion in the colonies.

136–7. Jean Alphones Turretin to Society, Kalends, Jan. 1709 (Latin), presenting his *De Variis Christiana Doctrina Fatis*.

138. Turretin to Secretary, 22 Jan. 1709 (French), enclosing (136–7).

139. Secretary to Turretin, Westminster, 24 Jan. 1709. Turretin's work was presented to the society by Bonet.

140–4. Osterwold to G. Nichols, Neuchatel, 10 Mar. 1709 (Latin), referring to previous correspondence with Secretary.

145–50. Memorial of Leonhard (Latin), relating some religious developments in Switzerland. Written in 1708, but bears testimonial to Leonhard by Antonius Klingle dated 20 May 1709.

151. Picket to William Nichols, 20 May 1709 (Latin), expressing respect for Church of England.

152–3. Leonhard to Secretary and to Society, 20 May 1709 (Latin), relating to religious affairs in Switzerland and referring to (145–50).

154–7. Testimonials to Hager (Latin). Latest date, 14 June 1709.

158–9. Delius to Treasurer, Halleren, 25 June 1704 (French, with translation), asking him to pay 31 guilders to Secretary to remit to Delius in payment for printing translation of Bishop of Chichester's sermon.

160. Bassagne to Secretary, Rotterdam, 30 July 1709 (French), concerning religious affairs.

161–2. Testimonial to Hager (German), bearing various signatures, 5 Dec. 1709.

163–4. Picket to Secretary, Geneva, 15 Jan. 1711 (Latin). Three copies of complimentary address to society.

165–6. Daniel Ernest Fablons to Society, Berolini, 20 Jan. 1711 (Latin), giving some account of a similar society on the Continent.

167–8. Bassnage to Secretary, La Haye, 31 Mar. 1711 (2 copies, French). He has dedicated a book to the society.

169. Leonhard to Secretary, 22 June 1711 (French), relating efforts to propagate the Gospel on the Continent.

170. Mattheus Christophers to Secretary, Amsterdam, —— June 1711 (Dutch), relating to religious affairs.

171–3. Johann Friedrich Hager to Secretary, Ansberg, 15 Aug. 1711, concerning his work with the Palatines (German, with translation).

174. General letter to foreign members, Nov. 1711 (copy, French), acknowledging correspondence.

175–6. Johannes Angelus Berniera to Society, undated (Latin), concerning religious affairs.

177. Undated English version of some ecclesiastical calendar.

178–83. Undated scheme for education of Danish Prince.

184–5. Undated account of some Protestant ministers in Bohemia.

186–8. Undated memorial (attributed in *notation* to Cockburn) proposing to set up Church of England worship in Holland.

189. Undated form of subscription for support of worship of Church of England in Amsterdam. Subscriptions to be paid to Bishop Compton.

190. Members of the English congregation in Amsterdam.

191. English–Dutch church calendar.

192–3. Extract from letter of Tronchin and Turretin, undated, urging provision of English worship for benefit of English merchants in Leghorn.

194. Undated account of conversion from Roman Catholicism of Antonio Alverado, Professor of Divinity in Toledo.

195–6. Undated account of Lubominsky.

197. Undated translation of part of letter of Scherer relating to Leonhard.

198. Undated petition to Society of brothers Appia for books to be used in their work.

199. Undated certificate for Leonhard, initialled by Secretary.

CHINA

200–1. Extract from letter of supercargoes in China, 30 Apr. 1791, recommending appointment of chaplain at 'factory'.

INDIA

202–3. Extract from charter of East India Company, 5 Sept. 1698, requiring them to maintain a minister and schoolmaster in their colony on St. Helena.

204–9. Copies of the same extract.

210. J. Broughton to —— ('My Lord'), Bartel's Buildings, Holborn, 21 Jan. 1752, saying that he has laid project of a charity school at Bombay before a committee of (S.P.C.K., *Notation*) and the members expressed approval, but deferred action because of slim attendance and absence of treasurer, Dr. Denne.

211. Trustees of Bombay Charity School to Bishop of Oxford, 6 Dec. 1754. Acknowledging his effort to secure aid of S.P.C.K., as related in his letter of 1752, receipt of which was delayed.

212. P. Byfield to Bishop of Oxford, Bombay, 8 Feb. 1755, describing progress of charity school.

213. Do. to do., Bombay, 10 Mar. 1756, concerning the school.

214. Do. to do., Bombay, 20 Jan. 1757. More about the school.

215. Do. to do., Bombay, 8 Apr. 1758, concerning the school.

216. William Johnson to Archbishop of Canterbury, Calcutta, 21 Aug. 1784. Relating his efforts, as chaplain of East India Co., to secure erection of church in Bengal.

217–18. D. Brown and other ministers to the Archbishop of Canterbury, Calcutta, 10 Sept. 1787, urging missionary effort among the natives.

219. William Johnson to Archbishop of Canterbury, Calcutta, 10 Sept. 1789, reporting completion of church and his own projected return to England.

220–3. Thomas Blanshard and other chaplains to the Earl of Cornwallis, Governor General, Calcutta, 20 June 1788 (copy received 5 Aug. 1789), urging missionary effort.

224. Do. to Archbishop of Canterbury, 2 Jan. 1789, Calcutta, enclosing (220–3).

225–6. J. Owen to G. Sharp, Calcutta, 12 Mar. 1789, enclosing a copy of (220–3).

227–8. D. Brown and other ministers to Archbishop of Canterbury, Calcutta, Sept. 1789, urging missionary effort.

229. Fragment of an act against 'Papists', dated 24 June 1791.

230–8. Proposals for propagating the Gospel in the East Indies, attributed to Major Mitchell and dated 17 Mar. 1800 in *notation* (cf. 260).

239–50. *The Pentateuch in Five Languages*, by Francis Gladwin. Calcutta, Cooper & Upjohn, 1791. Specimen pages, with note of presentation from Sir Charles Broughton Rouse to the Archbishop of Canterbury, Calcutta, 1 Feb. 1792.

251. Wilberforce to the Archbishop of Canterbury, Palace Yard, 18 May 1793. Clauses relating to religious institutions were admitted to the India bill with Mr. Dundas's approval and little opposition.

252–3. Undated statement of salaries paid to East India Co. chaplains.

254–9. Religious clauses referred to in (251).

260. M. Mitchell to Archbishop of Canterbury, St. George's Place, Hyde Park, 17 Mar. 1800, transmitting (230–5).

261–4. Another copy of the proposals.

265. Archbishop of Canterbury to Henry Guillam, Judge of the Supreme Court of Judicature, Madras: Lambeth House, 31 May 1803. Countersigned 'B. London'. They have confirmed reappointment of Dr. Kerr to post at Fort St. George, but assure Guillam that they are convinced of his good intentions in opposing it.

266–78. A Proposal for Establishing a Protestant Mission in Bengal and Bahar. Undated (2 copies).

279. Undated resolutions declaring it the duty of the East India Co. to maintain chaplains at its stations.

280–4. Undated regulations governing the Bombay Charity School.

VOLUME X

AMERICAN COLONIES AND U.S.A.

GENERAL

1–4. Draft of an order for establishing an American episcopate in the reign of Charles II, copied from document found among Fulham Papers by Bishop of London in 1776.

5. Testimonial to George MacQueen, signed by Vincent Edwards and others, Embleton, Northumberland Co., 19 Mar. 1701.

6–20. Memorial of George Keith concerning state of religion in the colonies, 14 Sept. 1701 (4 copies).

21. List of books supplied to Keith for use in his mission.

22–3. Secretary to Keith, Petty France, Westminster, 30 June 1703 (copy). Convinced that Keith does not run any risk of incurring penalties of Toleration Act. Glad to hear of favourable disposition to Church in New England. Suggests appointment of suffragan bishop (crossed out). A number of documents sent by Keith have not been received. Society has agreed to name Talbot as a missionary.

24–5. Extracts from colonial correspondence prepared for presentation to meeting, 27 Feb. 1701/2.

26. Bishop of Gloucester to Archbishop of Canterbury, Gloucester, 6 Oct. 1703, certifying that he has given Charles Smith permission to go to America.

27–9. Testimonial of sundry clergymen to Thomas Tye, 15 Nov. 1703 (Latin).

30. List of gifts by Col. Nicholson to colonial churches through 1703.

31. Testimonial of David Denoon, M.D., to Alexander Stuart, 1 Feb. 1703/4.

32–3. List of books delivered to Dr. Bray for the society by B. Tooke, from library of Mr. Dedwell, 6 June 1704.

34–5. George Keith to Society, asking payment for missionary services from 25 Mar. 1702 to 14 Aug. 1704.

36–7. Keith's account of benefactions of Col. Nicholson to colonial churches, 3 Nov. 1704.

38–9. List of missionaries in service in 1704.

40–1. List of books for a missionary's library, approved by society, 15 Mar. 1705.

42. Testimonial of several ministers to Christopher Buckton, Stamford, 10 Apr. 1705.

43–4. List of missionaries with dates of appointment through July 1705.

45. Secretary to (Keith), Petty France, Westminster, 25 Oct. 1705 (copy), asking for information concerning his agreement with Talbot.

46. Do. to Missionaries, Petty France, Westminster, 6 Nov. 1705 (copy) to accompany package of printed instructions.

47. Charles Masham to Treasurer, St. Helena, 24 Nov. 1705, reports arrival and receipt of books from society.

48–9. Memorandum of payments from treasurer prepared by George Keith for Committee, 20 Feb. 1705/6.

50. List of letters (by names of addressees) sent to colonies by Mr. Livingston, 3 May 1706.

51. Bishop of Carlisle to (Bishop of London?), Rose, 20 May 1706, recommending an unnamed Episcopal clergyman from Scotland.

52. Secretary to Turner, Petty France, Westminster, 28 May 1706 (copy), saying that, on recommendation of Bishop of London, society is prepared to consider employing him as a schoolmaster.

53. Do. to do., 25 June 1706, saying he has not had a reply to previous letter.

54–8. Testimonials to Cordiner, 3 and 10 Sept. 1706.

59–63. Lists of missionaries sent to plantations through Lady Day, 1707.

64. Testimonial of Gideon Johnston and others to James Adams, former schoolmaster in Castlemere, 18 Aug. 1707.

65. Testimonial of Henry Sanford to Adams, Castlesagh, 20 Aug. 1707.

66. Testimonial of the Bishop of Elphin and others to Adams, 26 Aug. 1707.

67–8. Bishop of London's proposals for an American suffragan, dated Dec. 1707 in *notation* attributed in further *notation* to Archbishop Tenison.

69. Answers of sundry Presbyterian clergy to queries whether certain ministerial acts constitute a violation of the Rule of Order of the Church of Scotland, London, 9 Aug. 1708.

70. Testimonial to James Reynolds, 20 Jan. 1708/9.

71. Geo. St. George to Archbishop of Dublin, Cariuk, 28 Jan. 1708/9, asking him to recommend Reynolds to Bishop of London.

72. P. Mahon to Archbishop of Dublin, Cavetowne, 28 Jan. 1708/9. Testimonial to Reynolds.

73. Testimonial to Reynolds from Bishop of Killmore and Ardagh, 19 Feb. 1708/9 (Latin).

74-5. Testimonials to Robert Sinclair, 20 and 23 June 1709.

76. Secretary to Governors of Plantations where the society has missionaries, Westminster, 24 Sept. 1709 (copy), asking them to 'encourage' missionaries to observe rule requiring regular correspondence with society.

77. Do. to missionaries, Westminster, 26 Sept. 1709 (copy), enjoining compliance with the same rule.

178. Testimonial to Samuel Colby from Bishop of Killmore and Ardagh, 29 Nov. 709.

79. Secretary to Gov. Tynte, Petty France, Westminster, 26 Dec. 1709 (copy), introducing Hassel.

80. Shute to Secretary, 1 Jan. 1711/12, reporting satisfactory preaching by Philips.

81. John Humphreys to Secretary, H.M.S. *Shoreham*, Spithead, 13 July 1712. Hopes to sail with first fair wind.

82-3. Testimonials to Rowland Ellis, 19 and 20 Sept. 1711.

84. Edward Brace to Secretary, Bigleswade, 8 Nov. 1711, offering his services as factor in connection with Codrington Estate.

85-6. J. Hare to Secretary, London, 5 Dec. 1711. Testimonial to Charles Bradley.

87. James Vernon to Secretary, 16 Dec. 1711. Testimonial to Philipps.

88-9. Report of Attorney General (P. Yorke) and C. Talbot on Bishop Gibson's first petition for jurisdiction, 27 Jan. 1725.

90-8. Copies of Bishop Gibson's petition and commission, 1726-7, with some later notes on ecclesiastical jurisdiction in the colonies.

99-104. Copy of Bishop Gibson's commission, 9 Feb. 1726/7 (Latin).

105-6. Proposal that Bishop of London share colonial jurisdiction with other bishops. Attributed in *notation* to Bishop Sherlock.

107–35. Memorial of Bishop Sherlock reviewing history of colonial jurisdiction and proposing appointment of colonial bishops (2 copies).

136–9. Abstract of the foregoing memorial, dated 1749–50 in *notation*.

140–73. Account of the American colonies drawn up for the Bishop of London by Dr. (William?) Smith, London, 1762.

174–9. Thoughts on the present state of the Church of England in America, 1764 (June). Anonymous, but writer of unsigned *notation* says he has seen original with corrections in Archbishop Secker's hand.

180–2. Some notes concerning suffragan bishops copied from H. Wharton, *Anglia Sacra*.

183–4. Suggestions concerning ecclesiastical jurisdiction in the colonies, attributed in *notation* to Dr. Bentham, 1765. Refers to (180–2).

185–6. Account of legacies bequeathed to S.P.G. for support of American bishops. Last legacy, by Archbishop Secker, is dated 4 Apr. 1768.

187–8. Petition to the King for colonial bishops from convocation of clergy in New York and New Jersey, New York, 12 Oct. 1771.

189–92. Samuel Seabury, Samuel Cooke, and Charles Inglis on behalf of clergy in New York to Chandler, Cooper, Vardill, and Boucher (Loyalist clergy in England), 28 Oct. 1780. Note that clergy of New York had named the four addressed as their agents to petition for American bishops in 1777, and present further arguments for an American episcopate.

193–6. Memorial of society to Lord Sydney, Secretary of State for the Colonies, undated, but evidently written shortly after the recognition of American independence, making proposals for the establishment of the Church in the King's remaining dominions.

197. Copy of printed statement of John Wesley concerning his appointment of Coke and Asbury as superintendents of the American Methodists.

198–9. Petition of John Jeffreys to the King, 15 Feb. 1785, asking that lands be granted to society in Quebec or New Brunswick to replace some he had given it in New York before American Revolution.

200–9. Petition of clerical and lay delegates to General Convention to the archbishops and bishops, Philadelphia, 5 Oct. 1785, requesting consecration of American bishops (5 copies).

210. Draft of reply from archbishops and bishops, 27 Feb. 1786. Note by Archbishop says reply was given to Mr. Adams for transmission to convention on that date.

211–13. Unsigned draft of letter discussing the American petition, attributed in *notation* to Archbishop of York (2 copies).

214–15. Draft of reply to committee of General Convention, Jan. 1786.

G

216–17. William White, Francis Hopkinson, and Samuel Powell to Archbishops, Philadelphia, 24 July 1786, acknowledging receipt of reply on behalf of committee.

218–28. Notes on variations in the 'Philadelphia Liturgy' (proposed American Prayer Book of 1786).

229–30. Bequests to society for American episcopate. Similar to (185–6), but signed by Wm. Morice, Secretary, Gower St., 21 Mar. 1791.

231. Table showing comparative figures for society's missions, 1783 and 1792.

232. Undated list of places proposed by Bishop of Nova Scotia for new missions. Same sheet contains notes of expenditures through 1795.

233. Extract from 'Dr. Bray's Narrative'.

234. Extract from minutes relating to missionaries, for Lord Lovelace (*notation*).

235–6. Undated notes concerning missionaries. Names from early eighteenth century.

237–8. W. Glover to Bishop of London, undated, minimizing ecclesiastical differences.

239–42. The Case of His Majesty's Subjects, Members of the Church of England in America. Undated. An appeal for bishops.

243–4. Undated draft of an appeal for the conversion of Negroes.

245–6. Undated draft of a petition for colonial bishops.

247–8. Undated list of books for a missionary library.

249–59. State of religion in the plantations, undated. Attributed in *notation* to the 'Governor of New England'.

260. Undated fragment proposing a 'Board of Superintendence' for the colonial churches.

261. Undated fragment noting churches in some colonies.

262–3. Undated considerations on the state of the missions.

264. Undated list of books for a missionary's library.

265. Undated statement of books supplied to the society.

266. Draft of an account of religion in the plantations.

267–8. Undated list of maps of the plantations.

269. Undated testimonial to Henry Rooke by J. Searle.

270. Copy of undated letter from Secretary (Chamberlayne) to missionaries, with society's printed instructions.

271. Undated list of officers of Queen's Bench.

VOLUME XI

AMERICAN COLONIES

CANADA

1–2. Henry Newman to Secretary, London, 18 Mar. 1704, reporting sending a parcel of newspapers to Jackson in Newfoundland at request of society.

3–4. Testimonial to Jacob Rice, 21 June 1704 (Latin).

5. Rice to (Secretary?), St. John's Harbour, N.F., 28 Nov. 1704, complaining of the climate, the people, and the Army.

6. Testimonial of William Foulkes and Phillip Phillips to Rice, 17 May 1704.

7–8. Petition of sundry inhabitants of Sussex County, DELAWARE, to Bishop of London, 6 Mar. 1705/6, asking for a minister. (Misplaced here).

9. John Jackson to Newman, 16 Aug. 1706, asking financial aid.

10. Do. to Society, London, 17 Oct. 1706, asking aid.

11–12. Do. to do., 20 Dec. 1706, asking aid.

13–14. Do. to Committee, 23 Dec. 1706, asking aid.

15. Do. to do., 3 Mar. 1706/7. Another appeal.

16. Do. to Secretary, 21 Mar. 1706/7, asking him to find out if the Archbishop has applied to the Lord Keeper in his behalf.

17. Do. to do., Cecill-Court, 16 July 1708, asking aid.

18. Jacob Rice to Society, 20 May 1709, asking continuance of support.

19–20. Jackson to Society, 21 Oct. 1709, asking aid.

21. Certificate of merchants trading with Newfoundland to faithfulness of Rice. 21 Oct. 1709.

22–3. Testimonial to Rice from three clergymen, 21 Nov. 1709.

24. Extracts from address of the Chapter in Quebec to the King, 1763, asking appointment of a (Roman Catholic) bishop.

25–6. Extracts from letter of Mrs. Brooke to Bishop Terrick, 24 Jan. 1765, describing conditions among Roman Catholics in Quebec.

27. Copy of part of letter of Revd. Mr. De Vaux to Mr. Peckell, 6 Apr. 1765, discussing problems of Protestant clergymen in Quebec.

28–9. Queries humbly submitted to the friends of Protestant episcopacy in North America, sent to unnamed writer of *notation* by Dean Tucker of Gloucester, June 1765. Propose sending an Anglican bishop to Quebec.

30–6. Anonymous proposals for setting up Church establishment in Canada, London, 3 Apr. 1786.

37–41. Bishop Inglis to the Archbishop of Canterbury, Halifax, 13 Sept. 1788, describing a visitation through Nova Scotia and New Brunswick, and relating a controversy with Secretary Morice of S.P.G. over support of missionaries in his diocese.

42. Granville Sharpe to Archbishop of Canterbury, Leidenhall St., 27 Dec. 1789. He is forwarding a letter from the Chief Justice of Canada and quotes other correspondents relating to proposal of statehood for Vermont, and relations of Bishops White, Seabury, and Provoost.

43. Managers of the fund for building college at Windsor to the Duke of Portland, Halifax, 26 Dec. 1794. Unsigned copy attested by Bishop Inglis. Cost exceeded estimate, though building was made of wood instead of stone, because competent stonemasons could not be obtained.

44. Will. Knox to (Archbishop of Canterbury), Soho Sq., 3 Feb. 1795. As recently appointed agent for New Brunswick, he is seeking to promote their application for a bishop.

45. Certificate of Bishop Inglis, Clermont, N.S., 9 Apr. 1799, saying that he has given Robert Stanser permission to visit England. Testimonial to Stanser from three parishioners of St. Paul's, Halifax, on same sheet, 18 Apr. 1799.

46–7. Bishop Inglis to the Archbishop of Canterbury, Clermont, N.S., 25 Mar. 1799. If the archbishop thinks his son too young for the office of commissary, he proposes Archibald Paine Inglis, former superintendent of diocesan seminary. He has declined applications to ordain naval chaplains (only in deacon's orders) and requests for ordination from the West Indies. Beardsley, S.P.G. missionary in New Brunswick, has become involved in a bigamous marriage. Houseal, missionary to German congregation in Halifax, has died and a German preacher is no longer needed, as they all speak English.

48. Do. to do., Clermont, N.S., 18 Apr. 1799, sent by Stanser, who may be seeking a cure in England. If he does not return to Halifax, Bishop Inglis asks that a replacement be sent. If he does return, he should be given an appointment as chaplain to the garrison.

49. Testimonial to Stanser from wardens and vestry of St. Paul's, Halifax, 26 Apr. 1799.

50. Stanser to the Archbishop of Canterbury, Bulwell, near Nottingham, 2 Aug. 1799. His wife having been safely delivered of a boy, he is planning to return to his parish, but asks the archbishop's help in obtaining a larger allowance from the government.

51. Do. to do., Halifax, 21 Feb. 1800, reporting safe arrival after a stormy voyage. Prices are high because of the return of the Duke of Kent and continuance of the war.

52. Do. to do., Halifax, 22 July 1800. Refers to new regulations concerning marriage licences and asks for a chaplaincy.

53. Bishop Inglis to Archbishop, Clermont, N.S., 26 July 1800. He is seeking allowance for a commissary in Nova Scotia in addition to the one now in New Brunswick. He has corresponded with the governor, Sir John Wentworth on the marriage licence issue, and had some personal conferences with him on the same subject. Urges chaplaincy for Stanser, but fears opposition from the Duke of Kent, who favours a rival applicant.

54–5. Do. to do., Clermont, N.S., 11 Sept. 1800, introducing his son, John, who is visiting England before being ordained.

56. John Inglis to the Archbishop, Mortimer St., 6 Feb. 1801, giving some information concerning chaplaincies in dockyard and garrison at Halifax.

57. Bishop Inglis to Archbishop, Fredericton, 20 Apr. 1801, urging provision of chaplain for dockyard and naval station.

58. Do. to do., same date. As (57) was meant for public perusal, he writes this to thank the archbishop for favours to his son, whom he has urged to return promptly because of disturbed state of public affairs.

59. John Inglis to Archbishop, London, 27 May 1801, seeking appointment as missionary.

60. C. Willoughby to Archbishop, Windsor, N.S., 5 June 1801, thanking him for aid in securing increase in his stipend from society.

61. Robert Stanser to Archbishop Halifax, 27 June 1801, asking his aid in obtaining chaplaincy at the naval hospital in opposition to the Duke of Kent's candidate, Wetherell.

62. John Inglis to the Archbishop, London, 29 July 1801. He is preparing to return to Nova Scotia.

63. Do. to do., London, 4 Aug. 1801. Thanking him for favours, asking his recommendation to the governor for Stanson and Willoughby, referring to efforts to secure an endowment for King's College, and enclosing (64).

64. A proposal for the support of Church and college in Nova Scotia by a land grant.

65. Recommendations concerning the issuing of marriage licences in Nova Scotia, dated 4 Aug. 1801 in *notation*. In John Inglis's hand.

66. John Inglis to Archbishop, Falmouth, 12 Aug. 1801. Thanks to the archbishop's introduction to Admiral Whitehead, he is to sail with the fleet when it leaves for Halifax.

67. Memorial of Governors of King's College, Windsor, to the Duke of Northumberland, Principal Secretary of State, 16 Sept. 1801, applying for a charter.

68. Memorial of Bishop Inglis to the Archbishop of Canterbury, Clermont, N.S., 1 Oct. 1801, asking for four additional missionaries.

69–70. Bishop Inglis to the Archbishop, Clermont, N.S., 1 Oct. 1801. Reports the return of his son, and refers to (67 and 68). Letter will be presented by Pidgeon, the society's missionary at Fredericton, who is obliged to return to England for his health. Stanson is still seeking a chaplaincy. Supports his son's recommendation of a land grant for Church.

71–2. Governors of King's College to the Archbishop, Halifax, N.S., 20 Oct. 1801, asking his support for their petition.

73–4. John Inglis to the Archbishop, Halifax, 20 Oct. 1801, reporting safe arrival. Since his return he has been involved in a controversy over the issuing of marriage licences to an 'Anabaptist' preacher.

75. Do. to do., Halifax, N.S., 7 Nov. 1801. Governors of the college have feed Scrope Bernard to expedite the charter.

76. Minutes of Governors of King's College, Windsor, 14 Sept. 1802, on receipt of royal charter.

77–8. Bishop Inglis to the Archbishop, Clermont, N.S., 28 Sept. 1802, reporting receipt of charter and describing affairs of the college. Has appointed his son, recently married, as commissary, on receiving a special grant for the purpose.

79–111. Printed statutes of King's College, ratified 18 July 1803, with signatures of governors and MS. notes of exceptions by Bishop Inglis.

112. Undated petition of merchants trading with Newfoundland, asking appointment of an S.P.G. missionary.

113–16. Undated list of parishes on the St. Lawrence River with sketch map showing their locations.

117–48. Manuscript autobiography of C. Griffin, an S.P.G. missionary, dated Bridgeton, N.S., 13 Mar. 1826, and ending with a request for an increase in salary.

149–52. Undated observations on Griffin's petition.

CONNECTICUT

153. Timothy Titharton to ——, Stratford, Conn., 8 Nov. 1705, criticizing Independents.

154–6. Sundry inhabitants of Stratford to George Muirson, 1 June 1706, asking him to officiate among them.

157. George Knell and Timothy Titherton to Muirson, Stratford, 29 June 1706, acknowledging his reply, in which he apparently agreed to come to them if he could.

158–59. Beginning of incomplete letter apparently written by Stratford group to Muirson in 1706, referring to a visit by him and Col. Heathcote.

160–1. Caleb Heathcote to —— ('Worthy sir'), Stratford, 1 Jan. 1707, asking him to present Stratford's plea to the society.

162–3. Timothy Titherton to Muirson, Stratford, 6 Feb. 1706/7, giving names of persons baptized on 2 Sept.

164–5. Sundry inhabitants of Stratford to Muirson, 27 Mar. 1707, asking him to try to obtain allowance for a missionary.

166–7. Memorial of Quakers to the Queen, asking disallowance of law against them in Connecticut. Referred to Lords Commissioners of Trade and Plantations, 8 Apr. 1705. Read 17 Apr. 1707 (*notation*).

168–9. Answer of Sir Henry Ashurst, agent of the colony, read 4 May 1707 (*notation*), says law was passed 32 years ago to suppress 'ranters', is generally regarded as obsolete, and Quakers do not show that any Friends have been prosecuted under it.

170–2. Counter-reply of the Quakers, read 5 June 1707 (*notation*).

173–4. Counter-reply by Ashurst, read 27 June 1707 (*notation*).

175–8. Counter-reply of Quakers, read 2 Oct. 1707 (*notation*).

179–80. Disallowance of the act, 11 Oct. 1707.

181–2. Unsigned memorandum to society, apparently by Heathcote, 18 June 1708, speaking of his visit to Stratford with Muirson and urging aid.

183. Samuel Johnson to the Archbishop of Canterbury, Stratford, Conn., 12 Nov. 1766, acknowledging the archbishop's efforts on behalf of colonial bishops and presenting some arguments for them.

184. Undated account of the state of the Church in Connecticut, referring to visit of Muirson and Heathcote and asking for a missionary.

185. Undated fragment containing a note to the effect that the society does not think it should 'meddle with' affairs in Connecticut unless it receives an application from that colony.

186–7. Undated notes relating to Bishop Seabury's consecration and problem of providing a third bishop for the United States.

DELAWARE

188. Certificate of Principal (Jonathan Edwards) and fellows of Jesus College, Oxford, that Henry Nichols has been appointed to one of two fellowships in that college, established by Sir James Germain, whose holders are required to serve in the plantations if called to do so by the Bishop of London, 13 May 1703. On sheet containing printed instructions as to type of recommendation required by the society of those seeking appointment as missionaries.

189–90. Petition of inhabitants of Dover Hundred, Del., to Bishop of London, 30 Aug. 1703, asking for a minister.

191. Testimonial of James Chalmers and David Crawford to George Ross, London, 1 Mar. 1704/5.

192. Subscription for support of a minister by residents of Apoquimininck, 4 Sept. 1705. Indicates that they have built a church.

193–4. Petition of inhabitants of Apoquiminick to the society for a missionary, —— 1705. (Date partly torn off.)
NOTE: (xi. 7–8 belongs at this point).

195–6. Vestry of Dover Hundred to Society, 20 Mar. 1705/6, asking further allowance for Thomas Crawford because of long illness.

197. Thomas Crawford to Secretary, Dover Hundred, 3 Apr. 1706, reporting work in his cure.

198. Do. to do., Dover Hundred, 8 Apr. 1706, with similar information.

199–200. George Ross to Secretary, Newcastle, 17 May 1706. Reporting conditions in his parish.

201. Crawford to Secretary, Dover Hundred, 13 June 1706. Requests Prayer Books.

202–3. Testimonial to Thomas Jenkins, 28 June 1706.

204. Birth certificate and testimonial to William Black, signed by John Sharp, J.P., Dumfriesshire, Scotland, 21 Sept. 1706.

205. Secretary to Ross, Petty France, Westminster, 2 June 1707 (copy). Criticizing him for not writing oftener. Evans, who was supposed to acquaint the secretary with conditions in that area has been prevented by illness from visiting England as expected.

206. Jenkins and Black to Secretary, Torquay, 13 Aug. 1707, reporting difficulties in sailing for America.

207. Jenkins to Secretary. On board *Ruby*, Spithead, 30 Aug. 1707, reporting further difficulties.

208. Black to Secretary, Spithead, 30 Aug. 1707, concerning the same.

209. Jenkins and Black to Secretary, Portsmouth, 28 Oct., 1707, report further difficulties and refer to Cordiner's capture by the French.

210. Secretary to Black, Petty France, Westminster, 20 Jan. 1707/8. Society has authorized him to draw on the treasurer for £10.

211. George Ross to Secretary, Newcastle, 19 July 1708, reporting conditions in his parish and arrival of Black and Jenkins.

212–14. Jenkins to Secretary, Newcastle, 26 Aug. 1708. He has settled there instead of at Apoquiminick, where he was sent.

215. Thomas Crawford to Bishop of London, Kent County, Del., 20 Aug. 1708, asking his help in securing a larger allowance from society (copy). With note from Bishop Compton, Fulham, 20 Jan. 1708/9, asking that request be presented to the committee.

216. Secretary to Ross, Windsor Castle, 28 Aug. 1708, rebuking him for not reporting.

217–18. Crawford to Secretary, 31 Aug. 1708, Kent Co., Del., reporting conditions in his parish, which he estimates to be fifty miles long.

219. Secretary to Black, Petty France, Westminster, 6 Sept. 1708, criticizing him for not reporting his arrival and accusing him of being hotheaded and covetous, besides being Scotch. Letter is sent by Mr. Evans, who is presented as a good example (copy).

220. Do. to Jenkins, Petty France, Westminster, 6 Sept. 1708, indicating that unfavourable reports of his and Black's character come from (Francis?) Philips.

221. Do. to Black, Petty France, Westminster, 16 Feb. 1708/9 (copy). He is directed by the society to ask Black to report on the station juggling of Nichols, Ross, and Jenkins. Nichols has been dismissed by the society.

222. Do. to Jenkins, Petty France, Westminster, 15 Feb. 1708/9 (copy). Society has approved report of committee holding that local support promised at Apoquimininck was sufficient to justify his being sent there. As he has violated the society's orders against changing stations without permission, he will receive no further payments until he has satisfied them in this matter.

223. Do. to Ross, Petty France, Westminster, 15 Feb. 1708/9 (copy). He will receive no more money from the society because of his unauthorized removal from Newcastle to Chester.

224–5. Parishioners at Apoquiminick to Bishop of London, 7 Mar. 1708/, reporting that Jenkins has returned to them and asking renewal of the society's allowance. Even when residing at Newcastle, he preached among them frequently.

226–7. Jenkins to Secretary, Apoquiminick, 23 Mar. 1708/9, excusing his removal, and implying that he had not received society's instruction against changing stations before he did so. Accuses Col. Quarry of inciting Apoquimininck to present a memorial against him. (This presumably preceeded 224–5).

228. Secretary to Ross, Petty France, Westminster, 3 June 1709 (copy). He can expect no further aid from the society until he has given a better justification of his change than he has so far.

229. Jenkins to Secretary, Apoquimininck, 20 June 1709, pleading for reinstatement.

230. Parishioners of Apoquiminick to Secretary, 5 Sept. 1709, reporting death of Jenkins in Philadelphia, 30 July 1709. Evans arranged the funeral and Talbot preached the sermon.

231. Secretary to Jenkins, Petty France, Westminster, 24 Sept. 1708 (copy), informing him that society has restored his allowance.

232. Secretary to vestry of Apoquiminick, 6 Jan. 1708/9 (copy). On learning of Jenkins's death, the society has directed Black, the missionary in Sussex, to serve them.

233. Secretary to Black, Petty France, Westminster, 6 Jan. 1708/9 (copy), informing him of his appointment to Apoquiminick. Indicates that Black reported being driven from his former post by the French, and that Col. Nicholson confirmed the report.

234. Secretary to vestry at Newcastle, Petty France, Westminster, 7 Jan. 1709/10 (copy), introducing Robert Sinclair, who has been appointed to replace Ross.

235. Do. to do., Petty France, Westminster, 27 Jan. 1709/10 (copy), asking them to put Sinclair in possession of the society's library.

236–7. Sinclair to Secretary, Newcastle, 7 Dec. 1710. Parish is divided between a pro- and anti-Ross party.

238. Vestry at Apoquiminick to Secretary, 11 Dec. 1710. They ask appointment of another missionary, as Black refuses to serve them, having accepted a cure in Ackamack, Va.

239–40. Vestry at Newcastle to Secretary, 2 Apr. 1711, asking increased allowance for Sinclair.

241. Secretary to vestry at Apoquiminick, Petty France, Westminster, 21 Apr. 1711 (copy), announcing appointment of Club as their missionary.

242. Do. to Club, Petty France, Westminster, 21 Apr. 1711, informing him of his appointment to Apoquiminick, and that Humphreys, who brings this letter, will replace him at Oxford, Pa. (copy).

243. Jacob Henderson to Secretary, Apoquiminick, 20 May 1711. On advice of the governor, Col. Quarry, Evans, and Talbot, he is residing at Apoquiminick and serving that parish and Dover Hundred.

244–5. Vestry at Apoquimincik to Secretary, 24 June 1711, asking appointment of Henderson as their missionary. Indicate he had originally been sent to Dover Hundred.

246. Secretary to Henderson, Petty France, Westminster, 24 July 1711. On recommendation of Gov. Gookin, the society is transferring him to Lewes.

247. George Ross to Secretary. On board the *Hector*, in sight of Sandy Hook, 18 Sept. 1711. He has got that far on his return from England.

248–9. Vestry at Newcastle to Society, undated, asking continuance of support for Ross.

250. Justices of the peace of Kent Co., Del., to the Society, 1 Oct. 1709, testifying to good conduct of Crawford.

GEORGIA

251–3. Comments by Bishop Terrick and Bishop Greene on proposed charter of Whitefield's college in Georgia, May 1767.

254. Northington to the Archbishop of Canterbury, 27 Aug. 1767, concerning the same.

255. Archbishop of Canterbury to the Earl of Northington, Lambeth, 28 Aug. 1767 (draft). The archbishop disapproves of the second draft of the charter, because it does not require the head of the college to be a member of the Church of England, but he wants Northington to say this and not make the archbishop responsible for the rejection.

256. George Whitefield to the Archbishop, Tottenham Court, 1 Sept. 1767, asking if the Lord President has acted on his petition. *Notation*, apparently by the archbishop, says that he replied by servant that he expected an answer from the Lord President any day.

257. Archbishop to Whitefield, 18 Sept. 1767. Draft of note accompanying letter from the Lord President.

258. Whitefield to the Archbishop, Tottenham Court, 13 Oct. 1767. Through a series of mistakes, the archbishop's letter with that of the Lord President has just reached him.

259–60. Do. to do., Tottenham Court, 16 Oct. 1767. Defends omission of the requirement as many, probably a majority, of the contributors are dissenters, and governor and council of Georgia have approved the draft of the charter.

261. Do. to do., Tottenham Court, 11 Nov. 1767, asking archbishop to send papers relating to the orphanage by bearer, and suggesting that he examine the charter of the College of New Jersey.

262–3. Do. to do., Tottenham Court, 12 Feb. 1768, stating his intention of publishing his correspondence with the archbishop on the subject of the college.

VOLUME XII

MARYLAND

1–2. John Gilbert to the Bishop of London, Plymouth, 23 Apr. 1702, introducing Samuel Magaw, a Scotch clergyman, who is in need of assistance, having been driven into Plymouth by unfavourable winds while on his way to visit a kinsman who is a minister in Dover.

3–4. Testimonial to John Sharpe from clergymen of Maryland, Annapolis, 26 Apr. 1704.

5–6. Extract from Maryland act of 3 Oct. 1704 declaring that slaves are not manumitted by baptism.

7. Testimonial of several residents of Somerset County, Md., that price of tobacco there has been low for the past five years.

8. Cordiner and Jenkins to Secretary, Portsmouth, 28 Apr. 1707, reporting difficulties in getting passage to America.

9. Cordiner to Secretary, Portsmouth, 17 June 1707, concerning the same.

10. Do. to do., Portsmouth, 9 July 1707, concerning the same.

11. Do. to do., aboard *Chester*, Spithead, 4 Aug. 1707. He has sailed, but his ship was ordered back.

12. Cordiner to the Bishop of London, on board *Chester*, Spithead, 30 Aug. 1707. His ship has been ordered to convey the King of Portugal to Lisbon and then sail for Virginia.

13–14. Do. to Secretary, on board the *Chester*, Spithead, 15 Oct. 1707. His ship has not sailed yet, but is ordered to do so with the first favourable wind. He asks relief.

15. Secretary to Cordiner, Petty France, Westminster, 20 Sept. 1707 (copy). Society has voted to advance one 15th of their salaries to him, Black, and Jenkins.

16. Cordiner to Secretary, Portsmouth, 26 Oct. 1707, acknowledging grant and speaking of courtesy shown him by gentlemen in Portsmouth, particularly the mayor (Irving) and vicar (Ward).

17. Do. to do., Dinan, 17 Oct. 1707. He has been captured by the French.

18. Do. to Mr. Linton, Dinant, 7 Feb. 1707/8, reporting his hardships as a prisoner.

19. Do. to Secretary, Precott Court in St. John's St., 5 June 1708, acknowledging favours from the society.

20–1. Do. to the Committee, undated, but referred to in (19), asking them to intercede with the Queen for his relief, as he lost all his possessions when captured.

22–39. Do's. account of his adventures as a prisoner, undated, but dealing with events of 1707/8.

40–1. Do's. memorial to the Society, asking further relief. Says that he is preparing to enter some business.

42. Jonathan Evans and Robert Walker to Bishop of London, on board the *Ruby*, Spithead, 30 Aug. 1707. Ship was ordered back to Spithead after starting its voyage.

43–4. Walker to Secretary, 18 Sept. 1707. He has given up sailing on the *Ruby* and is seeking another opportunity. He has been sent to Maryland as a schoolmaster by the Bishop of London.

45–6. Do. to do., Portsmouth, 1 Oct. 1707, asking aid.

47. Secretary to Mr. Herbert, Petty France, 9 Mar. 1707 (9) (copy), asking aid for Cordiner.

48–9. Robert Keith to the Society, 4 Apr. 1708. His salary having been stopped for failure to sail to America, he offers explanations.

50. Certificate of James Hindman, 27 Apr. 1708, that Keith had engaged passage and was preparing to sail with him, when he received notice of his dismissal by the society.

51. Keith to members of the Committee, 21 May 1708, referring to (49–51).

52. Undated memorandum of Mrs. Keith, asking that aid be given to her and her children if her husband remains in Maryland.

53–5. Case of Robert Keith (2 copies).

56–7. Additional memorial of Robert Keith.

58–59. Memorial of Mary Keith to the Archbishop of Canterbury, asking relief.

60. Another petition of Keith to the society.

61–2. Henry Nichols to Society, St. Michael's Parish, Talbot Co., Md., 13 Sept. 1708, explaining his removal from Chester, Pa.

63–4. William Black to Secretary, Annapolis, 7 June 1709, explaining that he had to flee his parish in Delaware because it was raided by a French privateer.

65–6. Black to the Bishop of London, Annapolis, 7 June 1709, with a similar account.

67. Jacob Henderson to Secretary, *Reserve*, in the Downs, 28 Dec. 1710. They are waiting for a favourable wind. He acknowledges gift from the society.

68–9. Do to do., Kicotan, Va., 21 Mar. 1710/11. He has got that far and is waiting for an opportunity to get to Dover, Del. Mr. Wallace, the minister at Kicotan, with whom he is staying, advanced £5 to Jenkins on a bill on the society which has been protested. Wallace has had a report from Urmston of the death of James Adams, the society's missionary in North Carolina.

70. Alexander Adams to the Bishop of London, Stepney Parish, Somerset County, Md., 2 July 1711, asking him to obtain a grant from the society because of Adams's extra labour in supplying vacant parishes and the low price of tobacco.

71–2. Do. to Secretary, Stepney Parish, 2 July 1711, asking for an allowance.

73–4. Undated account of George Trotter's mission to Maryland, beginning in 1697 and ending with his return to England in 1706.

MASSACHUSETTS

75–6. Extracts from the charter of the Company for the Propagation of the Gospel in New England and Parts Adjacent, 1661.

77. George Keith to Secretary, Boston, 12 June 1702, giving an account of his missionary tour.

78. P. Gordon to Secretary, Boston, 13 June 1702, giving an account of the voyage over and noting that Keith has been joined in his mission by the ship's chaplain, John Talbot.

79. Keith to Secretary, Boston, 7 July 1702, reporting that Talbot has joined him.

80–1. Samuel Myles to the Bishop of Gloucester, Boston, 8 July 1702. He has sought to promote the Church in surrounding towns by lending books, and has drawn a bill on the society for £30 expenses in lodging Keith.

82. Do. to do., Boston, 3 Aug. 1702, asking his aid in obtaining an answer to petitions sent home for ministers.

83–4. Christopher Bridge to Keith, Boston, 17 Nov. 1702. Reports forwarding letters of Keith to London and arrangements for printing Keith's answer to Mather. (Addressed to Keith in Philadelphia.)

85. James Honeyman to Society, Boston, 16 Nov. 1703. He has arrived in Boston after a long voyage, his ship having had to wait for a convoy.

86. Certificate of James Roissie, Master of the *Portsmouth Galley* that Honeyman took passage on his ship in April, 1703, but that sailing was delayed by want of a convoy.

87–8. John Brown to Archbishop of Canterbury, Swansea, 23 Feb. 1703, asking that a missionary be sent to Swansea in response to previous petitions.

89–92. J. Dudley and others to the Archbishop of Canterbury, Boston, 4 Jan. 1703/4. Testimonial to Bridge who is visiting England with Myles's permission. (2 copies).

93–4. Myles to Dr. Beveridge, Boston, 4 Jan. 1703/4, introducing Col. Charles Hobby. Bridge did not have his permission to return, not having met the conditions he set, and he asks that someone else be sent in his place.

95–6. Do. to the Archbishop of Canterbury, Boston, 5 Jan. 1703/4, introducing Col. Hobby and asking replacement of Bridge.

97–8. Do. to Beveridge, Boston, 26 Feb. 1703/4, introducing Mr. Barclay, who can tell him all about Bridge.

99–101. Bridge to Society, London, 15 June 1704, giving his version of the affair. Because of the precariousness of his salary from the Privy Purse, his supporters tried to get him a salary from the vestry, but in the end all he got was permission to return to England to try to arrange better payment of his official salary.

102. J. Dudley to Myles, Roxbury, 10 Dec. 1703 (copy, enclosed with (99–101), asking for a vestry meeting to consider advancing Bridge's salary, pending official payment. On same sheet: Myles to Bridge, Boston, 22 Dec. 1703, consenting to Bridge's return, on condition that he draw a bill to Myles for £50.

103–4. Edward to Thomas Bromfield, Boston, 4 Oct. 1704, giving account of a society lately founded to promote religion in New England.

105. Myles to Bishop of London, Boston, 16 Oct. 1704. Testimonial to Muirson, who is going home for orders.

106–7. Testimonial to Muirson from wardens and vestry in Braintree, 19 Oct. 1704.

108. Secretary to ——, Petty France, Westminster, 23 Jan. 1705/6 (copy), asking for information about Corporation for the Propagation of the Gospel in New England.

109. Myles to Gardner, Boston, 25 June 1706. Although Bridge is supposed to be going to Narragansett, Myles sees indictions that he plans to remain in Boston.

110. Henry Newman to the Secretary, Lyon, 19 Aug. 1706, recommending that Bridge be sent to Rhode Island.

111. Daillé to Secretary, Boston, 8 Sept. 1706 (Latin), requesting books.

112. Bridge to Secretary (?), Boston, 7 Oct. 1706. Believes that a number of Harvard students are about to conform to the Church.

113. Daillé to the Society, Boston, 8 Oct. 1706, asking aid.

114. Myles to Secretary, Boston, 9 Oct. 1706, asking society's help for French congregation in Boston.

115–16. Dudley to Secretary, Boston, 10 Oct. 1706, making similar request.

117. Bridge to Secretary, Boston, 15 Oct., 1706, supporting this request.

118. Myles to Secretary, Boston, 15 Oct. 1706, asking that society refund money advanced to Rawlins to enable him to come home for orders.

119. Henry Caner to the Archbishop of Canterbury, Boston, 16 Oct. 1766 (misplaced, because of misreading of date), urging appointment of a bishop, referring to plans for Indian mission and to controversy over New Hampshire grants.

120–1. Edward Bromfield to Secretary, Boston, 24 Feb. 1707. Enclosing some books published by his society and referring to work of Ryhans Billings (Congregational?) minister at Little Compton and of Elias Neau in New York.

122–3. Myles to Secretary, Boston, 4 Mar. 1707. Bridge has had conflicting orders from the society, directing him to Narragansett and from Bishop Compton directing him to (Newport) Rhode Island.

124. Secretary to Daillé, Petty France, Westminster, 25 Mar. 1707 (copy). Committee has resolved that Daillé is not eligible for an allowance because his congregation has not conformed to the Church of England and because he was not sent abroad by the society. A similar action was previously taken with respect to Bondet in New York.

125. Do. to Myles, Petty France, Westminster, 6 June 1707 (copy), explaining refusal of Daillé's request. The Bishop of London is having difficulty in finding a well qualified clergyman to replace Bridge as Myles's assistant.

126–7. Myles to Secretary, Boston, 15 Aug. 1707, seeking to collect money advanced to Rawlins and noting that Bridge has been ordered to Narragansett.

128–9. Duplicate of (126–7).

130. Henry Head to Honeyman, Little Compton, 20 Dec. 1707, asking if he has any news of the coming of a minister from England.

131. John Brown to Myles, Swansea, 19 Jan. 1707/8, reporting local sickness.

132. Myles to Secretary, Boston, 12 Mar. 1707/8, saying that Honeyman will inform him how basely he (Myles) has been used by Bridge.

133-4. Extract from a letter of Thomas Barclay to Bishop Compton, Boston, 4 Mar. 1707/8, giving a pro-Myles account of the Myles–Bridge controversy.

135-6. Gov. Dudley to Bishop Compton, Boston, 27 May 1708 (copy). Honeyman is returning to wait on the bishop. Dudley hopes that his and Bridge's assignments can be adjusted satisfactorily, as they are both good men.

137. Secretary to Myles, Windsor Castle, 4 Aug. 1708 (copy). Society can only repay his advance to Rawlins by deducting it from Rawlins's salary when he enters their service. State of the society's finances precludes any reconsideration of Daillé's application. The Bridge–Honeyman controversy has been settled by the committee, but the secretary accuses Myles of having written contradictory letters on the subject.

138-9. Gov. Dudley to Bishop Compton, Boston, 20 Aug. 1708, expressing his support for Myles, and promising to do his best to maintain peace in the congregation.

140. Paul Dudley to the Secretary, Boston, 25 Mar. 1709, testifying to good character of Bridge.

141-2. Abstract of several testimonials to Bridge received by Henry Newman from correspondents in Massachusetts. Latest date, 26 Mar. 1709.

143-4. Myles to Secretary, Boston, 22 Sept. 1709. He is sending copies of letters from governor and vestry to the Bishop of London relating to their parochial controversy.

145. Bridge to Secretary, Boston, 26 Oct. 1709. He is on his way to Rye, and has written the lieutenant-governor of New York and the church wardens to inform them of his mission.

146-7. Myles to Secretary, Boston, 16 Dec. 1709. Bishop Compton writes that the society is pressing him to appoint an assistant at Boston, but Myles would be content to remain without one, and see the money used to supply nearby missions.

148. William Brattle to Henry Newman, Cambridge, 3 Sept. 1711, protesting inaccuracy of article in Society's printed report concerning Braintree.

149. Leverett to Secretary, Cambridge, 1 Nov. 1711 (extract in secretary's hand), complaining of the same article, which states that the churchwardens and vestry in Braintree, in their testimonials to Muirson, declared that they were without a pastor, and asked that William Barclay be sent to them.

150. Do. to do., Cambridge, 12 Nov. 1711. Says there is only one person in Braintree who can be called a Churchman.

151. Gov. Dudley to Secretary, Boston, 13 Nov. 1711. Inquiries he has made at request of Society have satisfied him that charges against Honeyman in Rhode Island are groundless, and that Honeyman has behaved well for the past three years.

152–61. Petition of clerical and lay deputies to General Convention, 8 Aug. 1789, to Archbishops of Canterbury and York, asking their assent to the consecration of Edward Bass as Bishop of Massachusetts by White, Provoost, and Seabury.

162–3. Copy of letter of Bishop White to the clergy of Massachusetts and New Hampshire, Philadelphia, 10 Aug. 1789, relating to this matter.

164–5. Undated address of the vestry of King's Chapel, Boston, to the Bishop of London, saying that they prefer to do without an assistant.

166–7. Undated recommendations that King's Chapel, Boston, be aided by society, as it needs enlarging, requires two ministers, and the payment of the assistant's salary from the privy purse is precarious. Payment of arrears was cancelled by death of William III.

168. Myles to Gardner, Boston, Sept. ——, asking him to secure secretary's support for unspecified petition. Postscript instructs him to burn this and other letters.

169. Secretary to Governor of New England, undated draft, saying that society will defray expenses of students who come home for orders, if they are qualified.

NEW JERSEY

170–1. Talbot to Gillingham, Newcastle, 10 Apr. 1703 (copy). On way to his mission. Letter is chiefly an unfavourable account of religion in the colonies, with special strictures against the Quakers.

172–3. Do. to do., Virginia, 3 May 1703. He is visiting friends there. Keith is at his daughter's house. Reports beginnings of several churches in New Jersey and Pennsylvania (copy).

174–5. Lewis Morris to Dr. Beveridge, Trenton, 12 July 1703, asks appointment of a minister for Monmouth County, where the labours of Innis and of Keith and Talbot have brought a number of people into the Church.

176–9. Talbot to Secretary, Philadelphia, 26 Aug. 1703. Acknowledges appointment by society, gives some account of Keith's mission, and praises Gov. Nicholson for his incorruptibility and his zeal for the Church. Identifies recipient of (170–3) as Richard Gillingham, Vicar of Chigwell in Essex.

180–3. Do. to do., Philadelphia, 1 Sept. 1703. Repeats some of the information in (176–9), and asks for books, as the parcel he had with him is lost. Urges sending bishops. Keith plans to return in spring. Both this and (176–9) are being brought by John Thomas.

184. Wardens of Burlington to Archbishop of Canterbury, 1 Sept. 1703. Having built a church, they ask for aid in securing Prayer Books and furnishings.

185–6. Talbot to Secretary, New York, 22 Feb. 1704. Refers to a conference of some of the clergy held at the instance of Lord Cornbury and Col. Nicholson. Defends Nicholson against critics. Notes conversion of some Quakers.

187. Parishioners of Burlington to Society, 2 Apr. 1704, reporting Talbot's settlement among them.

189–90. Talbot to Secretary, Philadelphia, 7 Apr. 1704. Notes that Keith is returning. Praises work of Alexander Innes and hopes that society will aid him. Notes that Honeyman's settlement has been delayed by a scandal, and refers to a number of other clergymen.

191–6. Do. to Whitfield, 20 Oct. 1704. Speaks of attending a meeting of clergy of New York, New Jersey, and Pennsylvania in New York, which has sent an address to the society. Reports conditions in Burlington, refers to several missionaries, and pleads for a bishop.

197–8. Do. to Society, London, 14 Mar. 1705, asking to be appointed missionary in Burlington, having lost his living in Gloucestershire. He came home partly to promote plea for a bishop.

199. John Brooke to Secretary, Elizabeth, 20 Aug. 1705, reporting his arrival. On advice of Cornbury, he has settled in Elizabeth to serve that and neighbouring towns.

200. Thomas Crawford to Secretary, Burlington, 7 Nov. 1705, asking to be transferred from Dover Hundred, Del., because it is an unhealthy location.

201. Brooke to Secretary, Elizabeth Town, 23 Nov. 1705. He has assembled a congregation at Piscataqay and recommends sending a missionary there.

202–3. Do. to Archbishop of York, Elizabeth Town, 23 Nov. 1705, reporting arrival and successful beginning.

204. Secretary to Rudman, Petty France, Westminster, 2 Mar. 1705/6 (copy). He made a mistake in drawing on the society under the impression that he had been employed as a missionary, but, in view of good reports of his work, society has voted to pay him £30 for the current year, plus a gift of £20.

205. Do. to Brooke, Petty France, Westminster, 22 Apr. 1706 (copy), announcing the dispatch of a parcel of books and informing him of the society's rule that all missionaries must give an exact account of local contributions.

206. Daniel Leeds to Keith and Talbot, Burlington, 28 Apr. 1706, speaking of two islands in the Delaware which, as a test of the main current convinces him, are on the Jersey side and therefore belong to the Crown, which he thinks might be persuaded to give them to the Church in Burlington.

207. Secretary to Moore, Petty France, Westminster, 3 May 1706 (copy). Because his negotiations with the Indians, to whom he was sent, failed, society has appointed him and Talbot to serve alternately in Burlington and as itinerants in North Carolina. (New Jersey?)

208. Brooke to Archbishop of York (?), Amboy, 11 Oct. 1706. Complains that society is not paying him what they promised when they transferred him from Long Island.

209–15. Do. to Secretary, Amboy, 11 Oct. 1706, reporting on his work in several places and complaining that his allowance is less than the £100 which he says was orally promised him by the Archbishop of Canterbury and other members of the committee.

216–19. Printed remonstrance of New Jersey Assembly to Governor Lord Cornbury, 8 May 1707, and the Governor's response. The grievances are of an administrative nature, some of them relating to the subordination of New Jersey to New York. No ecclesiastical issues are mentioned.

220. Secretary to Talbot, Petty France, Westminister, 8 June 1707 (copy). Asking him to personally deliver letters in a packet that will be given him by Capt. Hamilton, and urging him as senior missionary to set an example of moderation.

221. Do. to Moore, Petty France, Westminister, 9 June 1707 (copy of letter sent by Talbot). Informing him of his appointment as missionary at Hopewell, with an allowance of £60. He has been supplying for Talbot. Enjoins him to make regular reports, including an account of local contributions, in accordance with the society's order.

222. Talbot to Secretary, *Reserve* at Spithead, 23 June (1707). Ship required to return to port by Dunkirk squadron.

223–4. Thorogood Moore to Secretary, Burlington, N.J., 17 July 1707. Refers to some bills drawn on the Treasurer.

225–6. Talbot to Secretary, Burlington, 24 Aug. (1708? *Notation* gives year as 1707, but contents seem to require later year.) It is nine months since he saw Moore and Brooke off from Boston and he fears they are lost. He sees their troubles as providing argument for a bishop. He returned through Connecticut, where he notes that Muirson has gathered forty communicants.

227. Do. to do., Lisbon, 14 Sept. (1707). His ship has been driven in there on its way to New England. Mentions difficulties of Black and Cordiner.

228–33. Printed reply of New Jersey Assembly to Lord Cornbury's answer to its remonstrance, 24 Oct. 1707.

234–5. Talbot to Secretary, Rhode Island, 13 Dec. (1707). Reports his safe arrival. Refers to flight of Moore and Brooke and to Bridge–Honeyman dispute.

236. Do. to do., New York, 10 Jan. (1708). He has got this far, but cannot get to New Jersey because of ice. On his way from Rhode Island he preached to a congregation of two or three hundred in Stratford. Refers to Col. Heathcote as the finest gentleman he has met in America.

237. John Hamilton to Secretary, Burlington, 13 Jan. 1707/8. A testimonial to Honeyman, who will deliver it.

238. Talbot to Secretary, Westchester, 14 Feb. (1708). Still prevented by weather from proceeding to New Jersey. He gives some account of Muirson's work in Connecticut.

239–41. Secretary to Talbot, Windsor Castle, 6 Aug. 1708 (copy). Speaks of differences of opinion between them, voices suspicion that Talbot had selfish motives for returning to England, and urges him to moderation. Mentions reports that he has preached in parishes of neighbouring clergy against their wishes.

242. Do. to Capt. Hamilton, Petty France, Westminster, 6 Sept. 1708, asking him to keep an eye on the society's missionaries.

243. Henry Shute to Secretary, 28 Sept. 1708, reporting satisfactory preaching by Vaughan.

244. Talbot to Secretary, Rhode Island, 13 Dec. (1707?). It is dated 1708 in *notation*, but reference to departure of Moore and Brooke points to earlier year.

245–6. Petition of Edward Vaughan to the committee, undated, but refers to preaching test reported in (243). Asks some allowance from the society for his expenses as, at the urging of Mr. Evans, he came to London to seek appointment as missionary though under canonical age for ordination to the priesthood.

247–8. Testimonial to Vaughan from clergy in the Diocese of Landaff, where his father, Robert, is rector of Woolves Newton. Undated, but seems to belong with papers for 1708.

249. Secretary to —— Bass, Petty France, Westminster, 24. Jan. 1709/10 (copy), asking him to counsel and report on missionaries. Postscript refers to some land that Bass has advised the society to purchase in the province.

250. Do. to do., Petty France, Westminster, 22 Feb. 1709/10 (copy). (*Notation* identifies Bass as Secretary of New Jersey.) Asking further information about the lands referred to in (249) and speaking of a proposal to buy a house in Burlington as a possible future residence for a bishop. This plan must be kept secret, lest the price go up.

251. Do. to Talbot, Petty France, Westminster, 25 Feb. 1709/10 (copy), accusing him of intemperate language in speaking of his opponents.

252–5. J. Bass to Secretary, Burlington, 23 May, 1711. Giving some account of condition of the Church in New Jersey and Delaware and a description of the land referred to in (249).

256. Secretary to —— Sharpe, Petty France, Westminster, 24 May 1711 (copy). Committee has approved some recommendations of his for safeguarding its books, but cannot purchase his books for the use of missionaries, as they are not on the list approved by the society.

257. Do. to Vaughan, Petty France, Westminster, 24 May 1711 (copy). He cannot expect an augmentation of his allowance as Halliday has been sent to assist him.

258–9. Halliday to Secretary, Amboy, 5 Aug. 1711. He serves Amboy and Piscataway, having a larger congregation in the latter town. He has had some difficulty with those who are holding subscriptions raised to build a church under Moore in Amboy.

260–1. Bass to Secretary, Burlington, 9 Aug. 1711, referring to the house in Burlington and to the dispute in Amboy.

262–3. Vaughan to Secretary, Elizabeth Town, N.J., 12 Oct. 1711. He has had a dispute with Col. Townley over land supposedly donated for a church in Elizabeth. Criticizes Halliday's conduct in Amboy.

264. Undated description of Elizabeth, attributed to Col. Nicholson.

265. Undated fragment listing towns in New Jersey.

266. Lewis Morris to Secretary, undated, referring to Keith's mission.

267. Notes on a memorial of Moore concerning things he thought necessary for his mission.

268. List of furnishings desired for the Church in Burlington.

269–70. Undated account of religion in East Jersey, attributed to Col. Morris in *notation*.

VOLUME XIII

NEW YORK, 1700–1706

1–2. Extract from statement of 'Praying Indians' (those converted to some form of Christianity) to the Commissioners for Indian Affairs at Albany, 28 June 1700. Reproaches English with not instructing Indians in Christianity.

3–4. Letter of Lords Commissioners of Trade and Plantations to Archbishop of Canterbury, Whitehall, 25 Oct. 1700, recommending establishment of a fund to support ministers of the Church of England among Indians.

5. William Vesey to Samuel Myles, New York, 10 Feb. 1702. Refers to an effort of Bridge to obtain a chaplaincy held by Vesey, to inquiries concerning Honeyman and Col. Quarry, and asks Myles to send a cask of wine and a cask of pickle sturgeon. Says Talbot defended Myles against some who favoured Bridge. (Year may be 1703. Reading uncertain.)

6–7. Testimonial of Thomas Tipping to John Bartow, 28 May 1702.

8. Testimonial to Bartow by several clergymen, 2 Apr. 1702. (Latin.)

9. Testimonial to do. from William Stephens, Vicar of Lynton in Cambridge-shire, 3 June 1702. Bartow has been his assistant and has kept a private school in Lynton for four years.

10. Testimonial to do. from parishioners of Pampisford, Cambridgeshire, where he was vicar for four years, 10 June 1702.

11. Testimonial to do. from Thomas Harris, rector of Dutford, 10 June 1702.

12. Testimonial to do. from Henry Smyth, Rector of Hildersham, 13 June 1702.

13. Bartow to Society, London, 25 June 1702. About to leave for Portsmouth, he asks an advance for expenses.

14. Do. to Secretary, Portsmouth, 7 July 1702, asking for an advance. His passage cost £8.

15. Do. to Secretary, Portsmouth, July 1702, asking that society establish a credit for him in New York.

16. Extract from a letter of Samuel Thomas to Dr. Bray, Rye, 17 Aug. 1702, complaining of ill usage of Captain, who will not allow him a cabin to sleep in, though he paid over £10 for passage.

17. Thomas to Bray, Rye, 17 Aug. 1702. The letter from which (16) is extracted, describing difficulties at start of voyage.

18. Bartow to Whitfield, New York, 7 Oct. 1702. He has arrived safely, but finds much sickness in town. He has met Col. Heathcote, who has shown him great kindness.

19-20. Extracts from letters of missionaries to various correspondents from Nov. 1702 to Mar. 1704, testifying to zeal of Col. Nicholson on behalf of the Church.

21. George Keith to Secretary, New York, 11 Dec. 1702. Speaks of Talbot's joining in his mission and refers to a letter of Lord Corbury to the justices of the peace against the Quakers.

22-3. Testimonial of Rector (Vesey) wardens and vestry of Trinity Parish, New York, to good behaviour of Keith during his mission.

24. Order of Queen in Council, 3 Apr. 1703, directing the Archbishop of Canterbury to make arrangements for sending missionaries to the Iroquois as a means of confirming their allegiance to England.

25. Honeyman to Secretary, Portsmouth, 10 May 1703, reporting difficulties in sailing.

26-7. John Bartow to Secretary, Westchester, N.Y., 25 May 1703. Describes operation of provincial establishment act and reports a legal dispute over land in Westchester.

28. Elias Neau to Treasurer, New York, 10 July 1703 (French), reporting work with Negro slaves.

29. Translation of (28).

30. Lord Cornbury to the Bishop of London, Burlington, 23 Aug. 1703, introducing (John) Thomas who is returning for priest's orders, having been assistant and schoolmaster in Philadelphia.

31–2. Testimonial to Charles Smith from clergy of the Diocese of Worcester, 6 Sept. 1703.

33–8. Printed copies of amendments to the laws governing Trinity Church, New York, dated 2nd and 3rd years of Queen Anne.

39. Testimonial of James Chalmers and David Crawford to William Urquhart, 4 Feb. 1703/4.

40. Lord Cornbury to the Society, New York, 21 Mar. 1703/4. Testimonial to Keith, who is about to return to England.

41. Do. to the Bishop of London, New York, 21 Mar. 1703/4. Another testimonial to Keith.

42. Lewis Morris to Keith, Trenton, 4 Apr. 1704, praising his work.

43–4. Heathcote to Secretary, Manor of Scarsdale, 10 Apr. 1704, describing religious conditions in Westchester.

45. Neau to Treasurer, New York, 15 Apr. 1704 (French), describing his work.

46. Honeyman to Dr. Beveridge, 15 Apr. 1704, reporting his settlement in Jamaica, N.Y.

47. Do. to Secretary, Jamaica, 15 Apr. 1704, describing his initial work there.

48. Translation of (45).

49. Bartow to Secretary, Westchester, N.Y., 24 May 1704. Reports arrival of Pritchard, scandal (which he disbelieves) relating to Honeyman, and death of Lockier.

50. Thomas Pritchard to Secretary, Mamaroneck, 6 June 1704, reporting on his work.

51. Do. to do., Rye, N.Y., 18 June 1704. Reports baptizing two adults and having a large class of catechumens.

52–5. Neau to Treasurer, New York, 22 June 1704 (French, with translation), reporting on his work.

56–7. Honeyman to Secretary, Jamaica, N.Y., 26 June 1704. Urquhart has been sent to replace him, on the basis, he says, of a single charge against him.

58. William Thomson to Henry Shute, Richmond, 28 July 1704. Testimonial to C. Buckton of Stamford.

59–60. Neau to Treasurer, New York, 4 July 1704 (French, with translation), reporting on his work.

61–2. Urquhart to Shibs, New York, 4 July 1704. Urges sending a bishop. Is told that a number of Harvard students might conform to the Church of England if ordination was available. Local residents find the society ignorant of geography, as some of its published reports place Rhode Island in New York and Long Island in New England. Vesey complains that Neau is negligent in church attendance. Scandal around Honeyman seems to have arisen because he persisted in lodging at a certain house after Vesey had advised him that it was a place of ill fame.

63–4. Neau to Secretary, New York, 29 Aug. 1704 (French, with translation). Vesey has challenged his canonical right to function as a catechist, since he is a layman and a merchant.

65–6. Do. to Dr. Woodward, New York, 15 Sept. 1704, referring to this dispute and giving some account of his catechizing.

67–8. Do. to Secretary, New York, 15 Oct. 1704 (French, with translation), relating to the same controversy.

69–70. John Lydins to Society, New Albany, 28 Aug. 1704 (Dutch, with translation), giving some account of his work among the Indians.

71–9. An account of the state of the Church in New York, New Jersey, and Pennsylvania as it was laid before the clergy convened in New York, 5 Oct. 1704. Also includes New England, though it is not named in heading. Honeyman is placed in Newport.

80–1. Bartow to Society, Westchester, N.Y., 10 Oct. 1704. Books donated by the society have been gratefully received by those whose residence is too remote for regular church-attendance.

82–4. Address of the convened clergy to the Bishop of London and the Society, New York, 17 Oct. 1704. Request books to distribute, especially those dealing with controversial issues.

85. Vesey to the Archbishop of Canterbury, New York, 26 Oct. 1704. Recommends appointment of Muirson as catechist to replace Neau. Neau is a worthy and good man, but he is an elder of the French congregation and a merchant. He does not communicate with the Church of England, and he does not speak good English.

86. Heathcote to the Bishop of London, New York, 23 Oct. 1704, recommending appointment of Joseph Cleator as schoolmaster.

87. Do. to Secretary, New York, 23 Oct. 1704, making the same recommendation.

88. Duplicate of (87).

89. Thorogood Moore to Secretary, New York, 24 Oct. 1704. He reached New York in August. He recommends continuance of Neau as catechist, but believes that Muirson could also serve usefully as assistant to Vesey and schoolmaster.

90–1. Vesey to the Secretary, New York, 26 Oct. 1704. Praises Neau, but thinks catechist should be at least in deacon's orders and again recommends Muirson for the post.

92. Urquhart to the Secretary, New York, 1 Nov. 1704. Describes conditions in Jamaica and recommends Muirson.

93-4. Pritchard to Secretary, Rye, N.Y., 1 Nov. 1704. Reports conditions in his parish and asks that he be given the same allowance (£50) as Bartow and other missionaries.

95-6. Cornbury to Secretary, New York, 6 Nov. 1704. Corrects some errors in the society's printed report. Muirson was sent as schoolmaster for Albany, but as there was no allowance for a schoolmaster there, Cornbury held him in New York, where the legislature had provided an allowance. He is now going home for orders.

97-9. Neau to Secretary, New York, 6 Nov. 1704. He has carried out a promise made to Moore by resigning his post in the French church and conforming to the Church of England (French, with translation).

100. Cornbury to Secretary, New York, 6 Nov. 1704. Duplicate of (96).

101-4. Neau to Treasurer, New York, 20 Dec. 1704 (French, with translation). Mentions that he became acquainted with the Book of Common Prayer while still in his 'dungeon'.

105-9. Account of the state of the Church in New York in 1704, signed by C. Congreve.

110. Testimonial of the Earl of Crometie to Aeneas Mackenzie, 29 Jan. 1704/5.

111. Heathcote to Secretary, 23 Feb. 1705, Manor of Scarsdale. As Muirson's appointment as catechist is causing dissent in Trinity Church, he recommends sending him to Staten Island.

112-13. Vesey to the Society, New York, 26 Feb. 1705, making the same recommendation. He no longer needs an assistant, as Cornbury has directed the chaplain (Sharp) to assist him and has designated Club as schoolmaster.

114-16. John Thomas to the Society, New York, 1 Mar. 1704/5. He has been settled in Hempstead for two months, but finds that most of the people are Independents or Presbyterians, with some Quakers. His position would be precarious were it not for the support of Lord Cornbury.

117-19. Thorogood Moore to Secretary, Albany, 8 Mar. 1704/5. Reproduces an exchange of speeches with representatives of the Indians, but is not sure of acceptance. Recommends an allowance for Eburne, who ministers on the Isle of Shoals. Reports opposition to Muirson in New York.

120-2. Thomas to Secretary, Hempstead, N.Y., 26 May 1705. He still meets with opposition, but has won over some dissenters.

123. Bartow to Secretary, New York, 26 May 1705. Complains of slowness in payment of allowance. Col. Morris has presented a bell to the church in Westchester.

124-5. Thomas to Secretary, Hempstead, 27 June 1705. Complains of stubbornness of Independents in resisting conversion, though he and Urquhart, the only other Church minister on the island, have made some gains.

126-7. Urquhart to Secretary, Jamaica, N.Y., 3 July 1705. His position has become more tolerable since the arrival of Thomas. Requests prayer books.

128-9. Thomas and Urquhart to the Society, Jamaica, 4 July 1705, repeating the same information as (124-7) and praising Lord Corbury.

130-1. Petition of residents of Oxford, Pa., for a missionary, 19 Aug. 1705. (Misplaced.)

132-3. John Thomas to Society, Hempstead, 23 Aug. 1705. He serves Hempstead and Oyster Bay, and lacks prayer books and church furnishings in both places. Has difficulty in obtaining sponsors in baptism, as people object to performing that office.

134. John Barclay to Keith, New York, 7 Sept. 1705. Brooke gives most of his time to Elizabeth, where the local (Independent?) minister died recently, after suffering a stroke while reading a rebuke to his congregation for going to hear others.

135-7. Neau to Secretary, New York, 3 Oct. 1705 (French, with translation). He has resumed his catechizing, with the support of the society and with Vesey's approval.

138-9. List of masters and mistresses who send their slaves to Neau for catechizing (French, with translation).

140. Abstract of a letter from New York (writer not given), 22 Oct. 1705, relating to Moore's mission to the Indians. Moore has returned to New York saying that he had received no reply to his address to the Indian chiefs. He was told (by whom?) that he had followed the wrong procedure. He should have obtained authority from Lord Cornbury to tell the Indians that he had been sent by Queen Anne in answer to their requests.

141-4. Samuel Eburne to Secretary, New York, 25 Oct. 1705. Having read in the printed report of the society that a grant was made to the minister on the Isle of Shoals, he is submitting evidence that he is that minister (2 copies).

145. Aeneas Mackenzie to Secretary, Staten Island, 8 Nov. 1705. He has been well received by the English third of the population. The other two-thirds are Dutch and French.

146-9. Heathcote to Secretary, Scarsdale, N.Y., 9 Nov. 1705. After acknowledging election to society, he gives an account of the religious situation in the province and especially in Westchester.

150-1. Do. to do., same date. Two copies of a note reporting the sending of (146-9).

152-3. John Thomas to Secretary, Hempstead, 9 Nov. 1705. Pleads again for prayer books.

154-5. An abstract of (146-9), apparently in the same hand.

156-7. Address of missionaries in New York and New Jersey to Society, New York, 12 Nov. 1705. Having persuaded William Bradford to print an edition of the Prayer Book, with Tate and Brady, they ask society to make him a grant. They note that Bradford was bred a Quaker, but is now a Churchman, and assert that he suffered business losses because of his conversion.

158-60. Thorogood Moore to Secretary, New York, 13 Nov. 1705. Having left Albany because he could not obtain any answer to his address to the Indians, he gives some reasons why he thinks the society should concentrate its work on the English population.

161-3. Thomas and Urquhart to the Society, New York, 14 Nov. 1705. They have received a gift of prayer books for use in Jamaica, but ask more for distribution among the people there and in Hempstead.

164. Urquhart to Secretary, 14 Nov. 1705. He has received some furnishings and books through Neau. Refers to a predecessor, Stuart, who absconded because of debt.

165. Moore to Secretary, New York, 14 Nov. 1705. Suggests that he be sent to Burlington as Talbot is going to England.

166-71. Neau to Secretary, New York, 15 Nov. 1705. Repeats information in (135-7), with similar lists of masters.

172-3. Muirson to Secretary, Rye, N.Y., 21 Nov. 1705. When he returned from England, Lord Cornbury sent him to Rye to replace Pritchard, who had cut his own throat. He has visited Connecticut, where he found a number of people favourably disposed to the Church.

174. Vesey to Secretary, New York, 21 Nov. 1705. Willing to accept Neau now that he has the Bishop of London's licence. Repeats that he had no objection to him personally, as he was a 'glorious confessor of our most holy religion'. Muirson has gone to Rye. He was asked to collect the society's books held by Gordon, but they are unmarked, so the matter will have to be settled with Gordon's brother. Asks an allowance for Huddleston, schoolmaster in New York.

175-7. Cornbury to Secretary, New York, 22 Nov. 1705. Recommends sending a missionary to Suffolk County, on the end of Long Island. He took the chaplain at the fort with him on a recent visit on Long Island, who read services in Brookhaven. He has authorized Moore's going to Burlington, but speaks of trying to make things 'easier' for him at Albany on his next visit. Muirson is settled at Rye and Mackenzie on Staten Island.

178. Muirson to Secretary, Rye, N.Y., reporting on his work. He has drawn a bill on the society for £25, anticipating an allowance of £50.

179-80. John Sharpe to Secretary, 24 Nov. 1705, Fort Anne, New York. He accepted the chaplain's post after serving a half year in New Jersey. Recommends sending a missionary to Suffolk County and giving aid to Rudman, Hepburn, and Bondet.

181. Cornbury to Secretary, New York, 27 Nov. 1705, recommending an allowance for Huddleston.

182. Heathcote to Secretary, Manor of Scarsdale, 20 Dec. 1705. The people at Rye are building a stone church. He recommends allowance for Huddleston.

183. Robert Livingston to Secretary, 20 Dec. 1705, asking aid for Lidins at Albany.

184–5. Robert Gardiner and Thomas Lillibridge to Keith, Newport, R.I., 12 Dec. 1705 (misplaced), protesting transfer of Honeyman. They say that he was charged with 'base actions' when chaplain of a man-of-war.

186. Abstract of several letters received from Heathcote in 1704–5 summarizing a number of recommendations for promoting the Church in Westchester.

187. Livingston to Secretary, 31 Jan. 1705/6. He has been told by recent arrivals from New York that Moor has no intention of returning to Albany. Recommends sending of pious books for the use of the inhabitants.

188. James Gordon to Secretary, Haronby, 5 Feb. 1705/6. Asks that a list of the society's books held by his deceased brother be sent to Vesey, so that the rest of his library can be disposed of. Describes work of charity schools in Haronby.

189. Neau to Secretary, New York, 1 Mar. 1705/6 (French), reporting on his work. Letter will be delivered by Evan Evans.

190–1. Extract of the society's minutes relating to Neau up to 21 Mar. 1706.

192–4. Thomas to Secretary, Hempstead, 7 Apr. 1706. People are building a new church. Quakers are numerous in the county.

195. Do. to do., Hempstead, 10 Apr. 1706. Repeating information in (192–4) and asking for books for distribution.

196. Heathcote to Secretary, New York, 16 Apr. 1706. 200 persons have been baptized in Rye and about 20 or 30 added to communion since Muirson's arrival. Muirson plans to visit Stratford, where he has learned that there are a number of churchmen, and Heathcote will accompany him. Heathcote recommends an allowance to Bondet, on condition that he assist Bartow.

197. Secretary to Heddleston, Petty France, Westminster, 18 Apr. 1706 (copy). Committee has decided that society should not grant a regular allowance to a schoolmaster not appointed by it, but has voted him a gift of £10.

198. Do. to Cornbury, Petty France, Westminster, 18 Apr. 1706 (copy). A missionary will be sent to Suffolk County as soon as 'conveniently maybe'. If Moore's mission to the Indians fails, he will be joined to Talbot in the care of Burlington. Richard Townsend has been appointed schoolmaster on Staten Island at request of Mackenzie.

199. Copy of (197).

200. Secretary to vestries of Thomas and Urquhart, Petty France, Westminster, 22 Apr. 1706 (copy, with spaces for names left blank), expressing satisfaction at cordial relations reported between minister and vestries.

201-2. Neau to Secretary, New York, 30 Apr. 1706 (French, with translation). Finds that some masters fear that they will lose control of their slaves if they are baptized.

203. Secretary to Bradford, Petty France, Westminster, 3 May 1706 (copy), asking him to send specimens of his edition of prayer book.

204. Do. to Mackenzie, Petty France, Westminster, 3 May 1706 (copy), informing him of Townsend's appointment and of a shipment of books.

205. Do. to Neau, Petty France, Westminster, 3 May 1706 (copy, French). Mentions acts of Maryland and Virginia declaring that baptism does not emancipate slaves.

206. Do. to Thomas and Urquhart, Petty France, Westminster, 3 May 1706 (copy). Society has voted to send them prayer books and the Bishop of London has secured a gift of a large church Bible, Prayer Book, and book of homilies for each of their churches from the Queen. They should account to the treasurer for books received.

207. Do. to Vesey, Petty France, Westminster, 3 May 1706 (copy), asking his continued support for Neau. Society has asked the Archbishop of Canterbury to apply to the Queen to direct the passage of declaratory laws similar to those referred to in (205).

208. Do. to Bondet, Petty France, Westminster, 24 May 1706 (copy). Society has voted him a gift of £10, but cannot grant him a regular allowance unless his congregation conforms to Church of England, although he himself is episcopally ordained.

209. Do. to Muirson, Petty France, Westminster, 24 May 1706 (copy). Queen is giving a pulpit and communion table to the church at Rye, and society is donating prayer books.

210. Do. to Heathcote, Petty France, Westminster, 5 June 1706 (copy). Society approves his effort to get larger official stipends for the ministers in Westchester, and does its best to secure the appointment of a suffragan, as he has recommended. Society fears that it might be a breach of the Toleration Act for it to intrude in Connecticut, unless requested by the inhabitants (crossed out).

211. Do. to Sir Jeff. Jeffries, Petty France, Westminster, 27 June 1706 (copy), asking by what ship books delivered to him for shipment to Pritchard were sent, and if Pritchard left any estate.

212. Do. to Urquhart, Petty France, Westminster, 3 Aug. 1706. Asking him to deliver to Muirson society's books which he secured on departure of Stuart.

213-14. Bartow to Secretary, New York, 8 Aug. 1706. Society has withdrawn his allowance, leaving him in great distress.

215-16. Do. to do., 14 Aug. 1706, about the same matter.

217. Bartow to (Bishop of London?), Westchester, 16 Aug. 1706. Allowance was stopped because he had been in service three years.

218–20. Petition of wardens, justices, and vestry of Westchester, 27 Aug. 1706, asking continuance of Bartow's allowance.

221–4. Printed copy of acts passed by 7th session of the General Assembly of New York, beginning 17 Sept. 1706 (2 copies). Act for raising money to fortify the City of New York; act for raising a fund for the defence of the frontiers; act to encourage baptism of slaves. All children of slave mothers to be slaves in perpetuity; no slave to be admitted witness against a freeman.

225–6. Muirson to Secretary, Rye, 2 Oct. 1706. Church in Rye is nearing completion. He has visited Connecticut and preached in Stratford. He is informed that there are many unbaptized persons in Connecticut, as the Independents will only baptize the children of those who are in full communion with them.

227–8. Huddleston to Revd. John Postlethwaite, New York, 9 Oct. 1706. Grateful for the gift of £10, but would still like a regular allowance.

229–30. Bartow to Secretary, New York, 4 Oct. 1706, pleading for restoration of allowance.

231–2. Do. to do., 12 Oct. 1706. Reports sending (222–4). Says that charges against Honeyman in Newport were brought by a turbulent person, who had previously caused trouble for Lockier.

233. Robert Livingston to Secretary, New York, 14 Oct. 1706. Reports safe arrival. His son-in-law, Capt. Vetch, who has been in business in Massachusetts, has been 'excessively' fined by the government there and is going home to seek a remission of the fines.

234–5. Joseph Cleator to Secretary, Dartmouth, on way to New York, 29 Oct. 1706. Ship was driven into port by bad seas and the enemy.

236–7. Neau to Secretary, New York, 28 Nov. 1706. He has procured passage of act printed in (222–4), and has asked Vesey and Sharpe to preach occasionally in favour of instruction of slaves.

238–9. Huddleston to Postlethwaite, New York, 21 Nov. 1706, asking him to support a petition that he is presenting to the Bishop of London.

240. Bradford to Secretary, New York, 12 Dec. 1706. He has sent a copy of his edition of the prayer book and is now sending a copy of his Philadelphia Almanac, which the Quakers are trying to discourage by promoting a rival.

241. Cleator to Society, Dartmouth, 23 Dec. 1706. Captain hopes to be able to sail in three weeks.

VOLUME XIV

NEW YORK, 1707–undated

1–2. Vesey to Secretary, New York, 23 Feb. 1707/8, expressing regret at having reported the scandal concerning Honeyman, which he now believes was generated by a 'scandalous wretch'. (Letter is dated 1707, but *notation* makes it 1707/8.)

3–4. Heathcote to Secretary, New York, 24 Feb. 1707, giving an account of Muirson's work in Connecticut. Not having heard from Cleator, he presumes that he is dead or has declined the post.

5. Neau to Secretary, New York, 1 Mar. 1706/7 (translation), reporting on his work.

6–9. Muirson to Secretary, Rye, 4 Apr. 1707, reporting on his work.

10. Secretary to Cornbury, Petty France, Westminster, 5 Apr. 1707 (copy), informing of two new rules of society: that missionaries are to receive one quarter's payment after notice of dismissal by society and that society will require assurance of local support before starting a new mission.

11–12. Neau to Secretary, 9 Apr. 1707 (French, with translation), mainly a testimonial to Evan Evans, against whom calumnious reports have been sent to England.

13. Heathcote to Secretary, New York, 14 Apr. 1707. Mentions another visit of Muirson to Connecticut, and speaks of an Independent (?) minister named Reed who will come to England for orders if assured of employment by the society.

14. Bartow to Secretary, Westchester, 15 Apr. 1707, seeking restoration of his allowance.

15–16. Clergy of New York area to Society, New York, 3 Apr. 1707, asking restoration of Bartow's allowance.

17–18. Thomas to Secretary, Hempstead, 21 Apr. 1707, reporting on his work.

19. Muirson to Secretary, Rye, 22 May 1707, reporting on his work.

20. Secretary to Thomas, Petty France, Westminster, 2 June 1707 (copy), recommending peaceful persuasion as the means to win over Quakers and other dissenters.

21. Do. to Heathcote, Petty France, Westminster, 3 June 1707 (copy). Society might name Bondet as assistant to Bartow, if Heathcote can show that Bartow wants an assistant, and that Bondet can preach in English, and will conform to the liturgy. Cleator has been delayed in sailing.

22. Do. to Neau, Petty France, Westminster, 3 June 1707 (copy). He has sent one of Neau's letters, describing his work, and a copy of his catechism to Osterwald.

23. Do. to Livingston, Petty France, Westminster, 6 June 1707 (copy), thanking him for delivering letters and other material sent by him.

24–5. Do. to Muirson, Petty France, Westminster, 6 June 1707 (copy), urging caution in his work in Connecticut.

26. Do. to Huddleston, Petty France, Westminster, 6 June 1707 (copy). £10 gratuity granted him by society and £10 worth of books are being sent by Postlethwaite.

27. Do. to Bartow, Petty France, Westminster, 7 June 1707 (copy). The three-year rule which led to the discontinuance of Bartow's allowance was adopted in the hope that local support would be sufficient within that time. Having found by experience that it is not, they have adopted the rule that missionaries will serve at the society's pleasure.

28. Heathcote to Secretary, Manor of Scarsdale, 18 June 1707. Cleator has arrived, to Heathcote's surprise, as letters explaining his delay had miscarried.

29–30. Cleator to Secretary, Rye, N.Y., 14 July 1707, reporting arrival.

31–2. Neau to Secretary, New York, 22 July 1707 (French, with translation). Number of catechumens has increased since the Dutch minister has preached in favour of instructing the slaves. Neau has fitted up a schoolroom in his house, so that he can teach them by candlelight, as they are at work during the day.

33–5. Do. to do., New York, 24 July 1707 (French, with translation), repeating some of information in (31–2) and adding that he has drawn on the treasurer for his salary. Postscript recommends Bondet.

36–7. Bondet to Secretary, New Rochelle, 24 July 1707 (French, with translation), seeking payment of arrears that he says are due him from the society.

38–9. Huddleston to Postlethwaite, New York, 30 July 1707, seeking allowance from the society and referring to financial affairs of himself and his brother Thomas.

40. Do. to Secretary, New York, 30 July 1707, seeking allowance.

41. Do. to Society, undated, but evidently sent with (40), petitioning for an allowance. He has been schoolmaster in New York for 18 years.

42–5. Thorogood Moore to Secretary, Fort Anne, N.Y., 27 Aug. 1707. He is a prisoner in the fort, having been arrested and accused of rebellion for refusing to obey a summons from Cornbury (doubting its legality) and continuing to preach when inhibited by Lt. Gov. Ingoldsby.

46. Unsigned note, dated New York, 28 Aug. 1707, apparently enclosed with (42–5), saying that Moore was suspended for rebuking Ingoldsby for immorality.

47. Neau to Secretary, New York, 28 Aug. 1707 (French), saying that Moore was arrested for rebuking Ingoldsby's immorality.

48–9. Moore to Secretary, Fort Anne, Aug. 1707 (copy), repeating the information in (42–5). This copy will be brought by Brooke if he succeeds in reaching Boston without being arrested.

50–1. Neau to Secretary, New York, 26 Sept. 1707. Brooke is also confined.

52. Urquhart to Secretary, New York, 30 Sept. 1707, reporting on his work in Jamaica and his efforts to secure books sent to Stuart.

53. Huddleston to Secretary, New York, 18 Nov. 1707, reporting that he has drawn on the society for its gratuity.

54–9. Cornbury to Secretary, New York, 29 Nov. 1707 (2 copies). Moore escaped with the aid of Brooke while Cornbury was in Albany. Informed that Bartow has been accused of misconduct in letters to the Bishop of London, Cornbury attests to his innocence.

60. Joseph Johnson to Moore and Brooke, 29 Nov. 1707, expressing hope for their safe arrival in England and enclosing copy of assembly's remonstrance to Cornbury (xii. 216–19?).

61–2. Bartow to Secretary, New York, 1 Dec. 1707. Acknowledging his restoration to the society's employ and reporting on his work.

63. Law. Cleator to Secretary, 3 Dec. 1707, concerning payment of his father's stipend.

64–9. Heathcote to Secretary, 18 Dec. 1707, Manor of Scarsdale, outlining a plan for providing schoolmasters for the colonies (5 copies).

70–3. Urquhart and Thomas to the Secretary, Jamaica, 22 Dec. 1707. Acknowledge gift of books and furnishings and report enlargement of church in Hempstead and building of one in Oyster Bay (2 copies).

74–5. Heathcote to Secretary, 24 Dec. 1707, Manor of Scarsdale, urging the sending of a bishop to the colonies (2 copies).

76. Lewis Morris to (Moore and Brooke?), Morrisania, St. John's Day (26 Dec. 1707). Letter seems to have been meant to reach them in Boston, for it refers to an effort by the New York authorities to have them held in Massachusetts, and gives an account of controversies with Cornbury following their flight.

77. Cleator to Secretary, Rye, N.Y., 27 Dec. 1707. He has requested the treasurer to pay his salary to his wife or her order.

78. Vesey to the Bishop of London, New York, 29 Dec. 1707, defending Honeyman, who is under attack by Gardner in Newport. Though Vesey admits that he was 'too hasty to believe' the report against Honeyman when he was chaplain of a man-of-war in New York, he has since learned that the woman who brought it was a 'scandalous wretch'.

79. Heathcote to Secretary, Manor of Scarsdale, 30 Dec. 1707. Careful inquiries have convinced him of Honeyman's good character.

80. Huddleston to Postlethwaite, New York, 30 Dec. 1707, introducing the son of the late attorney-general, Shelton Broughton, and asking Postlethwaite to introduce him to the secretary, to whom he will report on Huddleston's work.

81–8. Muirson to Secretary, Rye, N.Y., 9 Jan. 1707/8 (2 copies). He has only received £18 (currency) of his official salary of £50 since he came, having refrained from pressing for full payment, as the people were building a church. He admires Neau, and is happy to confer with him about the instruction of Indians and Negroes, but there are only a few of either in his parish. The few Indians there are tell him that they will not become Christians because of English hypocrisy. Cornbury has been recalled. Muirson hopes his successor will secure legislation against the immoralities that are rife in the province. He has tried being nice to the Independents, but they are not nice to him. Letter will be brought by Broughton.

89. Do. to Myles, Rye, 14 Jan. 1707/8. He has been warned by Myles that Bridge's intrigues may extend to New York. He hopes to see Myles in the spring to consult him about raising a subscription to build a church in Stratford.

90–1. Heathcote to Secretary, New York, 16 Jan. 1707/8, urging that naval chaplains have more authority (2 copies).

92. Do. to do., Manor of Scarsdale, 23 Feb. 1707/8, urging a bishop for the colonies.

93–6. Bondet to Secretary, 28 Jan. 1707/8, New Rochelle, N.Y., thanking society for gift of £20 (2 copies).

97–8. Urquhart to Secretary, Jamaica, L.I., 4 Feb. 1707/8, reporting the murder of a local resident, William Hallett and his family, by an Indian, abetted by a Negro woman slave.

99. Muirson to Secretary, Rye, N.Y., 20 Feb. 1707/8, sent by Honeyman, whom he supports in his controversy with Bridge. Controversy shows need for a colonial bishop.

100–1. Bartow to Secretary, Westchester, 28 Feb. 1707/8, supporting Honeyman. Postscript notes that Talbot has departed for Burlington, but that Barclay is still at Boston.

102. Secretary to members of committee to wait on Gov. Lovelace (of New York) in the interests of the society, Petty France, Westminster, 7 June 1708, calling a meeting at house of the Bishop of Bangor.

103–4. Cleator to Secretary, Rye, N.Y., 11 June 1708, reporting on his work since his arrival.

105–6. Huddleston to Secretary, New York, 15 July 1708, giving an account of his work and inquiring if the society has acted on his petition for aid.

107. Secretary to Morris, Petty France, Westminster, 21 July 1708 (copy). Though the language is not entirely clear, it appears that Morris had asked the secretary to use his influence to secure the appointment of Heathcote as governor, but that the request arrived too late for action.

108. Do. to Cleator, Petty France, Westminster, 24 July 1708 (copy), saying that payment of his salary will be made in accordance with his request (77).

109–10. Do. to Bartow, Petty France, Westminster, 26 July 1708 (copy). He is sending copies of resolutions reinstating Bartow, who has been subject of some accusations now held to be groundless. Secretary refuses to name accuser or state accusation, but warns Bartow that the society has spies over him, some of whom are nearer than he thinks.

111–14. Do. to Heathcote, Windsor Castle, 2 Aug. 1708 (copy). Society has resolved to send Muirson to Connecticut as soon as a replacement can be found for Rye, and Nicholson has pledged 25 guineas for one year toward his support. As Muirson is both young and a 'North Briton', Heathcote is urged to counsel him to 'qualify his zeal' if he goes to Connecticut. If Reed (13) comes to England for orders and is qualified, secretary is sure society will employ him and contribute to his passage, but it cannot undertake to support his family. Secretary agrees with Heathcote's commendation of Evan Evans. Explains Cleator's delay in arriving and asks Heathcote to be sure that he reports regularly. Heathcote's request that society seek Cornbury's recall following the Moore–Brooke incident arrived after the recall had been ordered. Society cannot do anything for Bondet at present, but will ask the Bishop of London to ask Gov. Lovelace to give him some public aid. Society has decided Bridge–Honeyman dispute at Newport in favour of Honeyman.

115. Do. to Muirson, Windsor Castle, 4 Aug. 1708. Refers him to (111–14) for action in regard to Connecticut, but adds that society has hopes of persuading the government of that province to grant religious freedom to members of the Church of England (copy).

116. Do. to Neau, Windsor Castle, 5 Aug. 1708 (copy), giving Neau some advice about instructing Negroes, and asking if he knows why Brooke abandoned his parish and why Moore escaped from prison instead of following the more heroic example of the Presbyterian minister imprisoned by Cornbury.

117. Do. to Urquhart, Windsor Castle, 7 Aug. 1708 (copy). Asking for an account of Gordon's books, and advising him to consult with Neau about instructing the heathen in his parish.

118. Do. to Vesey, Windsor Castle, 16 Aug. 1708 (copy). Reports decision in favour of Honeyman and acknowledges Vesey's expression of regret at having first believed the scandal against him, but thinks Honeyman contributed to it by his own folly in returning a second time to lodge in the house where the scandal had arisen.

119–20. Neau to Secretary, New York, 24 Aug. 1708 (French), reporting on his work.

121. Secretary to Mackenzie, Windsor Castle, 28 Aug. 1708 (copy). Society has complied with his requests for Dutch prayer books and a schoolmaster. He is urged to make regular reports.

122. Secretary to Bondet, Petty France, Westminster, 6 Sept. 1708. Bills for £30 which he reports drawing on the treasurer cannot be honoured, as the society does not owe him anything. It has petitioned the authorities to secure a more regular payment of his salary from the province.

123. Heathcote to Bishop of London, New York, 6 Oct. 1708, giving recommendation for promoting religion in the colonies: 1. The appointment of a bishop. 2. Care in appointing governors of good character. 3. Supplying of edifying books. 4. The establishment of a college. 5. Supply craftsmen for building churches and schools, as such projects often fail from lack of labour.

124–5. Cleator to Secretary, Rye, N.Y., 18 Oct. 1708, reporting death of Muirson, who was the first person to be buried in the churchyard of the new church.

126. Will. Gordon to Secretary, 13 Dec. 1708. (Place not given but contents seem to indicate it was written in London.) He has just arrived from Carolina in weak health, but will wait on the society in a week.

127–8. Warrants issued by Cornbury for payment of Bondet's salary, but still unpaid, 6 Jan. 1708/9, as attested by Heathcote, Sharpe, Evans, and Neau (2 copies).

129. Secretary to Bartow, Petty France, Westminster, 1 Feb. 1708/9 (copy), referring to former letter (109–10?) as answering his inquiries.

130. Do. to Mackenzie, Petty France, Westminster, 1 Feb. 1708/9 (copy), rebuking him for failure to report.

131. Do. to Neau, Petty France, Westminster, 1 Feb. 1708/9 (copy). As auditors found four years' salary due to Neau, secretary hopes he has received it.

132. Secretary to Thomas, Petty France, Westminster, 1 Feb. 1708/9 (copy). Urges instruction of Indians and Negroes and asks for any examples he can obtain of the Lord's Prayer in Indian, as he is collecting versions in all languages.

133. Do. to Urquhart, Petty France, Westminster, 1 Feb. 1708/9 (copy). Still concerned about books held by Stuart.

134. Heathcote to Secretary, Manor of Scarsdale, 17 Feb. 1708(9). Hopes society will not insist on Bondet's returning his overdraft, as he cannot do so, unless the province pays him his arrears.

135. Cleator to Secretary, Rye, N.Y., 28 Feb. 1708(9), concerning the payment of his salary to his wife.

136. Bondet to Secretary, New Rochelle, N.Y., 22 Feb. 1708(9) (French), concerning his financial problems.

137–9. Neau to Secretary, New York, 27 Feb. 1708/9 (French), giving an account of his work and some further information about the Moore–Brooke affair. List of masters with number of slaves attending his classes appended.

140. Secretary to Heathcote, Westminster, 7 Mar. 1708/9 (copy). He has submitted some recommendations of Heathcote to the Lords Commissioners of Trade and Plantations, but without result, partly because Sir Gilbert Heathcote refuses to sponsor them.

141. Do. to Archbishop of Dublin, 21 Apr. 1709, Petty France, Westminster (copy), informing him that James Reynolds has been appointed missionary to Rye, N.Y.

142–3. Heathcote to Secretary, New York, 28 Apr. 1709, making some recommendations for the promotion of religion in the provinces.

144. Thomas to Secretary, Hempstead, N.Y., 30 Apr. 1709, urging that missionaries be given a chance to defend themselves against charges against them.

145. Testimonial to Bondet dated Boston, 24 May 1696, copy attested by clergy of New York area, 5 May 1709. Bondet was sent with a company of Huguenot refugees by the Corporation for the Propagation of the Gospel among the Indians. They settled in New Oxford (Mass.?), where Bondet ministered to both French and Indians (learning the Indian tongue), until the French, fearing the Indians, moved away. He then came to Boston.

146. Secretary to Lovelace, Petty France, Westminster, 6 May 1709 (copy), commending Vaughan and Reynolds to his protection.

147. Do. to Vesey, Petty France, Westminster, 6 May 1709 (copy), introducing Vaughan and Reynolds.

148–9. Bartow to Secretary, Westchester, 11 May 1709, reporting on his work. Mentions death of Muirson and arrival of Evans, who has gone on to Philadelphia, and refers to some other missionaries.

150. Secretary to Mr. Gilbert of Plymouth, Petty France, Westminster, 21 May 1709 (copy), enclosing (152) and asking him to deliver it to Reynolds.

151. Do. to Capt. Herriot, Petty France, Westminster, 21 May 1709 (copy), enclosing another copy of (152) and asking him to deliver it to Reynolds when, as is expected, he receives the Admiralty's order to put him ashore.

152. Do. to Reynolds, Petty France, Westminster, 21 May 1709 (copy), ordering him to return immediately to London to report to the society. Any letters given him for delivery in America should be turned over to Vaughan.

153–4. Lewis Morris to Secretary, New York, 30 May 1709. Reports death of Lord Lovelace on May 6 and again urges appointment of Heathcote. Cornbury, Nicholson, Quarry, and Ingoldsby are all seeking the post. Accuses Quarry of dividing the church in Philadelphia, by bringing in Ross from Newcastle. Speaks of his own efforts to bring his Dutch neighbours to a favourable view of the Church of England.

155–6. Certificate by sundry persons, Albany and New York, 30 May 1706, that Thomas Barclay has served faithfully at Albany since his arrival in 1707. Signers indentified in certification by Vesey, Sharpe, and Neau.

157. Secretary to Bondet, Petty France, Westminster, 6 June 1709, indicating that he has become a missionary and mentioning La Mothe as his principal sponsor in England.

158–9. Memorial of Thomas Barclay to the Bishop of London, describing his work with the garrison at Albany, among the Dutch at Schenectady, and with the Indians. (Undated, but refers to 155–6.)

160–1. Heathcote to Secretary, New York, 3 June 1709, reporting change of stations by Jenkins.

162–3. Neau to Secretary, New York, 6 June 1709, reporting on his work. Speaks of death of Lovelace and two sons and recommends Nicholson for post.

164–5. Bartow to Secretary, Westchester, N.Y., 10 June 1709. He has visited Amboy, while his congregation was supplied by Sharpe. He has received, at the hands of Nicholson, a letter written by the Archbishop of Canterbury to all the missionaries.

166–7. Thomas to Secretary, Hempstead, N.Y., 12 June 1709. He has persuaded about 35 dissenters to conform. In response to Secretary's wish to hear about heathen converted, he says that quite a few Negroes regularly attend his services, but that the few Indians in the neighbourhood are too 'sottish' to be reached.

168–9. Act of French congregation in New Rochelle, 12 June 1709 (French), acknowledging services of Bondet and stating that they have built a church which will always be used for services of the Church of England in English and French.

170. Heathcote to Secretary, Manor of Scarsdale, 13 June 1709. He went to New Rochelle, accompanied by Sharpe and Bartow, where the congregation presented (168–9) and declared their conformity to the Church of England in their presence.

171. Mackenzie to Secretary, Staten Island, 13 June 1709. Stating that contrary to some report that he believes has been sent to the society, the Brooks and Billop families have been his good friends.

172–3. Do. to do., same date, reporting on his work.

174–8. Urquhart to Secretary, Jamaica, N.Y., 15 June 1709 (2 copies), giving an account of Stuart's books. Muirson had married Heathcote's sister-in-law, a daughter of Col. Smith, shortly before his death, and has left a son, born posthumously.

179. Neau to Secretary, New York, 9 and 21 June 1709 (French, on same sheet). First letter reports on his work; second reports conformity of church in New Rochelle.

180–1. Cleator to Secretary, Rye, N.Y., giving an account of his work.

182. Secretary to Lovelace, Petty France, Westminster, 24 June 1709 (draft), announcing dismissal of Reynolds because of accusations of 'vile practices'.

183. Do. to Archbishop of Dublin, Petty France, Westminster, June 1709 (copy), reporting the same.

184–5. Cleator to Secretary, Rye, N.Y., 4 July 1709, enclosing list of scholars.

186. Neau to Secretary, New York, 5 July 1709 (French), asking that French books be supplied to church at New Rochelle.

187. Huddleston to Secretary, New York, 9 July 1709. He is submitting another petition for an allowance through Postlethwaite.

188. Neau to Secretary, New York, 5 Sept. 1709 (French), reporting on his work.

189. Robert Hunter to Secretary, London, 29 Sept. 1709. About to leave for New York as governor, he promises to support work of society.

190. Testimonial to Thomas Poyer by J. Philipps and J. Langhorne, 28 Nov. 1709.

191. Testimonial to Poyer by John Pember, 9 Dec. 1709. Poyer has been chaplain of H.M.S. *Antelope* and curate to Thomas Davids, rector of Haverfordwest, Pembrokeshire.

192. Secretary to Barclay, Petty France, Westminster, 11 Jan. 1709/10 (copy), informing him of his appointment as missionary and catechist at Albany.

193. Do. to Neau, Petty France, Westminster, 13 Jan. 1709/10 (copy). Letter will be brought by James Dupré, who accompanies Gov. Hunter as superintendent of the Palatines.

194. Do. to Bartow, Petty France, Westminster, 19 Jan. 1709/10 (copy), acknowledging letters from him.

195. Do. to Bondet, Petty France, Westminster, 19 Jan. 1709/10 (copy). Society has appointed him missionary with a stipend of £30 per annum.

196. Do. to Huddleston, Petty France, Westminster, 19 Jan. 1709/10 (copy). Society has granted him £10 for one year on condition that he teach 40 poor children.

197. Do. to Thomas, Petty France, Westminster, 19 Jan. 1709/10 (copy). Poyer is replacing Urquhart, who has died.

198. Do. to Bradford, Petty France, Westminster, 24 Jan. 1709/10 (copy). He failed to receive specimen pages of quarto edition of prayer book which Bradford sent.

199. Do. to Cleator, Petty France, Westminster, 24 Jan. 1709/10 (copy). Society is sending him some books.

200–1. Do. to Mackenzie, Petty France, Westminster, 24 Jan. 1709/10 (copy). His report and explanation, recently received, has led to his being forgiven for his failure to report for two years.

202. Do. to Morris, Petty France, Westminster, 24 Jan. 1709/10 (copy). Society has granted £50 for one year to Beyse for work in Harlem on Morris's recommendation.

203. Do. to Hunter, Petty France, Westminster, 22 Feb. 1709/10 (copy), asking him to examine property in Burlington.

204. Archbishop of Canterbury to Indian Sachems, 22 Mar. 1710 (copy). Long illness has prevented earlier answer to their petition. Assures them that society will send them two missionaries when certified that chapel and mission house are ready to receive them.

205. Secretary to Gov. Hunter, Petty France, Westminster, 3 May 1710 (copy), apparently in reply to a plea from Hunter for moderation on the part of missionaries, with special reference to Talbot.

206. Do. to Nicholson, Petty France, Westminster, 30 June 1710 (copy). Society has asked the Archbishop to apply to the Lord Treasurer for funds to support a mission to the Indians.

207. Bondet to Secretary, New Rochelle, N.Y., 8 Sept. 1710 (French), reporting on his work.

208. Secretary to Gov. Hunter, Petty France, Westminster, 28 Sept. 1710 (copy), sent by Halliday, who is to divide the East Jersey mission with Vaughan.

209. Do. to Bartow, Petty France, Westminster, 28 Sept. 1710 (copy). As Bartow has criticized society's action against Reynolds, he encloses copy of letter describing Reynolds's ill behaviour in the colonies, which, he says, coincides with reports of his misconduct in Ireland. Society is grateful to Vesey and Sharpe for supplying Urquhart's parish after his death, and may do something for Urquhart's and Muirson's widows.

210. Neau to Secretary, New York, 3 Oct. 1710 (French). Refers to a dispute that has arisen between conformists and non-conformists in Bondet's church.

211–12. V. Antonides to Hoefnagele, Midwout, 8 Oct. 1710 (copy), accusing Beyse of intruding in the Harlem congregation, without a call, though they have a regular minister, Du Bois.

213–14. Johan Freidrich Hager to Secretary, New York, 28 Oct. 1710 (German, with translation), reporting his arrival and the beginning of his work.

215. Bondet to Secretary, New Rochelle, 14 Nov. 1710 (French), reporting on his work.

216–17. Secretary to Neau, Petty France, Westminster, 14 Nov. 1710 (copy). Society is pleased to learn of safe arrival of Palatines and their charitable reception. Some French books have been sent to Bondet through La Mothe, and more will be.

218. Josua Kocherthal to Society, New York, 15 Nov. 1710 (German), asking aid and expressing willingness to use ceremonies of Church of England.

219. Barclay to Secretary, Albany, 7 Dec. 1710, reporting on his work. He preaches at Schenectady once a month. Only dissenters at Albany are of the 'Holland or Lutheran churches'.

220. Secretary to Bondet, Petty France, Westminster, 11 Dec. 1710 (copy), reporting sending of books and asking what progress he has made in bringing the rest of his flock to conformity.

221–3. Huddleston to Secretary, New York, 16 Jan. 1710/(11) (2 copies), requesting books for his poor scholars.

224. Secretary to Gov. Hunter, Petty France, Westminster, 7 Feb. 1710/11 (copy), thanking him for supporting Poyer in his suit and saying that, on recommendation of Hunter and Morris, society is continuing Beyse's stipend for another year, though he has not fulfilled their conditions.

225–6. Bartow to Secretary, Westchester, 31 Apr. 1711 [sic]. Regrets mistake in defending Reynolds, whom he did not know. Reports troubles of Poyer in Jamaica, where the dissenters have succeeded in interrupting payment of his official salary.

227. Poyer to Secretary, Jamaica, N.Y., 3 May 1711, with notitia parochialis. His official salary has not been paid.

228–9. Neau to Secretary, New York, 4 May 1711 (French), reporting on his work.

230. Mackenzie to Secretary, Richmond, N.Y., 4 May 1711. He has received a letter from the Bishop of London saying that he has concurred in his removal to Stratford. He has a church nearly finished on Staten Island.

231. P. Schuyler to Secretary, Albany, 4 May 1711. He is sending translations of the Lord's Prayer in Indian tongues, as requested. He visited the Indian country and laid out plans for fort and chapel, which he has submitted to Gen. Nicholson.

232. Hunter to Secretary, New York, 7 May 1711. Gives a favourable account of various missionaries, but thinks Talbot would have greater success if he had less warmth. Owner of house in Burlington, a minor, has been advised against selling.

233–4. Neau to La Mothe, New York, 7 May 1711 (French), giving some account of his work and of controversy in Bondet's church.

235. Halliday to Secretary, New York, 8 May 1711, reporting his arrival. Vaughan is to settle at Elizabeth, and Halliday will take Amboy and Piscataway.

236. Bondet to Secretary, New Rochelle, 16 May 1711, concerning the controversy in his church.

237. Secretary to Barclay, Petty France, Westminster, 24 May 1711 (copy). Though his reports were approved by the society, his account of his visit to the Indians gave offence to Nicholson, who said that it was misleading. Society is sending him some books. Pleased with his favourable report of neighbouring Dutch minister, Freeman.

238. Do. to Bartow, Petty France, Westminster, 24 May 1711 (copy), acknowledging his report.

239. Do. to Bondet, 24 May 1711, Petty France, Westminster (copy). They are sending him some books.

240. Do. to Bridge, Petty France, Westminster, 24 May 1711 (copy). Society has voted to give him £10 worth of books towards replacing the library he lost in moving. He is asked to find out what happened to books in Muirson's care. Secretary asks him for a private report on situation in Rhode Island, but it must be separate from his official report, as society will not believe anything he says about Honeyman.

241. Do. to Cleator, Petty France, Westminster, 14 May 1711 (copy), acknowledging his reports.

242. Do. to Hager, Petty France, Westminster, 24 May 1711 (copy). Society has voted him £10 for a surplice and books and is sending him 100 German prayer books.

243. Do. to Heathcote, Petty France, Westminster, 24 May 1711 (copy). Ross was captured by the French on his return to America and is still in their hands. Society has decided not to send Mackenzie to Stratford because of his report that the Staten Islanders are building a church.

244. Secretary to Kockerthall, Petty France, Westminster, 24 May 1711 (copy). The society is unable to give him an allowance because it is against their rules to employ anyone not sent by them.

245. Do. to Mackenzie, Petty France, Westminster, 24 May 1711 (copy). Society has ratified his agreement to employ two schoolmasters at £10 each, though he made it without their authorization.

246–7. Do. to Morris, Petty France, Westminster, 24 May 1711 (copy). Unfriendliness of Lutherans to both Anglican and Reformed, to which Morris has alluded, is also noted in Europe. Secretary attributes it to the Doctrine of Consubstantiation. Humphreys is returning in orders, to be missionary in Frankford, Pa., and schoolmaster in Philadelphia, Club being transferred to Apoquimininck, Del. Society cannot do anything for Connecticut, as it has made a rule not to start any new missions in the present state of its finances.

248. Do. to Neau, Petty France, Westminster, 24 May 1711 (copy). Society disturbed by his report that most Blacks in New York are still unbaptized. It is considering what to do for the conversion of those willed to it by Gen. Codrington in Barbadoes.

249. Do. to Poyer, Petty France, Westminster, 24 May 1711 (copy). He has sent a catalogue of Stuart's and Urquhart's books, but society now wants a list of those he actually has in hand. In addition to these they will send him books to the value of £10 on his posting a bond for their proper care. The books he brought with him are to be delivered to Beyse.

250. Do. to Thomas, Petty France, Westminster, 24 May 1711 (copy). Society has asked the governor to support Poyer against the dissenters, but their representatives in England have complained that Urquhart appropriated their meeting-house. Society has asked the Bishop of London to write to some missionaries who are not thought to be treating the dissenters politely enough.

251. Do. to Vesey, Petty France, Westminster, 24 May 1711 (copy). Society has continued Huddleston as schoolmaster and appointed Ross to Chester on Vesey's recommendation, but Ross has been taken prisoner by the French. Vesey is asked to comfort his wife and family.

252. Heathcote to Secretary, New York, 25 May 1711. Churches in the area are at peace, except in Jamaica. Stratford continues to solicit aid. He recommends David Clarke as schoolmaster in Westchester.

253. Secretary to Gov. Hunter, Petty France, Westminster, 8 June 1711. Asks him to check on Beyse, as society has a report that he has almost no congregation. Expresses uncertainty about justice of the dissenters' claim in Jamaica.

254. Table giving statistics for parish of Albany and Schenectady for 1710.

255. Secretary to Robinson and Reynolds (dissenting ministers), Petty France, Westminster, 18 June 1711 (copy). Their letter was the first time the society had heard the complaint (attributed to Mr. Mather) that Urquhart has seized the dissenters' church in Jamaica.

256. Do. to do., Petty France, Westminster, 30 June 1711 (copy). Committee has reported that it could not find anything in the records sufficient for a report on the Jamaica controversy, so an inquiry has been sent to Gov. Hunter. Secretary's own involvement in 'The Mine Adventure' and municipal business prevents a fuller account.

257. Do. to Gov. Hunter, Petty France, Westminster, 17 July 1711, (copy), inquiring about this dispute.

258. Do. to Mackenzie, Petty France, Westminster, 18 July 1711 (copy). Society has continued £10 per annum allowance for the two schoolmasters on Staten Island.

259–60. Thomas Barclay to Secretary, Albany, 12 June 1711, enclosing (254). He has had some success with Indians, with whom some of the Dutch ministers also continue to work.

261. Brief account of the Church in Jamaica, by George Ross, 26 July 1711. Basic issue is whether phrase 'Sufficient Protestant minister' in the provincial establishment act was meant to include regularly ordained dissenters. Holding that it did, vestry, controlled by dissenter, called Revd. Mr. MacNeash. Church was built by dissenters, but Cornbury seized it on the ground that it belonged to the Queen.

262–4. Bridge to Secretary, Rye, N.Y., 27 July 1711 (2 copies), enclosing notitia parochialis. Some people started holding irregular meetings in his parish. He had a conference with them at which they expressed difficulties concerning the perfection and divinity of Christ. The meetings were discontinued shortly after the conference. He wishes the society would direct its missionaries to hold occasional consultations. Urges laws against profanity and immorality. People at Stratford continue to appeal for help. Postscript to second copy, 21 Oct. 1711, acknowledges gift of Muirson's books from Col. Heathcote and of £10 worth of books from society.

265–6. Cleator to Secretary, Rye, N.Y., 6 Sept. 1711, acknowledging gift of books for distribution and enclosing list of scholars.

267–8. Hunter to Secretary, New York, 12 Sept. 1711. He has obtained promise of a refusal of the land in Burlington. Beys has promised to produce a certificate of performance of his duty. Halliday has been rebuked for loose conversation (though not accused of immorality) and has promised to reform, Vesey has persuaded Poyer to delay his action in Jamaica. Indians still ask for missionaries. They are now on an expedition into Canada under Col. Nicholson.

269–70. Extract from a letter of Revd. Mr. Odell, now assistant secretary to Sir Guy Carleton, to Chandler, New York, 29 Aug. 1783, referring to plan proposed by Sir Guy for appointment of a bishop for Nova Scotia.

271–4. Certificates and testimonials relating to election of Samuel Provoost as Bishop of New York, 21 Sept. and 11, 16, and 21 Oct. 1786.

275–6. Standing Committee of General Convention to the English bishops, Wilmington, Del., 11 Oct. 1786, acknowledging receipt of their letter and reporting its transmission to General Convention. Signed by Provoost as chairman.

277–83. Provoost's declaration of conformity, 28 Oct. 1786, attested by James Duane, Mayor of New York (2 copies).

284. Undated declaration of conformity to the Church of England by the French congregation in New Rochelle.

285–6. Undated petition of French residents of New Rochelle to the society for aid to Bondet.

287–8. Undated legal opinion concerning status of land in Westchester, allegedly escheated to the Crown and granted to the Church, but claimed by George Hoadly on the ground that he is the legal heir.

289–90. Undated recommendation by Evans, Sharpe, and Neau that Bondet be aided by society.

291–2. Second copy of (289–90) with signatures of Thomas and Urquhart added.

293–4. Undated letter of Bartow to Secretary giving an account of his work.

295–6. Undated petition of inhabitants and freeholders of Rye and Mamorenck to the Bishop of London on behalf of Cleator.

297. Undated fragment of letter relating to immorality in the Navy.

298. C. Smith to Society, undated. Unable to accept mission to Indians on terms offered.

299. Smith to Archbishop of Canterbury, undated but possibly preceding (298). He wants society's allowance augmented by royal bounty and payment to his wife guaranteed during her survival if he dies on mission.

300–2. Undated petition of Robert Livingston, Commissioner of Indian Affairs, to the Society seeking appointment of a missionary to the Indians.

303. Undated list of books left by Muirson. (Cf. 262–4.)

304. Heathcote to Secretary, undated, giving an account of his visit to Connecticut with Muirson.

305. Undated list of churches in the Province of New York.

306–7. Undated petition of wardens and vestry of Westchester for continuance of allowance to Bartow.

308–9. Undated petition of Rector, wardens, and vestry of Trinity Church, New York, for appointment of Huddleston as schoolmaster.

310–12. Undated petition of Huddleston for appointment.

313. Copy of (308–9).

314. Undated petition of Sebastian Vander Eycken to the Archbishop of Canterbury asking his endorsement for an appointment by the society as minister to the Dutch in New York.

315–16. Undated petition of justices, wardens, and vestry of Westchester for continuance of allowance to Bartow.

317. Undated petition of Palatines to Bishop of London asking continuance of Hager as their minister.

VOLUME XV

NORTH CAROLINA

1–2. Henderson Walker to Bishop of London, N. Carolina, 21 Oct. 1703, seeking a clergyman. Refers to Quakers as strongest group in province. Daniel Brett, first clergyman sent by S.P.G., behaved well for half a year, then began to behave scandalously.

3. Note by George Keith, London, 13 Oct. 1704, giving an unfavourable account of travelling conditions in North Carolina.

4. Opinion of House of Lords, 9 Mar. 1705, holding North Carolina Act regulating ministry invalid.

5. Testimonial of A. Middleton, Curate of St. Benedict's, Pauls Wharf, to William Gordon, 27 Sept. 1707.

6–7. Gordon to Secretary, Lyndhaven Bay, 1 Apr. 1708, reporting that he has reached there on his journey to North Carolina.

8–9. Wardens of Chowan Parish, N.C., to Society, 6 Aug. 1708, thanking society for books sent by Gordon and attesting to his faithful labour during his short stay among them.

10–11. Sundry residents of the parish to the Society, 24 Aug. 1708, praising Gordon and hoping for his early return.

12–13. Certificate of wardens, Chowan Point, N.C., 13 Sept. 1708, that if some of the vestry failed to sign the testimonial to Gordon, it was not because of opposition, but because they could not get to the meeting. (NOTE: This seems to refer to (10–11), though the signers are not therein identified as vestry.)

14. James Adams to Secretary, N. Carolina, 18 Sept. 1708. His work has been interrupted by political disturbances which he does not describe, as Gordon will report on them. Province is divided among Churchmen, Quakers, and a majority who have no religion. Quakers, though only 1/7 of population are the most influential group.

15. Certificate of Stephen Robins, Vicar of East Ham, and John Chifendale, Vicar of Barking, that John Urmiston discharged his duties as curate at East Ham, Essex County, faithfully for three years, 4 May 1709.

16–17. Gordon to Committee, undated but referred to in (18–21). After landing in Virginia he proceeded by a difficult overland journey to Chowan, where he was entertained by Mr. Glover, President of the Council, and began work, but shortly decided to return home because of ill health.

18–21. Do. to do., London, 23 May 1709. An account of politics and religion in North Carolina, seen in terms of conflict between the Church party and the Quakers.

22. Urmston to Secretary, East Ham, 28 Sept. 1709. He is unwilling to sail on the *Princess Anne* with the Palatines, as he believes that the voyage will be too rough for his family.

23. Do. to do., East Ham, 3 Oct. 1709, explaining that he will not be able to call on him until later in the week, and expressing doubts about his reception in North Carolina.

24–5. Copy of paper presented to the lower house of the Assembly of North Carolina, 11 Jan. 1709/10, by Wood, Maule, and (?), recommending amendments to the Church Act. Unidentified third party refers to himself in the first person as the one originally consulted.

26. C. De Graffenied to Bishop of London, New Bern, N.C., 20 Apr. 1711. Hasty departure from London to arrange for transportation of his Swiss colonists prevented his waiting on the bishop, but he asks him to receive them into the Church and grant them his patronage.

27. Urmston to Secretary, North Carolina, 17 July 1711. An insurrection against Governor Hyde has been suppressed by forces from Virginia. Mrs. Hyde, who is returning with the colonial Secretary, Knight, can supply details.

28–9. Testimonials to Giles Rainsford, both from Edward Grove, Chevington Parsonage, near St. Edmindsbury, 30 July and 7 Aug. 1711.

30. Rainsford to Secretary, Sheerness, 13 Dec. 1711. He has signed on the *Bedford Galley* to obtain passage to Virginia, but Capt. Andrew Lee says he must obtain an order from the Admiralty if he is to be released there and not held in service.

31. Do. to do., Chatham, 9 Jan. 1712. He has catechized the 'boys' with the captain's approval, and caused a woman kept on board by the warrant officers to be sent ashore.

32–4. Bishop of London to the Lords Commissioners of Trade and Plantations, Fulham, 19 Feb. 1759. Requested to comment on recent Church Act of North Carolina, he observes that it takes away the Crown's right of patronage, conferring it on the vestries, and sets up an uncanonical jurisdiction over the clergy in the form of a governing commission. He cannot say if it interferes with his colonial jurisdiction, because he is not sure that he has any.

35–43. Undated account of Blair's mission to North Carolina, following his ordination, 12 Apr. 1703. He covered most of the province, in spite of travel difficulties.

44–5. Undated petition of residents along Pamplico River, Bath County, N.C., to House of Lords, complaining that colonial government has refused them a minister.

46–7. Undated petition of wardens and vestry of Pascotank Parish, N.C., asking for a minister. They are at present being supplied by Richard Marsden.

PENNSYLVANIA

48–9. Testimonial to John Thomas from Andreas Rudman, Andreas Sandel, and Ericus Biörck, Philadelphia, 22 July 1702 (Latin).

50–1. George Keith to the Bishop of London, Philadelphia, 28 Feb. 1702/3, giving an account of his travels to date and mentioning Talbot's joining him.

52. Testimonial to John Thomas from Evan Evans, John Talbot, and three other ministers (Swedish?), Burlington, 18 Aug. 1703.

53. Keith to the Bishop of London, Philadelphia, 2 Apr. 1703, recommending Thomas, who has served as assistant to Evans and schoolmaster in Philadelphia.

54–5. Do. to Secretary, Philadelphia, 3 Apr. 1703, recommending Talbot and Thomas.

56–7. Testimonial to Thomas from Rector, wardens, and others of Christ Church, Philadelphia, 31 Aug. 1703. He is going home for priest's orders.

58–60. Keith to Secretary, Philadelphia, 4 Sept. 1703, giving an account of his visit to Virginia and North Carolina, from which he has just returned, and of his controversies with the Quakers.

61. Do. to do., Philadelphia, 14 Sept. 1703, recommending Thomas as a missionary.

62. Testimonial to Thomas Crawford from James Chalmers and David Crawford, London, 4 Feb. 1703/4.

63–4. Henry Nichols to Stubbs, Chester, Pa., 20 Mar. 1703/4, reporting his safe arrival on ship on which Gov. Seymour of Maryland was also a passenger. Gives favourable account of work of Keith and Evans. Latter has helped him by interpreting to the Welsh, as he does not yet speak their language.

65–6. Minister and vestry of Philadelphia to the Society, 7 Apr. 1704. Testimonial to Keith and Talbot.

67–8. Nichols to Treasurer, Upland, alias Chester, 30 Apr. 1704, reporting on beginning of his work. Asks that his stipend be laid out in goods in England, as he will get better value from it that way.

69–70. Rudman to Keith, Philadelphia, 10 May 1704. He is ministering to country churches and has drawn on Keith for a quarter's stipend (£12. 6s.), which he expects the society to refund.

71–2. Evans to the Bishop of London, New York, 17 Oct. 1704. He is in New York to attend a convocation of the clergy. Thomas has returned and is assisting him in Philadelphia. Recommends Muirson, who is returning for orders, and Rudman.

73–6. Copies of documents relating to claim of Swedish Church to lands in Chester, with opinion by J. Hooke, 18 Oct. 1704, that they are not sufficient to support title. Documents include copy of letter of Jasper Yeates to Gov. Nicholson.

77–8. Evans to Keith, Philadelphia, 25 Oct. 1704. He has had some success in converting Quakers through the use of Keith's writings.

79–80. Testimonial to Rudman from (Gov.) John Evans, Philadelphia, 20 Aug. 1705.

81. Rudman to Secretary, Philadelphia, 20 Aug. 1705. He is serving church in Frankford and asks aid of society.

82–3. Gov. Evans to Stubbs, Philadelphia, 24 Aug. 1705, defending Rudman against an attack by Edward Eaton.

84. Do. to do., Philadelphia, 23 Aug. 1705, recommending Clubb, schoolmaster at Philadelphia.

85. George Ross to Secretary, Philadelphia, 27 Aug. 1705, reporting his safe arrival and friendly reception by Evan Evans and the governor.

86. Thomas Crawford to Secretary, Philadelphia, 27 Aug. 1705, reporting his arrival.

87. Rudman to Treasurer, Philadelphia, 27 Aug. 1705, reporting that he has drawn on him for £50.

88. Petition of Rudman to Society, 1 Nov. 1705, asking aid for himself and church at Frankford.

89. Description of Christ Church, Philadelphia, signed by Evan Evans, 3 Nov. 1705.

90. Secretary to Nicolls, Petty France, Westminster, 2 Mar. 1705/6. Society is sending him some books as requested.

91–2. Nichols to Society, Chester, 10 June 1706. Sent by Evans, who is going home. Nichols has been two years in Chester. Local support has only come to half of the £60 currency a year that was promised.

93–4. Do. to Secretary, Chester, 21 June 1706, asking him to present (91–2) to the society and repeating complaint of inadequate local support. He is afraid that the three-year rule may lead to the loss of his support from the society.

95–6. Promissory note of Andrew Rudman to Evan Evans, 16 July 1706, for £100, to become due if bill for £50 on the society, cashed by Evans, is protested by treasurer.

97. Cleator to Treasurer, Rumney Bay, 1 Aug. 1706. He has got that far on his voyage and would like a letter of introduction to Col. Heathcote to be sent to him at Portsmouth.

98. Evan Evans to Secretary, Philadelphia, 19 Dec. 1706. He has to defer his intended trip to England (to defend himself against charges brought by members of his congregation) because he missed the Virginia fleet, but he plans to come in spring.

99–101. *Notitia Parochialis* of Henry Nicols for Chester, 17 Mar. 1706/7. Includes names of persons baptized, professors of the Church of England, and catechumens.

102. Testimonial of wardens, William Marten and William Davis, that Nicols has faithfully observed instructions of the society.

103. Secretary to Crawford, Petty France, Westminster, 4 June 1707 (copy). Agrees to his remaining at Dover Hundred, since his health is improved and he reports good relations with the people. Black is being sent to Sussex. Secretary complains that Crawford was more particular about his work in his letters to Stubs than to him.

104. Do. to Nicols, Petty France, Westminster, 4 June 1707 (copy). Society has passed a resolution rebuking him for complaining that he had not received the money from his fellowship when Dr. Edwards attests that he has done so. (Cf. vii. 261.)

105. Do. to Cols. Heathcote and Quarry, Petty France, Westminster, 1 July 1707 (copy). Society has voted to send 500 Bibles with Prayer Book annexed and 500 without to be distributed by 20 persons in the colonies and has directed him to seek their advice and assistance in this project.

106–7. Nicols to Secretary, Chester, 14 July 1707. Protests his innocence of all charges, without referring specifically to any.

108–20. Evan Evans's account of the state of the church in Pennsylvania, London, 18 Sept. 1707 (2 copies, with some variations). Ends with plea for a bishop. Evans himself was sent to Philadelphia by Bishop Compton in 1700.

121–2. Robert Quarry to Secretary, 12 Feb. 1707(8). Supports Cornbury against Moore and Brooke and criticizes convocation of clergy, which he believes acted against intentions of Nicholson, who financed it.

123–4. Evans to Society (London) 18 June 1708, in reply to an inquiry about prospects of Church in Connecticut. Shortly before leaving America, he accompanied Muirson to Stratford, where they had a good congregation. He believes Muirson would be a good man to send there.

125. Black to Secretary, Newcastle, 19 July 1708. He has got that far on his journey to Sussex, Del.

126. Secretary to Nicols, Windsor Castle, 5 Aug. 1708 (copy). Complains that Nicols has not answered society's rebuke reported in (104), and that he has made vague complaints about local opposition.

127–8. Do. to Col. Quarry, Windsor Castle, 6 Aug. 1708 (copy). Agrees with Quarry that clerical convocations may lead to disorder, and suggests sending a bishop as the remedy. Though Moore and Brooke are dead and Cornbury recalled, society would still like an exact account of that affair.

129. Talbot to Secretary, Philadelphia, Aug. 1708. Fears that Moore and Brooke are lost, and takes a gloomy view of state of church in New Jersey and Pennsylvania. Nicols has gone to Maryland.

130–1. Residents of Oxford, Pa., to Bishop of London, 21 Aug. 1708. Rudman has been supplying for Evans in Philadelphia for the past two years and Clubb has been supplying Oxford.

132–3. Rudman to Secretary, Philadelphia, 26 Aug. 1708. He is resigning Oxford to Club, because of lack of support. Complains that Evans deceived him by selling his bill on the society in Virginia, when he had promised to deliver it directly to the treasurer (96–7).

134. Secretary to Bradford, Windsor Castle, 28 Aug. 1708 (copy). He has never received specimen pages of Bradford's edition of Prayer Book, but suggests he see Heathcote and Quarry about the possibility of their buying from him instead of having books sent from England.

135. Do. to Crawford, Windsor Castle, 28 Aug. 1708 (copy), complaining of lack of reports.

136. Do. to Rudman, Windsor Castle, 28 Aug. 1708 (copy). Though his bill on the treasurer brought by Evans was unauthorized, the society agreed to pay it, but cannot give him any further increase in the present state of its funds.

137–8. Ross to Secretary, Chester, Pa., 2 Aug. 1708. He has come to Chester, and Jenkins is serving New Castle, partly as the result of tension between Ross and the New Castle congregation.

139. Secretary to Club, Petty France, Westminster, 28 Sept. 1708 (copy). Society unable to aid him at present, in spite of recommendation of Evans.

140. Do. to vestries of Chester and (with variations) of New Castle and Apoquiminck, Petty France, Westminster, 15 Feb. 1708/9 (copy), informing them of the society's rule against continuing the allowance of any minister who makes an unauthorized change of station.

141. Do. to Evans, Petty France, Westminster, 15 Feb. 1708/9 (copy), sending a copy of Rudman's letter about that bill (132–3) and asking for an explanation. As ship conveying Evans and Gov. Lovelace was reported lost, their friends were happy to learn that it was sighted off Rhode Island.

142. Do. to Nichols, Petty France, Westminster, 15 Feb. 1708/9 (copy), notifying him of his dismissal because of his removal to Maryland.

143. Do. to Rudman, 15 Feb. 1708/9 (copy), Petty France, Westminster, reporting the sending of his letter to Evans and saying that society will pay him a year's salary, if he returns immediately to Frankford.

144–5. Wardens and vestry of Trinity Church, Oxford, Pa., to Society, 5 Mar. 1708/9, reporting death of Rudman and asking that Clubb, who supplied them while Rudman was serving Philadelphia, be appointed as their minister.

146–7. Evans to Secretary, Philadelphia, 7 Mar. 1708/9, reporting safe arrival. Lovelace was seriously ill after arrival, but recovered sufficiently to attend the Assembly at Amboy. Rudman is dead. Clubb served Oxford faithfully, but his school in Philadelphia suffered. Jenkins has returned to his post since Evans's arrival.

148. Ross to Secretary, Chester, 9 Mar. 1709. He is preparing to return to New Castle, but hopes the society will allow him to move again if his health suffers.

149. Secretary to Crawford, Petty France, Westminster, 31 May 1709 (copy), enclosing a minute of the society relating to him.

150. Do. to Clubb, Petty France, Westminster, 3 June 1709 (copy). Society has voted to allow him £30 a year for work at Frankford and Oxford.

151–2. Evans to Secretary, Philadelphia, 16 June 1709. Ross is seeking a parish in Maryland and, failing that, will try to obtain post of schoolmaster and assistant in Philadelphia in spite of Evans's opposition.

153–4. Wardens and Vestry of Trinity Church, Oxford, to the Society, 16 June 1709, requesting allowance from Clubb.

155–6. Rector, wardens, and vestry of Christ Church, Philadelphia, to Society, 21 June 1709, attesting to Clubb's service at Oxford.

157. Clubb and wardens of Trinity Church, Oxford, to Society, 27 July 1709. Rudman served them only two years before going to Philadelphia, instead of three, as he alleged in letter to the secretary. Instead of paying, out of his pocket, for the installation of the glass donated to the church by the Queen, he sold it without authorization. He received £50 sterling a year from the church in Philadelphia while supplying for Evans.

158–9. Cha: Gookin to Secretary, Philadelphia, 27 Aug. 1709, reporting conditions in colony. Black has removed to Maryland. Crawford continues in Kent Co., Del. Ross has taken over the school in Philadelphia. Jenkins has died. Nichols has gone to Maryland. Party opposing Evans in Christ Church has hindered payment of his salary, and is supporting Ross. Gookin asks secretary to use his influence to get him continued as governor if Penn resigns his proprietorship to the Queen, as is rumoured.

160–3. Evans to Secretary, Philadelphia, 7 Aug. 1709 (2 copies), giving his account of the transaction concerning Rudman's bill. Says that party in Philadelphia put pressure on Clubb to get him to resign school to Ross. Evans and Talbot buried Jenkins in Christ Church. There is a rumour that Crawford has another wife in Scotland. Arrival of Vaughan reported from Boston. Clubb continues to serve Oxford.

164. Attestation by Gov. Gookin that Evans had assigned to Rudman a debt due him from William Hall in return for Rudman's bill, and that Hall produced receipts showing that the money was paid to Rudman, 29 Aug. 1709.

165–6. Gookin to Secretary, Philadelphia, 31 Aug. 1709, a shorter version of (158–9).

167–8. Vestry at Chester to Society, 1 Sept. 1709. Nichols served them three years before leaving for Maryland. There was some scandal concerning alleged familiarity with a married woman, but it was quieted by his own marriage. Money contributed for his support came to £60 (currency?) for each of first two years, but fell off to £40 in the third year.

169. Elizabeth Crawford, wife of Thomas, to the Society, dated 1709 in *notation*, saying that she is willing to join him, and asking that part of his salary be paid her for her present subsistence.

170. Secretary to Clubb, Petty France, Westminster, 12 Dec. 1709, confirming his appointment and saying that £10 worth of books are being sent him. *Notation*: Books have been delivered to Humphreys.

171. Do. to Crawford, Petty France, Westminster, 12 Dec. 1709 (copy). Claims on his salary advanced by his wife, her brother, and Crawford's attorney, Mr. Lind, have so impaired his reputation with the society that he is in danger of dismissal unless he can clear himself.

172. Do. to Evans, Petty France, Westminster, 12 Dec. 1709 (copy), asking for a report on Crawford, who is suspected of bigamy.

173. Do. to Gov. Gookin, Petty France, Westminster, 6 Jan. 1709/10 (copy), informing him of his election as a member.

174. Do. to Quarry, Petty France, Westminster, 28 Feb. 1709/10 (copy), asking him to investigate house in Burlington.

175. Do. to Gookin, Petty France, Westminster, 24 Sept. 1710 (copy), introducing Henderson, who is to replace Crawford at Dover Hundred.

176. Do. to Evans, Petty France, Westminster, 23 Sept. 1710 (copy), introducing Henderson, reproaching Evans for not writing, and asking reports on various missionaries. References to Crawford seem to indicate that the charge of bigamy was sustained.

177. Do. to vestry of Chester, 27 Dec. 1710 (copy), saying that Ross has cleared himself of charges and been restored to society's employment.

178–9. Talbot, Evans, Andrew Sandel (Swedish minister) and Vaughan to the Society, Burlington, 12 Apr. 1711. Recommend transfer of Sinclair from New Castle to Piscataqua or Stratford for his health. Also recommend aid to Biörck, Swedish minister in Pennsylvania, and an increased allowance to Clubb.

180. Secretary to Gookin, Petty France, Westminster, 26 Apr. 1711 (copy), introducing Humphreys, who is to replace Clubb (transferred to Apoquiminny) at Oxford.

181. Do. to Humphreys, Petty France, Westminster, 26 Apr. 1711 (copy), enclosing (180) for delivery to Gookin, as Secretary was out when Humphreys called to pay his respects before departing.

182. Do. to Sinclair, Petty France, Westminster, 26 Apr. 1711 (copy). Though society has consented to his return, because of ill health, secretary hopes that his reported recovery will induce him to stay.

183–4. Gookin to Secretary, Philadelphia, 21 May 1711. He has met with opposition of Christ Church vestry and others of Church party for approving bills concerning giving of evidence and one allowing religious societies to purchase estates.

185–7. William Smith to Sir William Johnson, 16 Mar. 1767 (copy), proposing a scheme for the conversion of the Indians. Its chief feature is the formation of combined white and Indian settlements, under the society's direction, one in New York and one in western Virginia.

188–9. Benjamin Rush to Granville Sharp, Philadelphia, 22 Apr. 1786. He presented Sharp's letter indicating favourable disposition of English bishops to the General Convention. Seabury has lately ordained 'five or six' Methodist preachers. One, Pilmore, is associated with Magaw at St. Paul's, Philadelphia.

190–9. Testimonials to William White's election and qualifications as Bishop of Pennsylvania, 1786.

200–1. Members of St. Paul's, Chester, Pa., to Society, undated, acknowledging services of Nichols.

202–3. Vestry and minister (Nicols) of St. Paul's to society, asking continued aid. Undated.

204–5. Evans, Talbot, Gookin, and Quarry to the Society, undated, asking them to authorize transfer of Henderson from Dover Hundred to Appoquiminy. He has met with opposition at Dover, partly from Presbyterians and partly in consequence of the Crawford affair. Moreover, the location is unhealthy.

206. The case of Andrew Rudman, signed by ministers of Pennsylvania, New York, and New Jersey, undated. Episcopally ordained in Sweden, Rudman was sent by the Archbishop of Uppsala to serve the Swedish congregation near Philadelphia. He served faithfully for five years, when he was replaced by another minister sent from Sweden. He was preparing to return when war broke out and Keith persuaded him to start serving the church at Oxford.

207. Undated statement by Ericus Biörck, minister of Swedish Church at Christeen, asserting that he also ministers to members of the Church of England along the Delaware, being prompted thereunto by the coming of 'Anabaptists'.

208–9. Undated testimonial of Swedish ministers to John Thomas (Latin).

210–12. Undated testimonial by Evans to service of Rudman at Oxford.

RHODE ISLAND, 1702–1707

213–14. John Lockier and wardens of church in Rhode Island (not otherwise designated) to society, 29 Sept. 1702, giving some account of the parish, which is four years old.

215. Honeyman to Dr. Beveridge, Rhode Island, 25 Nov. 1703, reporting his arrival. (Dated as shown in heading, but *notation* gives 1704, which seems more probable.)

216–19. Lockier, wardens, and others to society, Newport, 23 Dec. 1703, acknowledging gift of church furnishings and reporting addition of steeple to their building. State that Quakers continue to grow through immigration, but no longer make many converts.

220. Churchwardens, Robert Carr and Robert Lawton, to the society, 9 Oct. 1704, asking continuance of Honeyman, who was sent to them by Cornbury on death of Lockier. Indicate that a counter-petition has been sent by others.

221. Honeyman to Secretary, Rhode Island, 10 Jan. 1704/5, defending himself against charges.

222–3. Samuel Myles to Archbishop of Canterbury, Rhode Island, 23 Sept., 1705, introducing Gershon Rawlins, a candidate for orders, graduate of Harvard.

224–5. Anti-Honeyman petition, with numerous signatures, addressed to Society, Newport, 22 Dec. 1705.

226. Honeyman to Keith, Newport, 2 Feb. 1704/5, reporting that he has met with some opposition.

227–8. A similar petition to (224–5), 22 Dec. 1705, with some of the same signatures, but slightly different wording.

229–30. Robert Gardiner to Samuel Myles, Newport, 25 Dec. 1705. Since Bridge has come to Narragansett, the anti-Honeyman party is swinging to him.

231–2. Honeyman to Keith, Newport, 24 Jan. 1705/6, identifying Gardiner as leader of the opposition.

233. Do. to Talbot, Newport, 24 Jan. 1705/6, giving similar information.

234–5. Andrew Leaske to Society, 30 Jan. 1706, asking if society will pay £50 claimed by Honeyman as due him.

236. Honeyman to Secretary, Newport, 30 Apr. 1706, asking payment of stipend.

237. Robert Yate to Secretary, Bristol, 18 May 1706. Does not think society can anticipate much help from there. (NOTE: This is probably Bristol, England, though placed here in belief it was Bristol, R.I.)

238. Sundry residents of Newport to the Society, 24 Sept. 1706, thanking them for support of Honeyman and asking for a bell.

239. Copies of letters of clergy of New York area to the Bishop of London on behalf of Honeyman, one undated, one dated 7 Oct. 1706 and copy of address by sundry inhabitants of Narragansett to the Bishop, 3 Oct. 1706, acknowledging Honeyman's services to them in absence of regular minister. All on one sheet.

240–1. Another anti-Honeyman petition, Newport, 24 Sept. 1706, addressed to society.

242–3. A similar petition addressed to the Secretary, Newport, 24 Sept. 1706.

244. Pro-Honeyman petition, addressed to the Bishop of London, Rhode Island, 24 Sept. 1706 (copy).

245–6. Anti-Honeyman group to the society, Newport, 24 Sept. 1706, asking that Honeyman be sent to Narragansett and Bridge to Newport.

247–8. Two copies of (244).

249–50. Honeyman to the Bishop of London, Newport, 26 Sept. 1706, complaining that Bridge is seeking to supplant him.

251–2. Andrew Leaske to Society, undated, but referring to letter of attorneyship from Honeyman dated 29 Sept. 1706, asking payment of £50 claimed by Honeyman as due him. Leaske is Honeyman's uncle.

253. Honeyman to Secretary, Newport, 29 Sept. 1706, seeking payment of his salary.

254–9. More copies of pro-Honeyman petitions given before (239, 244).

260–1. Honeyman to Secretary, Newport, 8 Oct. 1706, a repetition of (253).

262–3. Do. to Bishop of London, 24 Oct. 1706, giving his side of the controversy.

264–5. Do. to Secretary, Newport, 24 and 26 Oct. 1706. Three copies of letters of similar purport to (253).

266–9. Do. to do., Newport, 28 Oct. 1706 (3 copies). He has received only £30 of his salary, and never did receive books that were sent him.

270–1. Do. to do., Newport, 8 Nov. 1706, expressing fear that previous letters have been lost.

272–3. A duplicate of (266–9) dated 4 Nov. 1706.

274. Address of four members of the church in Kingston, Narragansett Co., R.I., to the Bishop of London asking continuance of Bridge. Dated Nov. 1706 in *notation*.

275–6. Honeyman to Secretary, Newport, 19 Dec. 1706, complaining of intrusion by Bridge.

277–8. Residents of Newport to Society, 2 Feb. 1707, thanking them for appointing Bridge as their minister (2 copies).

279–80. Honeyman to Nicholson, Newport, 13 Feb. 1706/7, complaining of Bridge's intrusion.

281. Henry Newman to (Bishop of London?), Pallmall at the Black Lion, 14 Feb. 1706/7, opposing removal of Bridge from Narragansett to Newport. He was called to Narragansett by the Church people to keep dissenters from seizing the church building.

282–5. Residents of Newport to Society, 17 Feb. 1707, in support of Bridge against Honeyman (2 copies).

286–7. Bridge to Newman, Newport, 19 Feb. 1707. First he received a letter from the secretary telling him that his appointment to Narragansett was pending. Then he received a letter from the Bishop of London saying that the society had appointed him to Newport. On the advice of Gov. Dudley he has come to Newport, but Honeyman is opposing his takeover.

288–9. Honeyman to Secretary, Newport, 28 Feb. 1706 (7?), asking continuance of society's support but making no obvious reference to dispute with Bridge. May belong to earlier year.

290–1. Bridge to Secretary, Newport, Feb. 1707, conveying same information as (286–7).

292. Secretary to Bridge, Petty France, Westminster, 6 June 1707 (copy), informing him of his appointment to Narragansett as soon as the Bishop of London designated someone else as assistant in Boston. (NOTE: Though the date is as given, this reads like the letter referred to in 286–7.)

293. James Adams to Secretary, Bristol (R.I.?), 22 Nov. 1707. He and Gordon have got that far on the way to their missions.

294–5. Bridge to Secretary, Narragansett, 2 Dec. 1707. The people are unable, or unwilling, to provide him with a parsonage, and the church is unglazed, making it unusable in winter.

VOLUME XVI

RHODE ISLAND, 1708–undated

1. Bridge to Secretary, 3 Jan. 1708, Newport, accepting society's decision to remove him from Newport, but defending his own conduct by repeating information in (xv. 286–7).

2. Francis Foxcroft to Secretary, 10 Jan. 1708. Bridge has entrusted (1) to him for safe delivery and he is sending it by his son, Daniel. He believes that Bridge's removal will restore peace, but commends him, and thinks that his removal from Boston was a loss to the church there.

3–4. Robert Gardiner to Secretary, Newport, 24 Jan. 1708, protesting reappointment of Honeyman. Represents himself as first promoter of the Church in Newport. (NOTE: From the following documents it appears that (1–4), though dated 1708, belong to 1709, as they seem to refer to the settlement of the dispute.)

5–6. Petition of Bridge party to Gov. Samuel Cranston, Newport, 30 Jan. 1707/8, asking him to grant Bridge peaceable possession of the church, in opposition to Honeyman, as he has been appointed to the station by the Bishop of London (2 copies).

7–8. Honeyman to Bridge, 31 Jan. 1707/8, stating his side of the dispute.

9–10. Wardens and vestry of Newport to Society, 1 Feb. 1708, saying they cannot receive Honeyman, though they have been shown an order of the society restoring him.

11. Gov. Cranston to Bridge and Honeyman, Newport, 3 Feb. 1707/8. Repeats advice he gave at a private conference, that they should seek to reconcile their difference peaceably. It is his personal opinion that order of the Bishop of London appointing Bridge to Newport should be observed until reversed, but he does not have authority to intervene officially in ecclesiastical matters.

12. Certificate of Gov. Cranston, 5 Feb. 1707/8, that Bridge behaved soberly and properly at their conference.

13. Certificate by do., 6 Feb. 1707/8, that, before the church was broken into, he had told Lillibridge and Gardiner that Honeyman wanted the dispute to be referred to the proprietors or communicants of the church.

14–16. Anti-Bridge petition to the Bishop of London, 6 Feb. 1707/8, signed mostly by women.

17. Bartow to Whitfield, 28 Feb. 1707/8. He has heard from Honeyman that he is returning to England to present his case.

18. Affidavit of Thomas Lillibridge and Samuel Whitehair, sworn before Gov. Cranston, that they applied to Honeyman for the church keys before they broke in.

19. Affidavit of Saly Lillibridge, before Gov. Cranston, 28 Feb. 1707/8, saying that Honeyman declared, before her and her husband, that he would keep any other minister out of his pulpit.

20–1. Bridge to Stubbs, Newport, 29 Feb. 1707(8?), asking his support against Honeyman, who has gone to England to present his side.

22–3. Do. to Nicholson, Newport, 29 Feb. 1707(8?), seeking his support.

24. Affidavit of Robert Gardiner before Gov. Cranston, 4 Mar. 1707/8, saying that when told by the governor of Honeyman's proposal to refer the dispute to the communicants, he replied that while he did not approve of putting the Bishop of London's order to a vote he would consent, provided only the male communicants were allowed to vote.

25. Certificate of Gov. Cranston that he knows subscribers to a pro-Bridge petition to be masters of families and many of them freeholders, 4 Mar. 1707/8.

26–7. Pro-Honeyman petition to the Bishop of London, Newport, 5 Mar. 1707/8.

28–9. Honeyman to Secretary, Plymouth, 14 May 1708, reporting his arrival in England.

30–1. Do. to the Society, London, 4 June 1708, seeking reinstatement.

32. Newman to Secretary, 8 June 1708. He will wait on the committee that afternoon, presumably in Bridge's behalf, for a letter on the same sheet requests that if Bridge is returned to Narragansett, the society will consider transferring him to a better station at the first opportunity.

33–4. Honeyman to Secretary, 24 June 1708, stating his case.

35–7. Abstract from the minutes showing actions of the society relating to Bridge, 16 Aug. 1706 to 1 July 1708. They did first appoint him to Newport, but changed the appointment to Narragansett. Minute of 1 July 1708 orders secretary to inform him that his salary will be stopped unless he returns to Narragansett.

38–9. Honeyman to Secretary, London, 3 July 1708, asking that sealed notice of his appointment be delivered to an unnamed friend.

40. Secretary to Bridge, Petty France, Westminster, 24 July 1708, informing him of the decision. Notes that his letter of 2 Dec. 1708 (xv. 294–5) was dated from Narragansett and gave no indication of his intending to move to Newport.

41. Do. to Capt. Hamilton, Windsor Castle, 3 Aug. 1708, acknowledging a letter of Hamilton's which helped to clear Honeyman of scandal.

42–3. Honeyman to Evan Evans, London, 9 Aug. 1708, asking him to recommend to the society that, if Muirson is transferred to Stratford, society grant him an allowance of £100, as he cannot expect much local support. Note of concurrence signed by Evans.

44. Secretary to Capt. Steward, Petty France, Westminster, 16 Sept. 1708 (copy), thanking him for kind treatment of Adams and Gordon on their voyage to Virginia *en route* to Carolina.

45–6. Cranston to William Wharton, Newport, 12 Mar. 1708/9. Though he signed and sealed a testimonial to Honeyman's character, he did not intend to take part in the church dispute and regrets Honeyman's return, as he fears it will provoke further controversy (2 copies).

47. Do. to Bridge, Newport, 17 Mar. 1708/9, enclosing one copy of (45–6). Wharton is colonial agent for Rhode Island.

49. Honeyman to —— ('Reverend sir'), Newport, 24 Mar. 1708/9, reporting safe arrival after a difficult voyage.

50. Wardens and vestry of Newport to the Bishop of London, 28 Mar. 1709, complain that Honeyman broke into the church on his return without asking them for the keys.

51–5. Case of Christopher Bridge, London, 17 June 1709, reviewing the controversy and requesting payment of his bills (2 copies).

56–7. Bridge to Secretary, 2 and 14 July 1709, reviewing his controversies with Myles and Honeyman.

58–62. Petition of Honeyman to the Society, stating his case. Undated, but probably filed during his attendance on the society in 1708.

63. Secretary to Gov. Dudley, Petty France, Westminster, 20 Apr. 1711 (copy), asking him to investigate an anonymous complaint of scandalous conduct by Honeyman.

64. Do. to Adams, Petty France, Westminster, 24 May 1711 (copy), saying society has added £20 to his allowance in North Carolina (misplaced).

65. Do. to Col. Glover, Petty France, Westminster, 24 May 1711 (copy, misplaced), indicating continuance of Adams in North Carolina.

66. Honeyman to Secretary, 12 July 1711, acknowledging gift of books and altar piece.

67. Do. to do., Newport, 19 Oct. 1711, defending himself against anonymous charges referred to in (63).

68. James Manning to Granville Sharp, Providence, 26 July 1785 (copy). He has distributed Sharp's writings on ecclesiastical matters among Episcopalian acquaintances in Rhode Island and elsewhere. He is identified in heading of this copy as President of the College of Providence.

69. Do. to do., Providence, 13 Apr. 1786 (copy). Seabury has visited Rhode Island and confirmed there. It is reported that he has been invited to settle in Newport.

70. Andrew Leaske to Bishop of London, undated, asking help in collecting money claimed to be due to Honeyman from the society.

71. Do. to Society, undated, asking payment.

72–3. Do. to Secretary, undated, seeking payment.

74–5. List of subscribers to the church in Newport, undated, but containing names that appear on petitions of the Honeyman period.

76–7. Pro-Honeyman petition to the Bishop of London, undated.

SOUTH CAROLINA, 1702–1710

78–9. Samuel Thomas to the Treasurer, Carolina, 22 Mar. 1702 (3?), asking him to send some goods, all linen, no wool.

80. Do. to do., Plymouth, 8 Sept. 1702. He is ill and has been abused by some on the ship, but he has obtained permission to read prayers twice daily.

81–2. Do. to Dr. Woodward, Carolina, 10 Mar. 1703/4, with report to society on same sheet. He reached (South) Carolina in Dec. 1702 and was kindly received by Gov. Nathaniel Johnson. Reports on work since arrival.

83–4. Do. to Treasurer, 'From my study at Sir N. Johnson's in Carolina', 3 May 1704, reporting on his work and describing shortage of ministers in the colony.

85–8. Testimonials to Thomas Stackhouse, the last dated 23 Aug. 1704. He has been headmaster of school in Hoxam, diocese of York, and is son of John Stack-house, minister of St. Andrew, Auckland, County Durham.

89. Petition for aid from wife of a minister in Maryland. Name missing, but attested by George Keith, London, 9 Oct. 1704 (misplaced).

90–2. Testimonials to William Dun, formerly of the Diocese of Clogher, 24 Nov. 1704.

93–7. Testimonials to William Guy, last dated, 23 June 1705.

98–9. Testimonial to Francis Le Jau, formerly of Trinity College, Dublin, signed by Bishop Compton and others, 21 Nov. 1705.

100–1. Testimonials to Andrew Auchinleek, 15 and 20 Dec. 1705.

102–3. Robert Stevens to Society, Goose Creek, 21 Feb. 1705/6, complaining that new establishment act has led to ousting of Marston as Minister of St. Philip's, Charleston, and excludes dissenters from assembly.

104–6. Edward Marston to the Society, 'From my study near Charles Town', 25 Feb. 1705/6, complaining of his ouster.

107–8. Samuel Thomas to Secretary, Lavenham, 30 Mar. 1706, defending himself from an attack by Marston.

109. Lord Weymouth to Secretary, 12 Apr. 1706. Present disordered state of South Carolina gives little encouragement for sending missionaries there.

110–11. Abstract of Thomas's defence against Marston, undated, but probably presented about the same time as (107–8).

112–13. Francis Le Jau to Secretary, aboard the *Greenwich*, in Queen's Dock, near Plymouth, 6 May 1706, reporting delays in sailing.

114–15. Do. to do., *Greenwich*, in Plymouth Sound, 28 May 1706. Ship is now under orders to sail at the first opportunity.

116–17. Gov. Johnson and Council of S.C. to the Society, Charlestown, 16 Sept. 1706, thanking the society for aid, praising Thomas, and defending themselves against charges by Marston.

118. Testimonial to Robert Maule from Archbishop of Dublin, 1 Oct. 1706, with addition dated 10 Dec. 1706.

119. Secretary to Marston, Petty France, Westminster, 10 Oct. 1706 (copy). Society is returning Thomas to South Carolina, with new appointees, Dr. Le Jau, Dun, Auchinleek, and Hassel (the last as schoolmaster). Condition for sending them was repeal of a certain clause in the Church Act, but this has been annulled by the House of Lords. Criticism of Thomas arose out of his support for this act, but Society was satisfied with his explanation.

120–38. Church Act passed, 30 Nov. 1706 (2 copies).

139–40. Act to repeal all Church Acts prior to (120–38), including act requiring conformity to Church of England from members of the assembly.

141–4. Le Jau to Secretary, St. James, Goose Greek, 2 Dec. 1706. He reached South Carolina in October and was kindly received by the authorities. Thomas died shortly before his arrival. Auchinleek elected to stay in Bermuda.

145. Dun to Secretary, Charles Town, 6 Dec. 1706, reporting arrival. Auchinleek kept the books that he was supposed to carry to South Carolina with him in Bermuda.

146–7. Gov. Johnson and members of Council to Society, 26 Dec. 1706. Though they would like to be rid of Marston, they have offered him a country parish with the salary made equal to that at Charleston.

148–9. Le Jau to Secretary, St. James, Goose Creek, 15 Apr. 1707, reporting on his work.

150. Do. to Stubbs, St. James, Goose Creek, 15 Apr. 1707, reporting efforts to work with Indians, and controversy with dissenters.

151–4. Dun to Secretary, Charlestown, 21 Apr. 1707 (2 copies), reporting beginning of his work and asking that £30 of his stipend be sent in goods.

155–6. Secretary to Gov. Johnson and Council, Westminster, 30 Apr. 1707 (2 copies). Society is satisfied with adjustments in Church Act and is sending Maul to replace Thomas. New rule provides that missionaries will serve during pleasure of the society.

157–8. Do. to Le Jau, Petty France, Westminster, 2 June 1707 (copy), introducing Maul. Failure in New York has discouraged society from work with Indians. Copy of general instruction to missionaries to report local contributions on same sheet.

159–60. Do. to Dun, Petty France, Westminster, 2 June 1707 (copy). Dun's report was favourably received by Committee. No report has been received from Hasell.

161. Do. to Robert Stevans, Petty France, Westminster, 2 June 1707. His account of affairs in South Carolina differs so much from that given by the governor and council that the society is puzzled which to believe, but inclines to accept the official version. It is true that Thomas was originally sent as missionary to the Yammassees, but the war, which was then going on, prevented his going to them.

162. Archbishop of Dublin to Bishop of London, Dublin, 30 June 1707, recommending Gideon Johnston for post in Charleston.

163–4. Le Jau to Secretary, St. James, Goose Creek, 30 June 1707. He has been alarmed by a rumour that his wife and children were taken by the French on the way over. Thomas' widow is in distress. Le Jau is making preparations to catechize Indians and Negroes. Characterizes Marston as a trouble-maker.

165. Testimonial to Johnston from the Bishop of Killala and Achorny, 1 July 1707.

166–7. Le Jau to Stubbs, St. James, Goose Creek, 3 July 1707. Criticizes leaders of the 'Dissenting Party', and Marston.

168. Testimonial to Johnston from the Bishop of Tuam, Dublin, 21 July 1707.

169. Testimonial to do. from the Bishop of Elphin, 15 Aug. 1707.

170–1. Another testimonial to Johnston from the Bishop of Killala, 29 Aug. 1707.

172–3. Hasell to Secretary, Carolina, 6 Sept. 1707. He has supplied for Thomas since his arrival. He wrote from Bermuda by Holland, the minister, whose return was the occasion for Auchinleek's staying.

174–5. Nicholas Trott to Society, South Carolina, 13 Sept. 1707. Reports dissenting opposition to the establishment. Henry Gerard, a clergyman of the Church of England, much travelled and a good linguist, but with a poor delivery, has been stranded in South Carolina by shipwreck. Trott recommends him as missionary to the Yammassees. A postscript notes that Richard Marsden, recently arrived from Maryland, has become minister in Charleston.

176–7. Governor and Council to the Society, South Carolina, 19 Sept. 1707, reporting resistance to the collection of ecclesiastical taxes.

178. Le Jau to Stubbs, St. James, Goose Creek, 23 Sept. 1707. His family has arrived. His children seem to be over their acclimatization, but his wife is still ill. One woman in his parish has been arrested on a charge of witchcraft. Another, after being in delirium for two days, on apparently coming to, declared that she had been dead and related her experiences to a servant.

179–80. Do. to Secretary, St. James, Goose Creek, 23 Sept. 1707. Complains of low state of religion in province. His parish has recently completed building a new church.

181. Statistics of St. James's Parish, 23 Sept. 1707.

182–5. Dun to Secretary, St. Paul's, Colleton Co., 24 Nov. 1707. Reports arrival of Maul. An attempt to set parish boundaries failed in the assembly. His church is completed and furnished, but he is deferring Holy Communion until Christmas, as he finds the people ignorant of the nature of the sacrament (2 copies).

186–7. Maule to Secretary, Charlestown, 28 Nov. 1707. Governor has not yet assigned him to a parish. Marsden is in Charleston. Marston has a country parish. List of society's books left by Thomas enclosed.

188–9. Hasell to Secretary, Carolina, 30 Nov. 1707, reporting on his work. Ship on which one of his earlier letters was sent was captured.

190. Secretary to Gov. Johnson, Petty France, Westminster, 2 Dec. 1707 (copy). Society is sending Adams and Gordon to North Carolina. This letter will be brought by Gideon Johnston, whom the Bishop of London has appointed to Charleston, being assured by the governor's son and Col. Johnson, a member of the society, that the post was vacant.

191. Do. to Le Jau, Petty France, Westminster, 2 Dec. 1707, introducing Johnston.

192. John Wright to Robert Stevens, 10 Sept. 1707, saying that the late Gov. Moore told him that 'Parson Williams' was a chronic drunkard, who once christened a bear.

193–4. Thomas Smith to Stevens, 16 Jan. 1707/8. When he arrived in South Carolina with his father in 1683, there were two ministers professing to be of the Church of England. One was known as Rogers the Elder. The other was Atkin Williamson, a chronic drunkard whom some ill-disposed persons once induced to christen a bear. This was a matter of common report and Smith once heard the late Gov. Moore offer to swear that it was true. Williamson, though still a sot, was appointed by the gubernatorial party to replace Marston when he, as Smith believes, was illegally removed from Charleston.

195–6. Stevens to Secretary, Goose Creek, 3 Feb. 1707/8, enclosing (192–4) and reviewing the controversy over Marston and the church in Charleston. James Bires, who was sent to England to present the case, was taken by the French.

197–9. Governor and Council to the Society, 13 Feb. 1707/8. They are advised in letter from secretary brought by Maule that society approves of new Church Act, but they would like to have this approval presented in a more formal declaration. Maul has been appointed to a parish, as has Wood, who arrived with Maule, recommended by the Bishop of London, but without an appointment from the society. Marsden is serving Charleston.

200–1. Hasell to Secretary, Charlestown, 9 Mar. 1707. He is still supplying Thomas's former parish.

202–3. Le Jau to Secretary, St. James, Goose Creek. 13 Mar. 1707/8. He has been ill, though now recovered, and is afraid that some of his earlier letters have miscarried. Wood has not been well received in parish to which he was sent, though Le Jau thinks him a good man. Favourable references to other missionaries.

204–5. Do. to do., St. James, Goose Creek, 12 Apr. 1708. Repeats information in (202–3) in case it miscarries.

206–7. Governor and Council to Society, 15 July 1708. Hasel, who is going home for priest's orders, has functioned satisfactorily as deacon in St. Thomas's Parish, and they recommend his appointment as missionary.

208. Secretary to Auchinleek, Petty France, Westminster, 21 July 1708, rebuking him for deserting his mission. He has given a pestilence then raging in South Carolina as his excuse.

209. Do. to Gov. John Bennet, Petty France, Westminster, 21 July 1708. State of society's finances does not permit granting an allowance to Auchinleek in Bermuda.

210. Maule to Secretary, South Carolina, 21 July 1708. He was sent by governor to St. John's Parish on western branch of Cooper River. He cannot give exact statistics, as parish is not yet bounded, but he believes it contains about 40 Church families, 8 or 10 families of 'Anabaptists', and 2 or 3 of Roman Catholics. Clergy of province met together to thank the governor for his support.

211. Secretary to (John) Thomas (of Hempstead, N.Y.), Windsor Castle, 7 Aug. 1708 (copy), rebuking him for a too zealous proselytizing of dissenters and telling him to file his reports in approved form. (Misplaced here under impression it was addressed to Samuel Thomas.)

212–13. Certificate by Governor and Council, several ministers, and parishioners of Charleston, 16 Aug. 1708, that Richard Marsden, though duly elected rector of Charleston, voluntarily resigned in favour of the Bishop of London's appointee, Gideon Johnston (2 copies).

214–17. Marsden to Secretary, Charlestown, 23 Aug. 1708, giving his account of the situation and asking to be named a missionary (2 copies).

218–19. Extract from a letter of Josia Duprés to his son James, Carolina, 27 Aug. 1708 (French, with translation). Their minister, De la Pierre, has arrived in a destitute condition after a long voyage. They ask aid from their friends in London. The late Mr. Thomas stated that he studied with De la Pierre at the University of Dublin, and that he was one of the ablest students.

220–1. Ministers of South Carolina to the Society, Charlestown, 3 Sept. 1708, referring society to a statement of conditions in the province that they have sent to the Bishop of London by Chief Justice Trott.

222–3. Le Jau to Secretary, St. James, Goose Creek, 11 Sept. 1708, and Charlestown, 18 Sept. 1708. Recommends Hassell, who is returning for priest's orders. Dun is also going home, contrary to Le Jau's advice, and has been succeeded by Maitland, newly arrived. Though Marsden resigned Charleston to Johnston, the parish is still torn by dissension.

224–5. Do. to do., St. James, Goose Greek, 15 Sept. 1708, reporting on his work.

226–7. Dun to Secretary, Charles Town, 20 Sept. 1708. His parish contains about 300 adults, of whom about 80 profess the Church of England. There are 150 Presbyterians, 8 Independents, 40 'Anabaptists', 10 Quakers, and 12 with no definite affiliation. He is returning because of pressing business in Europe.

228–31. Johnston to (Bishop of London?), Charlestown, 20 Sept. 1708, expressing regret at coming to South Carolina, relating his difficulty in ousting Marsden, and giving an unfavourable account of the province and its people, except Gov. Johnson.

232. Maitland to Secretary, Charlestown, 16 Sept. 1708, asking for an allowance.

233–4. Le Jau to Secretary, St. James, Goose Creek, 15 Nov. 1708. He has done some work with neighbouring Indians, in spite of renewed illness. Maule, who is also ill, is the only other missionary remaining of those who came over with him.

235–6. Secretary to Le Jau, Petty France, Westminster, 24 Jan. 1708/9 (copy). He is unable to answer Le Jau's question about how to consecrate a church in the absence of a bishop, but hopes they will soon have one. The report of subscriptions to the society is confidential, and the contributors should not be told about it. He has transmitted a 'long and peevish' letter of Stevens to the Bishop of London and other members of the society.

237–8. Le Jau to Secretary, St. James, Goose Creek, 18 Feb. 1708/9. He and Maule are recovered, but Johnston is so ill the others have to supply his parish as best they can. Dun is reported in Virginia. Auchinleek has written him 'in great joy' at being restored to the society's favour.

239–40. Do. to do., St. James, Goose Creek, 18 Feb. 1708/9, reporting on his work and repeating some of the information in (237–8).

241. Maule to Secretary, South Carolina, 6 Mar. 1708/9, reporting on his work and acknowledging receipt of prayer books and tracts. Though he is fairly well now, he finds the climate unhealthy.

242. Secretary to Gov. Tynte (newly appointed), Petty France, Westminster, 9 Mar. 1708/9 (copy), asking him to secure the society's books formerly held by Thomas.

243. Tynte to Rev. Dr. Johnson (Johnston), 17 Mar. 1709(10?), saying he is sending an unspecified act for his consideration, and that it does not insist on the power of degradation, but only of deposition. Unsigned *notation*, possibly by Johnston, says that this was part of an effort to gain his support for the act.

244. Translated extract of letter from Escot, French minister in Charleston to Bonet, King of Prussia's resident in London, 24 Mar. 1709. Their colony of Santy (Santee?) has been erected into a parish and they are seeking a minister approved by the Bishop of London. His stipend will be £100 a year.

245. Tynte to Secretary, 2 Apr. 1709. Illness has delayed his acknowledgement of the secretary's letter (242).

246–9. Secretary to Le Jau, Petty France, Westminster, 25 July 1709 (copy). Letter will be brought by Gov. Tynte. Complains of not receiving reports from Maule. Wood has been granted an annual stipend of £50 for two years. Society deferred action of Trott's recommendation of Gerard as missionary to the Yammassees until Trott came to London, but learning from Hasell that Trott's visit has been deferred, they ask for more particulars about Gerard. Would some Spanish Testaments be useful among the Yammassees? Hasell has been appointed catechist and schoolmaster in Charleston. Asks particulars about Maitland and Fraser, who are seeking the society's support.

250. Do. to Proprietors of Carolina, 26 Sept. 1709 (copy), reporting a resolution of the society to discontinue sending missionaries to North Carolina unless an act of that province allowing vestries to dismiss ministers at will is revised.

251–2. Le Jau to Secretary, St. James, Goose Creek, 20 Oct. 1709. In baptizing slave he requires them to declare publicly that they are not seeking freedom, and gives them instruction in the duty of monogamy. He has been ill again, but is recovering. Johnston and Maule are ill.

253–4. Do. to do., St. James, Goose Creek, 4 Nov. 1709. Maule's house and most of his goods have been destroyed by fire.

255. Secretary to Johnston, Petty France, Westminster, 12 Dec. 1709 (copy), asking for elucidation of a recommendation in a letter of Johnston's to the Bishop of Sarum that clergy in South Carolina be 'naturalized'.

256. Do. to Le Jau, Petty France, Westminster, 12 Dec. 1709 (copy). Le Jau's questions about procedure in baptizing slaves have been laid before the Archbishop of Canterbury.

257. Do. to Maule, Petty France, Westminster, 22 Dec. 1709 (copy), rebuking him for infrequent reporting. Society has approved his appointment to St. John's.

258–64. Proposals for improving school and library in Charleston, unsigned, but possibly by Johnston. *Notation* at end says they were submitted to the governor at his request, 6 Jan. 1709/10.

265. Secretary to Maule, Petty France, Westminster, 20 Mar. 1710 (copy). Society has voted him a gift of £30 because of his fire losses. (Cf. 253–5.)

266–7. Le Jau to Secretary, St. James, Goose Creek, 13 June 1710, reporting work with slaves and relating some acts of wanton cruelty to Indian and Negro slaves. Act proposed six months ago and dropped to subject clergy to lay commission has been revived. An act that has been passed makes clergy responsible for repairs to their parsonages. Postscript dated 29 Oct. 1710 reports misconduct of Maitland with a Negro woman.

268–9. Maule to Secretary, 3 June 1710. Most of those in his parish profess to be of the Church of England, except for a few 'Anabaptists'. As even those professing the Church neglect the baptism of the children, he would like some tracts on the subject. He has baptized a few slaves.

270. Le Jau to Johnston, Goose Creek, 12 Aug. 1710, sending some books and pamphlets on loan. He has advised Maitland to consult Johnston concerning difference with his parishioners. Has been unable to obtain a copy of proposed act concerning clerical charges.

271. List of watchmen (in Charleston?) 2 Oct. 1710. *Notation* indicates it was sent as substitute for a list of parishioners.

272. Secretary to Le Jau, Petty France, Westminster, 18 Oct. 1710 (copy). Society has sent him a schoolmaster, Dennis. Asks him to inform Johnston and some other clergy that he will write as soon as he can. Asks him not to send a proposed present, as he does not receive them from missionaries.

VOLUME XVII

SOUTH CAROLINA, 1711–undated

1. Thomas Edwards to Secretary, Greek St., 3 Jan. 1711, introducing unnamed son of a country clergyman who desires a post in Carolina.

2. Secretary to the Carolina Proprietors, Petty France, Westminster, Jan. 1710/11 (copy), asking their support for a school which Johnston is trying to persuade the assembly to establish in Charleston.

3. Ralph Izard to Johnston, undated, but bearing *notation*, apparently in Johnston's hand, saying it was written before deaths of Gov. Tynte and Mr. Gerard. Izard and other members of the assembly are prepared to write to the society in Johnston's behalf. Occasion not stated.

4–13. Johnston to Secretary (?), 27 Jan. 1710/11. Assembly has added £50 to his salary during his incumbency, but he still seeks an allowance from the society. His congregation has been decreased by a number of deaths, and by the withdrawal of some dissenters. He continues to have a controversy with Marston. He is enclosing a note from Mr. Taylor (14), whom he has persuaded to seek orders. Reference seems to imply that he was formerly a dissenter. Various charges have been brought against Maitland, but no one will support them by oath. Later references in the letter seem to indicate that the 'dissenters' referred to are Presbyterians.

14. Ebenezer Taylor to Secretary, Charles Town, 6 Feb. 1710/11, stating his intention to sail home for orders.

15. Secretary to John Norris, Petty France, Westminster, 6 Feb. 1710/11 (copy). Society has expressed approval of his plan, reported in letter to Sir John Philips, of 'breeding up' his son to be a missionary to the Indians.

16. Do. to Wood, Petty France, Westminster, 7 Feb. 1710/11 (copy). Society is continuing his allowance, on Dr. Le Jau's recommendation.

17–18. Le Jau to Secretary, St. James, Goose Creek, 9 Feb. 1710/11, reporting on his work. As he fears that his Barbadoes correspondent, Col. Thomas Maycock, may have died, some of his letters sent that way may not have gone through.

19–21. Lists of burials and communicants in St. Philip's, Charleston, in 1710 and early 1711.

22–3. Fragment of a letter by Johnston describing his efforts to keep Capt. Flavel from defecting to the Presbyterians. Affidavit of Johnston before Chief Justice Trott, 15 Feb. 1710/11, saying that this was part of a letter that was to be sent to the secretary 31 Oct. 1710.

24. List of christenings in Charleston, 10 Apr. 1710 to 15 Feb. 1710/11.

25. Secretary to Madam Rhet, 10 Feb. 1710/11 (copy), thanking her for gift of communion plate to St. Philip's, and for kindness to Johnston during his illness.

26. Do. to Gignillat, Petty France, Westminster, 20 Feb. 1710/11 (copy). State of the society's finances makes it unlikely that they can aid him at present.

27. Do. to Hasell, Petty France, Westminster, 20 Feb. 1710/11 (copy), acknowledging his reports.

28. Do. to Sir Nathaniel Johnson, Petty France, Westminster, 20 Feb. 1710/11 (copy), thanking him and some others for kindness to Johnston. Seems to imply that Johnson is again governor.

29. Do. to Johnston, 20 Feb. 1710/11 (copy), Petty France, Westminster. Society has asked the proprietors to support his projected charity school (2). Prayer books for his use have been sent in care of Le Jau, because his letter suggested that he might be returning to England.

30. Do. to Le Jau, Petty France, Westminster, 20 Feb. 1710/11 (copy). Unable to answer his letters fully because society postponed action on them until the archbishop could be present. The society is seeking an act of Parliament for the conversion of Indians and Negroes.

31. Do. to L'Escot and Truilliart, Petty France, Westminster, 20 Feb. 1710/11 (copy), thanking them for kindness to Johnston and reporting sending of French prayer books.

32. Do. to Maule, Petty France, Westminster, 20 Feb. 1710/11 (copy), reproaching him for not acknowledging gift.

33. Do. to John Thomas (not the missionary), Petty France, Westminster, 20 Feb. 1710/11 (copy), thanking him for aid to Johnston.

34–5. Maule to Secretary, 4 Apr. 1711. He is seeking to persuade his parishioners to build a parsonage.

36–7. Le Jau to Secretary, St. James, Goose Creek, 12 Apr. 1711. He is sending secretary and treasurer a gift of Carolina rice. He questions accuracy of religious statistics in a pamphlet on the colony lately published in London, holding that it overstates the numbers of Presbyterians, Baptists, and Quakers, and errs in counting French Protestants among the Presbyterians.

38–9. Johnston to Secretary, 20 Apr. 1711. Maitland has died. Dispute with Marston continues. Maule has assisted Johnston in his illness.

40. List of those communicating on Easter, 1 Apr. 1711, probably enclosed with (38–9).

41. Johnston to Secretary, 21 Apr. 1711, introducing and recommending Taylor.

42–3. Le Jau to Secretary, St. James, Goose Creek, 30 Apr. 1711. Reports death of Maitland. The rest of the clergy are in fair health.

44. Rainsford to Secretary, Bury, Suffolk, 8 Feb. 1711, seeking an appointment.

45–6. Le Jau to Secretary, St. James, Goose Creek, 10 July 1711. Ship *Loyal Johnson*, by which he sent some earlier letters, was taken by privateers. Some removals from his parish have been more than offset by new arrivals from Barbadoes. Gignilliat has married an aged, wealthy French woman and seems unwilling to perform further clerical duty. Marston has visited the Yammassees and is seeking the support of the assembly for settling among them. Marsden is engaged in trade in Barbadoes.

47–8. Do. to do., St. James, Goose Creek, 14 July 1711, announcing arrival of Dennis.

49–50. James de Gignillat to Society, Goose Creek, 15 July 1711. Though he does not have a parish since his marriage, he proposes to supply vacant livings. He has translated the English catechism into French, and sent a copy to the society. Urges work among Indians.

51. Benjamin Bradly to the Secretary, 20 July 1711, introducing Giles Rainsford.

52. Secretary to Johnston, Petty France, Westminster, 4 Aug. 1711 (copy). Society has not yet acted on Johnston's application for aid, but probably soon will, especially as Mrs. Johnston is reported coming home to support it.

53. Do. to Governor and clergy of Carolina, Petty France, Westminster, 6 Aug. 1711 (copy), asking them to report on feasibility of a proposal to move Ross Reynolds, schoolmaster in St. Bartholomew's Parish, who has taught some young Indians free, nearer to the Yammassees, so that he can work among them.

54. Do. to Beyse, Petty France, 31 Aug. 1711 (copy), rebuking him for not reporting (misplaced).

55–6. Benjamin Dennis to Secretary, South Carolina, 3 Sept. 1711. He was delayed in his passage from Virginia to South Carolina by a revolt against Gov. Hyde of North Carolina led by Col. Cary.

57. Hasell to Secretary, St. Thomas's Parish, 4 Sept. 1711, reporting on his work, and saying that he is transmitting directions concerning parish libraries to other missionaries. Le Jau and Maul are well, but Dennis is ill.

58–9. Le Jau to Secretary, St. James, Goose Creek, 5 Sept. 1711. His parish is planning to build a school-house for Dennis's use, but such things go slowly in Carolina. He has written up a conference he had with some dissenters, and may print it.

60–1. Do. to do., St. James, Goose Creek, 18 Sept. 1711. He has not received the books sent in his care for Johnston. He has encountered some opposition to his efforts to convert the slaves.

62–3. Wardens and vestry of Christ Church Parish to the Society, 21 Sept. 1711, asking to be supplied with a minister. They were served for a time by Marston and later by Marsden, but both left. There is a Presbyterian minister in the parish.

64–5. Do. to Bishop of London, 26 Sept. 1711, making similar request.

66–7. Vestry of St. Andrew's parish, 1 Oct. 1711, seeking a minister following death of Alexander Wood.

68. Ebenezer Taylor to Secretary, on board the *Mary* in the Downs, 29 Dec. 1711. He fears that his ship, which has been sailing along the English coast, has missed the fleet with which it was to sail to America.

69. Copy of petition of St. Philip's, Charleston, to lower house of assembly, dated only 1710/11, asking for authority to rebuild church.

70–2. Testimonials to William Guy, 4–16 Jan. 1711/12.

73. Specimen lines in English, Latin, and Greek, signed by Guy, presumably as an exercise of some sort. Undated.

74. Another testimonial to Guy, Jan. 1711/12.

75–6. Undated petition of Guy to the Society. Having been designated by the society as schoolmaster in Charleston, and accepted by the Bishop of London for ordination to the deaconate, he asks to be supplied with books.

77. Undated petition of Daniel Mainadier to the Society. Though designated as missionary to Narragansett, he asks to be appointed to Christ Church Parish, S.C., having learned that it is vacant.

78. Mary Keith to the Archbishop of Canterbury, undated, asking relief. (Should be with Maryland documents.)

79. Undated petition of Mary Keith to the Society, asking aid.

80–7. Undated memorial of Samuel Thomas relating to Church in South Carolina and containing proposals for instruction of Indians and Negroes.

88. Undated testimonial to Thomas.

89–90. Stevens to the Society, Goose Creek, undated, criticizing Thomas for not staying among the Yammasees, though he had displaced Kendal, who had resigned St. George's Parish in Bermuda to work among them. Denies published reports that Thomas has instructed Negroes in Goose Creek.

91. Do. to Bishop of London, Goose Creek, undated, saying that he is entertaining Thomas at his plantation until Sir Nathaniel Johnson receives him as his chaplain.

92–8. Undated memorial of Thomas vindicating himself against charges brought by Marston, and explaining his reasons for not settling among the Yamassees.

99–100. Undated petition of Elizabeth Thomas, Samuel's widow, seeking relief.

101–2. Undated answers of Johnston to queries of the society, apparently related to his request for aid.

103–4. Undated 'case' of Johnston, indicating that he had refused an appointment to North Carolina and that there was some vacillation about sending him to South Carolina.

105. Undated copy of petition of dissenters in South Carolina to Moderator and General Assembly of the Church of Scotland, asking their aid in opposing South Carolina establishment act which, they say, inhibits dissenting ministers from baptizing or marrying. Declare that dissenters are a majority in South Carolina.

106–7. Gignillat to Secretary, undated, acknowledging letter saying society cannot give him an allowance at present (probably 26), offering a scheme for the conversion of the Indians, and giving a description of the province.

VERMONT

108–10. Report of a subcommittee to the committee of the Privy Council for plantation affairs, Whitehall, 2 June 1767, recommending that Governor of New York be ordered to desist from making grants in lands west of the Connecticut River (the present state of Vermont) in conflict with grants made by Benning Wentworth, governor of New Hampshire, including grant to the society.

111–15. H. Moore to Lords Commissioners of Trade and Plantations, New York, 16 Jan. 1766, transmitting a map of the region (2 copies of letter, one of map).

116. Samuel Peters to the Archbishop of Canterbury, Grosvenor Place, 12 Mar. 1790, reporting arrangements of General Convention of 1789, particularly relating to consecration to Edward Bass, Bishop-elect of Massachusetts, as related to him by American correspondents.

117–18. Request of a convention in Vermont to the Archbishop of Canterbury to arrange for the consecration of Samuel Peters as bishop of that state, 27 Feb. 1794.

119. Testimonial to Peters, signed by the Archbishop of Canterbury, 8 May 1794.

120. Peters to the Archbishop of Canterbury, 22 York St., Westminster, 16 July 1794, informing him of his election. Asserts that he was elected Bishop of Connecticut in 1784, but declined, and that he had entertained hopes of being named Bishop of Upper Canada.

121. Do. to do., 22 York St., Westminster, 25 June 1794. Two sets of credentials have both miscarried, but he encloses a copy of the address of the convention to the archbishop (presumably 117–18). Draft of archbishop's answer, on same sheet, 29 June 1794. As there are now three bishops of the English line in the United States, the act authorizing their consecration is no longer in effect.

122. Do. to do., 22 York St., Westminster, 30 June 1794, pleading for consecration on the ground of Vermont's remoteness from the rest of the country, and the difficulty of convening the American bishops. Draft of archbishop's reply, on same sheet, 2 July 1794, says he sees no chance of Peters obtaining consecration in England.

123. Finished copy of the archbishop's reply of which the draft appears on (121).

124–5. Archbishop of Canterbury to the Duke of Portland, Clarendon House, near Guilford, 12 Sept. 1794. In answer to an inquiry from the Duke, he repeats position stated in (121) and adds that Peters cannot obtain proper testimonials from America, as he has not resided there for several years.

126–7. A finished and slightly shorter copy of (124–5).

128–9. Peters to the Archbishop of Canterbury, 22 York St., Westminster, 4 Nov. 1794. Having been told by Mr. King that the Duke of Portland is of the opinion that the act of Parliament did not limit the number of bishops who could be consecrated, but that there was a further objection in that his consecration has not been approved by the civil authorities, he has obtained a certificate from the American minister, Pinckney, that the American government is not concerned in ecclesiastical matters.

130. John A. Graham to the Archbishop of Canterbury, 340 Strand, 18 May 1795. Identifying himself as 'agent of the church in Vermont', he pleads for the consecration of a bishop.

131. Do. to do., 340 Strand, 25 May 1795, having received an oral refusal from the archbishop he asks that the grounds be put in writing.

132. Archbishop of Canterbury to Graham, Canterbury, 17 June 1795, repeating his reasons for refusing to consecrate Peters.

VIRGINIA

133–4. Copy of act of 1667 declaring that the baptism of slaves does not entail their emancipation.

135–8. Two copies of notes on MS. Harl. B.M. no. 3790, saying that MS. shows that in 1672 the King named Alexander Murray, Rector of Ware Parish, Virginia, as bishop of Virginia, and that 'false calumnies' being brought against

Murray in Virginia, he asked a chance to vindicate himself, and a citation was issued announcing his intended consecration and calling on all objectors to come forward. Notes end at this point.

139–40. Richard Wathen to Maj. John Harper, Charles City Co., Va., 14 May 1683, relating to the title to a tract called the 'mill lands'.

141–2. More documents bearing on this title, contained in a letter of Mr. Keats to Thomas Symons, 28 May 1699.

143–9. Thomas Symons to Samuel Brewster, 4 Dec. 1702, with a number of documents supporting title of Richard Bond to these lands.

150. Francis Nicholson to the Bishop of London, Williamsburgh, Va., 11 Oct. 1703, introducing John Thomas, who is returning for priest's orders after serving as schoolmaster in Philadelphia, and John Moor, a leader of the church in Philadelphia, who is travelling with him.

151. Will. Urquhart to Secretary, Spithead, Hook of Holland. Ship on which he and Crawford are sailing has obtained a new mast and expects to sail soon for Virginia. Stuart had to go ashore because of illness.

152. Order in Council, 3 Mar. 1704, referring complaints of some members of the provincial council in Virginia against Governor Nicholson to the Lords Commissioners of Trade and Plantations.

153–4. Wardens, vestry, and other freeholders of Christ Church Parish, Kent Island, Va., to the Bishop of London, 18 Apr. 1704. Testimonial to John Sharpe, who has been their minister for two years.

155–6. W. Harrison to Secretary, Virginia, 23 May 1704, outlining steps that must be taken to claim the Bond estate, the principal one being to prove that George Bond is Richard's heir. Land is poor, but has the advantage of lying on a navigable creek, and having a water-mill, though that is in poor repair.

157–8. Nicholson to Secretary, 31 May 1704. A testimonial to George Keith.

159. Samuel Thomas to the Secretary, Portsmouth, 20 Apr. 1706, reporting various delays in sailing. Mr. Boon, who professes to be a supporter of the Church of England, has brought on board two dissenting ministers and a Scotch Presbyterian schoolmaster.

160–1. Le Jau to Secretary, on board the *Greenwich*, in the James River. 9 Sept. 1706. He has arrived there after a smooth voyage of ten weeks, and is being entertained by Mr. Wallace, rector of a neighbouring parish. He hopes to get to Williamsburgh to pay his respects to Commissary Blair.

162–3. List of parishes in Virginia, 25 Mar. 1707.

164. J. Wallace to Josiah Woodward, Elizabeth City Parish, 3 Apr. 1707. Only about 4 out of 40 clergymen in the province are regularly inducted, the rest being employed during the pleasure of their vestries.

165. Robert Walker to the Bishop of London, Portsmouth, 12 May 1707. His food has run out, apparently while waiting to sail. He has been supplied by Cordiner, but the latter's resources are also becoming exhausted.

166–7. James Adams to Secretary, Virginia, 19 June 1708. He and Gordon have reached Virginia on their way to North Carolina.

168. Black to Secretary, Kickatan, Va., 19 June 1708. He has reached there on his way to Pennsylvania (Delaware).

169–70. Hasell to Secretary, Virginia, 12 Oct. 1708, on his way to England (2 copies).

171. Halliday to Secretary, Virginia, 14 Mar. 1710/11. Having got thus far, he proposed to go to New York by land, but now has a chance to go there by ship.

172–5. William White to the Archbishop of Canterbury, Philadelphia, 11 Aug. 1789, with a copy to his reply to a request from Virginia for the consecration of David Griffith, saying that he does not feel free to consecrate until there are three bishops in the English line in America.

176–7 Wrappers.

178–9. William Wynne to the Archbishop of Canterbury, Doctors Commons, 27 Mar. 1790. He thinks more information is necessary before the Archbishop can reply to the request of General Convention that he approve the union of White and Provoost with Seabury to consecrate Bass. He is troubled by the fact that the convention asserted the validity of Seabury's orders.

180–207. Testimonials and other papers relating to the consecration of James Madison as Bishop of Virginia, 1790.

208–9. Undated request from vestry of unnamed parish, sent by Keith, asking continued aid of society. Placed here because of *notation* saying that it was from Virginia, but names of signers seem to show that it was from Chester, Pa.

210–13. Undated account of the foundation of William and Mary College, signed by S. Fouace (2 copies).

214–15. Unsigned, undated letter to governors of the College of William and Mary, relating to its affairs. *Notation* dates it 16 July 1722 and says it is in the handwriting of Archbishop Wake.

216–17. Jo. Keats to ——, 28 May ——, concerning title to Bond estate.

218. Undated note saying there are 13 vacant parishes in Virginia.

219. Undated account of religion in Virginia, attributed in *notation* to Mr. Keeble.

WEST INDIES

GENERAL

220. John Brooke to the Archbishop of Canterbury, 11 Nov. 1704, expressing his intention of going to the West Indies and asking to be recommended to the society for an appointment.

221–3. Memorial suggesting motives for improving the sugar colonies, addressed to the Archbishop of Canterbury by James Ramsey, Mr. Maudes, Downing St., 18 Mar. 1778. The proposal is to allow the slaves a minimum amount of self-government under an official Protector, restricting the authority of the master.

BAHAMAS

224–39. An act for establishing schools and providing schoolmasters in the several islands, 17 Dec. 1795.

240–50. Act for erecting and repairing of churches and maintaining of ministers, 24 Dec. 1795.

251. George Chalmers to the Archbishop of Canterbury, Whitehall, 15 July 1796, presenting the foregoing acts (224–50).

BARBADOES

252. Secretary to Governor Lowther, Petty France, Westminster, 6 Mar. 1710/11 (copy), asking his co-operation in obtaining possession of Codrington estate.

253. Robert Lowther to Secretary, Portsmouth, 17 Mar. 1710/11. He has received the 'exemplification' of the society's charter and will deliver to their attorneys. He fears that the conversion of the Negroes will prove a difficult task, because of the indifference or opposition of the masters.

254–5. Lowther to Secretary, Portsmouth, 27 Mar. 1710/11, with a catalogue that he and Nicholson made of books left with the minister in Portsmouth by one of the society's missionaries.

256–7. Benjamin Dennis to Secretary, *Reserve* in Carlile Bay, Barbadoes, 26 Mar. 1711. His ship put in there instead of going to Virginia, because it was running short of water. His wife bore a son on the voyage, apparently prematurely, as the result of being frightened by the sight of a privateer.

258. Bishop of St. Asaph to the Archbishop of Canterbury, Dartmouth St., 7 Apr. 1760. Committee on Barbadoes affairs has completed its work and he is submitting some documents.

259. List of members of subcommittee on Barbadoes, 1760.

260–1. Barbadoes managers to the Society, Codrington College, 28 May 1780, discussing changes in arrangements of the management of the plantation.

262. Undated draft of report of Barbadoes committee.

263–4. Undated, anonymous proposals for reviving the 'seminary of Learning' (apparently a preparatory school) in connection with Codrington College.

265–6. Undated list of Barbadoes clergymen signing an address to the King and list of churches damaged or destroyed in hurricane.

BERMUDA

267–8. Address of Governor, Council, and Assembly of Bermuda to the Society, St. George's, 10 Sept. 1706, asking aid for church. To be presented by their former minister, Thomas Holland.

269. Gov. Ben. Bennet to Society, 19 Sept. 1706, asking continuance of salary to Auchinleek.

270. Auchinleek to Secretary, 29 Oct. 1706, asking continuance.

271–2. Do. to do., 23 Dec. 1706, making same request.

273–4. H. Bennett to the Secretary, 5 Jan. 1708, transmitting a letter from the minister in Bermuda (Auchinleek?) and saying that he has received a favourable report concerning him from his brother, the governor.

275. Auchinleek to Secretary, 10 Feb. 1707/8, seeking aid.

276. Do. to do., 25 June 1708, asking aid.

277–8. Do. to do., 26 Mar. 1709. Though denied an allowance, he will be willing to serve the society's commands and hopes they may sometime restore him.

279–80. Jacob Rice to Secretary, St. John's, Newfoundland, 6 Nov. 1711 (misplaced), reporting conditions on his return.

JAMAICA

281. Samuel Eburne to the Society, Kingston, 12 Nov. 1705, requesting prayer books.

282–3. R. Tabor and Thomas Lloyd to the Secretary, Spanish Town, 5 Dec. 1707, describing religious conditions on the island.

284. Undated extract from Jamaica slave code, saying that no slave shall become free by becoming a Christian.

285. Thomas Lloyd to Secretary, 5 Dec. ——. Vestry has increased his salary since his arrival. Commissary Bennett has recently died.

LEEWARD ISLANDS

286–92. Undated abstract and other papers by Dr. Le Jau describing religious situation in Leeward and Caribbee Islands.

INDEX 1

NAMES AND TOPICS REFERRED TO IN THE SUMMARIES

Abraham (Indian), v. 263–8, 293–6.

Achenbach, viii. 91.

Ackamack, Va., xi. 238.

Adams, Alexander, iii. 46–53, xii. 70–2.

Adams, James: letters from, viii. 29, xv. 14, 293, xvii. 166–7; letters to, xvi. 64; testimonials to, i. 205, x. 64–6; death of, xii. 68–9; voyage of, xvi. 44; continuance of, in North Carolina, xvi. 65; sent to North Carolina, xvi. 190.

Adams, John, x. 210.

Adamson, John: letters from, vii. 34, 85–6, 95, 208; letters to, vii. 83; collection by, vii. 31.

Adderbury, Eng., vii. 66.

Albany, N.Y.: letters from, xiii. 69–70, 118–19, xiv. 219, 231, 259–60; missionaries in, i. 87–8; Barclay sent to, ii. 67–73, xiv. 192; Ogilvie sent to, v. 175–8; royal allowance sought for, vii. 184–5; Cordiner proposed for, vii. 187–8, 232, 235; schoolmaster proposed for, viii. 210; meeting in, xiii. 1–2; Moore leaves, xiii. 158–60, 175–7, 187; Cornbury in, xiv. 54–9; certificate from, xiv. 155–6; work of Barclay in, xiv. 158–9; statistics for, xiv. 254.

Albro, Samuel, viii. 63–4.

Alleyne, Abel, iv. 25–8, 37–40, 165–74, v. 95–100.

Alleyne, John, viii. 16.

Alverado, Antonio, ix. 194.

Amboy, N.J.: letters from, xii. 208–14, 258–9; dispute in, xii. 258–60; visited by Bartow, xiv. 164–5; Halliday to serve in, xiv. 235; assembly in, xv. 146–7.

Amoos, vii. 146–7.

Amsterdam, Ned.: letters from, ix. 19, 29, 32–3, 38–9, 43, 170; classis in, ii. 88; Church of England in, ix. 186–91.

Anglia Sacra (book), x. 180–2.

Annapolis, Md., v. 217–22, xii. 3–4, 63–4.

Annapolis Royal, N.S., ii. 209–12, iii. 121–6, 152–62.

Anne, Queen: grant sought from, iii. 72–8; address to, vii. 15–16; application to, vii. 112; promise from, vii. 217; postpones collection, viii. 119; authorizes collection, viii. 124, 126–7; aid sought from, ix, 72–3; disallowance sought from, xi. 166–80; intercession with, sought, xii. 20–1; order from, xiii. 24; request to, xiii. 140; gifts from, xiii. 206, 209; asked to direct legislation, xiii. 207; glass donated by, xv. 157.

Antelope (ship), xiv. 191.

Antonides, V., xiv. 211–12.

Ansberg, ix. 171–3.

Anwyl (min., N.S.), v. 223–8, 231–2, 282.

Apoquimininck, Del.: letters from, xi. 226–7, 229–31, 238, 243–5; Jenkins appointed to, i. 138–9, vii. 184; Black appointed to, ii. 96–9; Griffith recommended for, ii. 129–30; supply for, ii. 271; gift to Pugh in, iv. 123–6; death in, v. 3–8; Roberts recommended for, vii. 207; Jenkins proposed for, vii. 231; abandoned by Jenkins, viii. 88, xi. 212–14, 222; subscription in, xi. 192; petitions from, xi. 193–4, 224–5; Clubb sent to, xi. 241–2, xiv. 246–7, xv. 180; vestry in, xv. 140; transfer to, recommended, xv. 204–5.

Appia, Cyprian: gift to, i. 45–6; introduced, vii. 150; visit of, ix. 76–7; references to, ix. 84; petition from, ix. 198.

Appia, Paul; *same entries as for Cyprian.*

Archangel, Russia, ix. 34.

Archdeacons, vii. 25, 64, 69, viii. 33.

Arches, Deanery of, viii. 276–7.

Armagh, Abp. of: letters from, vii. 140, 243, 256, viii. 117, 155, 161, 185; letters to, vii. 134, 248–9, viii. 122.

Army (British), xi. 5.

Arnold, Jonathan: gratuity to, iii. 229–38, allowed to return, iii. 253–8; offer concerning, iii. 267–70; permitted to exchange, iv. 9–14; sent to Staten Island, iv. 15–20; charges against, iv. 41–4, v. 25–8; defence of, v. 75–80.

Arundel, Eng., viii. 70.

Asbury, Francis, x. 197.

Ashelworth, Gloucestershire, vii. 89, 100–1, 164.

Ashley River Parish, S.C., ii. 163–4.

Ashurst, *Sir* Henry, xi. 168–9, 173–4.

---

* As all but a few of the letters in the correspondence section, begining with vol. vii, are either written to or by Secretary Chamberlayne, I am using this general indication instead of listing the separate letters.

INDEX 2

NAMES APPEARING IN DOCUMENTS, BUT NOT MENTIONED IN SUMMARIES

(NOTE: Volume number followed by dashes and asterisk (e.g. v. – –*) indicates that a member is listed regularly among those present at the head of the minutes (vols. i–v).)

P

Q